RETIRE RICH WITH YOUR
ROTH IRA,
ROTH 401(k),
and
ROTH 403(b):

Investment Strategies for Your Roth IRA Explained Simply

BY MARTHA MAEDA

RETIRE RICH WITH YOUR ROTH IRA, ROTH 401(K), AND ROTH 403(B):
INVESTMENT STRATEGIES FOR YOUR ROTH IRA EXPLAINED SIMPLY

Copyright © 2011 Atlantic Publishing Group, Inc.
1405 SW 6th Avenue • Ocala, Florida 34471 • Phone 800-814-1132 • Fax 352-622-1875
Web site: www.atlantic-pub.com • E-mail: sales@atlantic-pub.com
SAN Number: 268-1250

Library of Congress Cataloging-in-Publication Data

Maeda, Martha, 1953-
  Retire rich with your Roth IRA, Roth 401k, and Roth 403b : investment strategies for your Roth
IRA explained simply / by Martha Maeda.
      p. cm.
  Includes bibliographical references and index.
  ISBN-13: 978-1-60138-321-1 (alk. paper)
  ISBN-10: 1-60138-321-5 (alk. paper)
  1. Individual retirement accounts--United States. 2. Retirement income--United States. I.
Title.
  HG1660.U5M345 2010
  332.024'01450973--dc22
                              2010000559

PROJECT MANAGER: Melissa Peterson • mpeterson@atlantic-pub.com
PEER REVIEWER: Marilee Griffin • EDITOR: Rebecca Bentz
PRODUCTION DESIGN: Holly Marie Gibbs • INTERIOR DESIGN: Harrison Kuo
FRONT & BACK COVER DESIGN: Jackie Miller • millerjackiej@gmail.com

Printed on Recycled Paper

We recently lost our beloved pet "Bear," who was not only our best and dearest friend but also the "Vice President of Sunshine" here at Atlantic Publishing. He did not receive a salary but worked tirelessly 24 hours a day to please his parents. Bear was a rescue dog that turned around and showered myself, my wife, Sherri, his grandparents Jean, Bob, and Nancy, and every person and animal he met (maybe not rabbits) with friendship and love. He made a lot of people smile every day.

We wanted you to know that a portion of the profits of this book will be donated to The Humane Society of the United States. *–Douglas & Sherri Brown*

The human-animal bond is as old as human history. We cherish our animal companions for their unconditional affection and acceptance. We feel a thrill when we glimpse wild creatures in their natural habitat or in our own backyard.

Unfortunately, the human-animal bond has at times been weakened. Humans have exploited some animal species to the point of extinction.

The Humane Society of the United States makes a difference in the lives of animals here at home and worldwide. The HSUS is dedicated to creating a world where our relationship with animals is guided by compassion. We seek a truly humane society in which animals are respected for their intrinsic value, and where the human-animal bond is strong.

Want to help animals? We have plenty of suggestions. Adopt a pet from a local shelter, join The Humane Society and be a part of our work to help companion animals and wildlife. You will be funding our educational, legislative, investigative and outreach projects in the U.S. and across the globe.

Or perhaps you'd like to make a memorial donation in honor of a pet, friend or relative? You can through our Kindred Spirits program. And if you'd like to contribute in a more structured way, our Planned Giving Office has suggestions about estate planning, annuities, and even gifts of stock that avoid capital gains taxes.

Maybe you have land that you would like to preserve as a lasting habitat for wildlife. Our Wildlife Land Trust can help you. Perhaps the land you want to share is a backyard—that's enough. Our Urban Wildlife Sanctuary Program will show you how to create a habitat for your wild neighbors.

So you see, it's easy to help animals. And The HSUS is here to help.

2100 L Street NW • Washington, DC 20037 • 202-452-1100
www.hsus.org

Trademark Statement

TABLE OF CONTENTS

Chapter 2: Roth Rules   39

Chapter 3: Strategies: Making the Most of Your Roth IRA   67

Chapter 4: Converting to a Roth   91

Chapter 5: Roth IRA Investments   111

Chapter 6: Principles of Investing   137

Chapter 7: Building and Maintaining Your Portfolio   153

Chapter 8: Doing the Research   179

Chapter 9: Self-directed IRAs   193

Chapter 10: Roth IRAs and Your Estate   219

Chapter 11: When You Inherit a Roth IRA   243

Introduction

S ince Roth IRAs (individual retirement arrangements) were created in 1997 by the Taxpayer Relief Act, financial advisors have praised them as an ideal vehicle for retirement savings. Income tax is paid on contributions before they go into the account, and all earnings from investments go to the owner tax-free during retirement. Roth IRAs are free of the cumbersome, mandatory withdrawals associated with traditional IRAs. They also present an opportunity to pass retirement savings on to your heirs without saddling them with heavy tax burdens. Several features of Roth IRAs make them suitable for other purposes, such as saving for education or the purchase of a home, accumulating wealth after retirement, and investing retirement savings in a business that you manage yourself. But Roth IRAs are not completely free of pitfalls. Like traditional IRAs, they are subject to a series of rules and restrictions that, if violated, can wipe out any advantage you might have gained from their tax-free status. If you already own a Roth IRA, or are thinking of opening one, you need an owner's guide to help you get the maximum benefit from it and keep it running smoothly. This book is your Roth IRA owner's manual.

The first chapters of the book explain the rules and regulations, contribution and income limits, restrictions on early withdrawals, and penalties for excess contributions and prohibited transactions — everything you need to know to successfully navigate the intricacies of Roth IRAs. You will also learn to weigh the advantages and disadvantages of traditional and Roth IRAs and to determine which type of IRA best fits your investment plans. You will find guidance on shopping for IRAs and learn what questions to ask before you sign a contract with an IRA provider.

Roth IRAs were designed to help working-class families save for retirement. Income limits prevent higher wage earners from contributing to Roths, and contribution limits ensure that Roth accounts do not grow too large. At the beginning of 2010, income limits for converting traditional IRAs or 401(k)s to Roth IRAs were lifted, ushering in a new era of large investment accounts accumulating tax-free earnings. The Internal Revenue Service (IRS) was hoping to encourage individuals with large balances in traditional IRAs and 401(k)s to convert, triggering an influx of deferred revenue for the U.S. government. Those who convert will have an unprecedented opportunity to generate wealth that can be passed on to their heirs free of income taxes. The stock market slump of 2008 added allure to this opportunity by drastically lowering the value of the investments in IRAs and 401(k)s. Their owners will be able to pay less income tax on the diminished balances as they transfer their assets to Roth IRAs, where they will regain value as the stock market recovers. Income limits still prevent wealthier families from contributing directly to Roth IRAs.

Two elements assure the growth of a Roth IRA: time and a sound investment strategy. A Roth IRA is only as successful as the investments it holds. Subsequent chapters of this book will review basic investment principles and discuss asset allocation, the building of a well-diversified portfolio, and strategies for protecting your investments while seeking growth. You will read about the different types of investments that can be held in a Roth IRA, and how to evaluate an investment before committing yourself. IRA providers offer a wide variety of structured investment plans, mutual funds, and opportunities for independent investors. The burden rests increasingly on the individual not only to set aside retirement savings, but to manage his or her own investment portfolio to maximum advantage. Learn to make the most of your Roth IRA by avoiding excessive fees and costly mistakes, and by planning properly for your retirement and for your heirs.

Self-directed Roth IRAs allow a hands-on investor to use specialized knowledge and experience to grow his or her own retirement savings. A self-directed IRA can be used to actively manage a portfolio of investments; buy, sell, and lease real estate; purchase tax liens; or deal in commodities. Learn the basics of setting up a self-directed IRA, how to assemble a staff of professional advisors when you need them, and how to avoid engaging in prohibited transactions that could result in the closure of your self-directed Roth IRA.

The final chapter addresses the challenges of saving for retirement during the current economic crisis and reveals some of the opportunities that exist for recovering losses. The book ends with a directory of resources to use in conducting your own research. Throughout the book you will find tips that emphasize important points or little-known details about Roth IRAs that could affect the choices you make. Many acronyms are associated with IRAs, so the full name, title, or term will be written out the first time it appears, and the acronym will be used throughout the rest of this book. *See Appendix B for a list of all the acronyms used in the book.*

Our rapidly evolving work environment is increasingly putting the individual at the forefront of retirement planning, as employers retreat from the responsibility of providing a secure retirement for their employees and the prospect of a worker having a lifetime career with one company diminishes. Do not be left behind. This book will equip you to take charge of your own financial future, whether you are taking your first small step or expanding a well-established foundation. Begin today to prepare for tomorrow.

Roth IRAs and Traditional IRAs

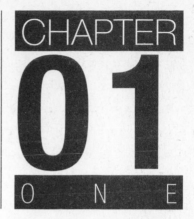

An individual retirement arrangement (IRA) is a special type of savings and investment account that increases the amount of money available to an individual in retirement by means of certain tax advantages. The U.S. Internal Revenue Service (IRS) strictly regulates these accounts to ensure they are not used for the wrong purpose by limiting the amount that can be contributed annually, imposing penalties for early withdrawal of funds, and enforcing a deadline for depleting the account after the owner's death. There are two types of IRA accounts: traditional IRAs and Roth IRAs. Income tax on contributions and earnings in a traditional IRA is deferred until the money is taken out of the account and the owner is required to make yearly withdrawals after retirement age. Contributions to a Roth IRA are subject to income tax in the year they are made, but no earnings in the account are taxed.

The rules governing IRA accounts change frequently and are sometimes adjusted for inflation or altered to compensate for the effects of specific events such as September 11, Hurricane Katrina, and the economic crisis of 2008-'09.

There are several varieties of IRAs, including employer-sponsored plans, individual accounts, plans for owners of small businesses, and even accounts for education savings. Most banks and financial institutions offer IRAs with specific investment choices, but an IRA can hold other types of financial instruments such as real estate and tax liens. Holders of IRAs may manage the investments themselves or follow a structured investment plan administered by a financial institution. An IRA is designed to fund an individual's retirement, but any balance remaining after the account holder's death can be maintained in a tax-advantaged account by his or her heirs.

History of IRAs

IRAs are relatively young: Congress introduced tax-advantaged retirement savings accounts for individuals in 1974. The first long-term IRAs did not begin to mature until after 2000, so there is little historical data to show how successful they are over a range of economic bubbles and declines. Roth IRAs are even younger; they were not created until 1997. The age of the oldest Roth IRAs is only a little more than ten years. Because the average working career lasts from 30 to 50 years, at least two decades must pass before economists can study exactly how tax-free earnings affect the growth of retirement savings.

Retirement in the United States

The concept of planned retirement developed in the United States during the 20th century. After the Dependent Pension Act of 1890 granted old-age pensions to all veterans over the age of 65 who had served in the Union army during the Civil War, the numbers of retired workers in the United States began to increase. Confederate states provided less generous pensions for Confederate veterans. Early in the 20th century, state and municipal governments began providing pensions for their employees, firefighters, and police officers. In 1916, 33 states offered pension for retired teachers; by 1934, 28 states provided support for the elderly indigent.

The American Express Company set up the first formal private pension plan in the United States in 1875. Railroads began offering pensions to employees who retired after 30 years of service, and other private companies saw pensions as a means of encouraging employee loyalty. Early pension plans were completely financed by employers and were either funded — meaning an investment account accumulated a balance from which employee payments were eventually drawn — or unfunded — meaning the company made guaranteed payments from cash they currently have. In a funded plan, balances were typically placed by pension fund managers in safe investments that produced a dependable return. These types of pension plans are also called "defined benefit plans" because they define a specific benefit for the employee at the occurrence of a specific life event such as retirement, disability, or death.

The 1926 Revenue Act further encouraged the establishment of pension plans by excluding income earned in pension trusts from taxation. Labor unions began organizing pay-as-you-go pension plans for workers in smaller companies that did not have retirement plans. These and other unfunded plans did not survive the Great Depression, but many independently funded private plans continued. The Social Security Act of 1935 extended benefits to those not covered by private pension plans. Even as social security expanded, private pension programs continued to grow. When wages were frozen during World War II, private pension plans became an incentive to attract workers in a tight labor market and a tax shelter from high wartime taxation rates. By 1960, 23 million people — nearly 30 percent of the nation's workers — were covered by private pension plans. In 1963, Keogh, or H.R.10, plans were established to allow self-employed individuals to save for retirement.

During the 1970s, many corporate entities realized that their pension plans would eventually become bankrupt and that they would be unable to provide retirement benefits. As average life expectancy increased, employers who chose to continue funding pension plans bore the risk that retired employees would outlive the funds allocated to them and the employer would have to make up the difference. The inability to quantify such a risk proved unacceptable to many businesses, and they began to look for ways to change the pension system. Congress began searching for solutions that would help businesses while protecting employees who had been promised a pension.

Over the last three decades, employers have attempted to eliminate the risk that a pension fund might perform poorly in the stock market and be inadequate for workers' needs by moving from defined benefit plans to defined contribution plans, in which the employer contributes a specified amount to a pension fund on behalf of an employee but does not guarantee the outcome. Plans such as the 401(k) — in which an employee makes tax-deductible contributions, sometimes with matching funds from the employer, and is given a selection of investments to choose from — are now popular.

Employee Retirement Income Security Act (ERISA)

In 1974, the Employee Retirement Income Security Act (ERISA) was enacted, requiring employers to follow funding requirements and to insure against unexpected events that could cause the insolvency of their pension plans. ERISA also introduced IRAs to encourage working individuals to save for their own retirements. A tax incentive allowed workers to reduce their taxable income by the amount they contributed to their IRAs, up to an annual limit. Workers could contribute whichever was less, $1,500 or 15 percent of their earned income. ERISA initially restricted IRAs to employees who were not covered by a qualified employer plan, including plans such as 401(k)s and 403(b)s. That provision was changed by the 1981 Economic Recovery Tax Act that permitted all working taxpayers under the age of 70 ½ to contribute to an IRA, regardless of their coverage under a qualified employer plan. It also raised the maximum annual contribution limits to the lesser of $2,000 or 100 percent of earned income.

Tax Reform Act of 1986

The Tax Reform Act of 1986, in a controversial move that some considered a setback for retirement funding, phased out the tax deduction for high-income wage earners who were covered by an employer retirement plan or had a spouse covered by an employer plan. The $2,000 annual contribution limit was retained for low-income wage earners, and those earning higher salaries were allowed to make non-deductible contributions.

Roth IRAs and Education IRAs

Roth IRAs were created by the Taxpayer Relief Act of 1997 (Public Law 105-34), allowing individuals to make non-deductible contributions to a retirement account and withdraw their earnings tax-free. Roth IRAs were named for Senator William Roth of Delaware, sponsor of the legislation, which was intended to encourage working Americans to save for their retirement and to add more flexibility to IRAs. By January 1999, over 7 million U.S. households had Roth IRAs.

The Taxpayer Relief Act also created Education IRAs, which allowed investors to save for qualified education expenses and raised the maximum income limit for which deductible contributions to IRAs were allowed. Different income limits were established for taxpayers covered by an employment-based plan, as well as taxpayers not covered by a company plan but whose spouses have a retirement plan through their employers.

Economic Growth and Tax Relief Reconciliation Act of 2001 (EGTRRA)

By 2000, it was clear that existing IRAs would be inadequate for the retirement needs of baby boomers. The Economic Growth and Tax Relief Reconciliation Act of 2001 (EGTRRA) made significant changes to the rules governing IRAs. Beginning in 2002, the limit on contributions was raised to $5,000. Workers ages 50 and older were allowed to make additional "catch-up" contributions of $1,000 per year to increase their account balances.

> ## *EGTRRA expired at the end of 2010*
>
> All of the provisions of EGTRRA expired December 31, 2010. Congress may once again make adjustments to IRAs. Current rules might only be enforced for a short time, so do not rely on them for long-term planning.

Tax Increase Prevention and Reconciliation Act of 2005 (TIPRA)

The Tax Increase Prevention and Reconciliation Act of 2005 (TIPRA: P.L. 109-222) eliminated the income limit for individuals converting a traditional IRA to a Roth IRA, which began in 2010. Those converting in 2010 will be given a one-time opportunity to stretch the payment of income tax on the conversion over two years, 2011 and 2012. Income limits for making contributions to a Roth IRA will remain in place. Congress expects individuals with high incomes who have accumulated large balances in traditional IRAs will opt to convert to Roths, bringing in a surge of revenue as deferred income taxes are paid.

Pension Protection Act of 2006 (PPA)

The Pension Protection Act of 2006, Section 824, allowed direct rollovers from eligible retirement plans to Roth IRAs. It also allowed a distribution from an eligible retirement plan of a deceased employee to be made directly to the IRA of a designated non-spouse beneficiary.

Roth IRAs and Traditional IRAs

IRAs are the U.S. government's method for motivating individuals to save for retirement and enabling them to save more. Technically, traditional IRAs allow a worker to invest more money during his or her working life by investing and profiting from funds that would otherwise have been paid as income tax. The government delays collecting the income tax until the individual reaches retirement age and the funds are withdrawn. Each year, an individual can contribute up to a certain amount — currently $5,000 — to one or more IRAs. If the individual's income does not exceed a specified limit, all of that amount can be subtracted from his or her income before calculating income tax for that year. People with higher incomes might be able to deduct part of their contributions. Anyone between the ages of 18 and 70 who has earned income can open a traditional IRA with a bank, credit union, or stock brokerage. Investing funds that would otherwise be paid as taxes for several decades allows an individual to accumulate more money for retirement. The federal government suffers no loss because it eventually collects the deferred income tax when the funds are withdrawn from the IRA.

Depending on the individual's tax bracket, the deferred income tax is 10 to 28 percent of the total amount being contributed. If you made the maximum 2009 contribution of $5,000 to a traditional IRA, you had $500 to $1,400 more to invest than if you had to pay income tax on that amount. According to a traditional IRA calculator created by KJE Computer Solutions (**www.dinkytown.net/java/RegularIRA.html**), if you are in the 15 percent income tax bracket and contribute $5,000 annually to a traditional IRA for a period of 20 years, at an assumed growth rate of 8 percent, then you would end up with $247,000 in your IRA account, compared to $210,000 in a taxable account. In reality, many factors affect the amount that accumulates in a tax-deferred account, including the amount that is contributed each year and the performance of investments held in the account.

Contributions to a Roth IRA are made after income tax has been paid on them. Unlike the earnings in a traditional IRA, which are taxed as regular income when they are distributed (taken out of the account), the earnings in a Roth IRA are tax-free income. Earnings are never taxed as long as the account has been in existence for more than five years and the owner is over 59½ years old when they are withdrawn; the withdrawal is made because of the death or disability of the owner; or $10,000 is withdrawn for the purchase of a first home. Originally, only individuals with lower earned incomes could contribute to Roth IRAs. In 2009, individuals with adjusted gross incomes (AGIs) greater than $169,000 could not contribute to a Roth IRA. Your AGI is the amount at the bottom of page 1 of your IRS Form 1040, U.S. Individual Tax Return.

Since the beginning of 2010, anyone could convert a traditional IRA or other qualified retirement plan to a Roth IRA, regardless of income, but the ability to contribute to a Roth IRA will still be subject to income limitations. After 2010, EGTRRA expired, and new contribution limits will be set for Roth IRAs.

Traditional and Roth IRAs are governed by many of the same rules and restrictions, such as annual contribution limits, the 59½ rule, penalties for early withdrawals and excess contributions, and exceptions. The most notable difference between traditional and Roth IRAs is the tax treatment they receive. Traditional IRAs allow you to defer income tax and invest a larger percentage of your income initially, but you pay income tax on both your contributions and your earnings when you take the money out. Contributions to a Roth IRA are taxed as income in the year the contribution is made, but all earnings can be withdrawn tax-free. *See Chapter 2 for more information on withdrawals.*

Traditional and Roth IRAs are designed as vehicles for retirement savings and not as tax shelters. The rules governing IRA contributions and withdrawals are intended to make them equitable and to prevent abuse. The primary purpose of an IRA is to provide retirement income during the lifetime of the owner, but IRS rules allow surviving spouses and heirs to continue receiving the tax benefits of IRAs for a limited period of time.

Anyone 18 or older who has earned income can contribute to a traditional or a Roth IRA. The owner of a traditional IRA must stop contributing in the year he or she becomes 70½ years old, then begin withdrawing a percentage of the money every year and paying income tax on it. The U.S. government does not want to defer the payment of income tax indefinitely, and it wants to ensure that income tax is paid on all the money in an IRA account within the owner's expected lifetime. If the owner of a traditional IRA dies before the account is depleted, his or her beneficiaries must continue withdrawing money and paying income tax on it. Because income tax has already been paid on contributions to a Roth account, the owner is not required to begin taking money out after reaching the age of 70½ and can continue making contributions as long as he or she is still earning income. When the owner of a Roth IRA dies, his or her beneficiaries do not have to pay income tax on the money when it is withdrawn.

Other Tax-advantaged Retirement Savings Plans

Tax-deferred retirement plans administered by employers existed before IRAs and share many of the same characteristics. The concept is the same: Invest now and pay income tax later. Income tax is deferred on contributions and earnings in a qualified retirement plan until the owner reaches the age of 70½, when he or she must begin to take annual distributions and pay taxes on them. There are several important differences in the regulations governing qualified retirement plans and IRAs, including higher contribution limits and stricter rules for distributions. Individual employers are required to comply with IRS guidelines but might place additional restrictions on their retirement plans, such as requiring that beneficiaries withdraw all funds within five years. In such cases, the retirement plan rules always take precedence over IRS regulations.

An individual can open an IRA with any bank or brokerage and select from a wide variety of investment options. Qualified retirement plans typically offer a narrower choice from a specific menu of mutual funds, sometimes supplemented with other investment opportunities.

Profit-sharing plans

The most common type of qualified retirement plan is the profit-sharing plan, in which employees are allowed to share in company profits and contribute some of those profits to their retirement savings. The term "profit sharing" refers to the structure of the plan. Company contributions to a profit-sharing plan are discretionary: The company can contribute to employee retirement plans even when it does not make a profit and is not required to make any contributions at all. Participants in a profit-sharing plan are permitted to take loans from their accounts, subject to plan rules.

The company must make contributions according to a set formula based on each employee's salary. Profit-sharing plans take several forms, including 401(k)s, stock ownership plans, and defined benefit plans.

401(k)s, solo 401(k)s, and Roth 401(k)s

Company 401(k)s and solo 401(k)s are qualified tax-deferred retirement plans that allow workers to make pre-tax contributions to an investment account. Income tax is deferred on the investment and earnings until they are withdrawn from the account. Strict restrictions are placed on withdrawals, including the same minimum age limit of 59½ for penalty-free withdrawals and required minimum distributions (RMDs) after the owner reaches age 70½. Employees pay income tax on their contributions to a Roth 401(k) plan, and qualified withdrawals are tax-free. Many companies offer matching contributions to 401(k)s or profit-sharing incentives to motivate employees to remain with the company longer. Participants in a 401(k) plan must select from among the investment options the plan provider offers. These plans typically offer a selection of mutual funds reflecting different investment styles, but in some cases, employees own company stock in their 401(k)s.

Solo 401(k) plans, established by the Economic Growth Tax Relief Reconciliation Act (EGTRRA) in 2002, are for self-employed individuals and owner-only businesses that have no full-time employees. An individual with sufficient income is allowed to make a substantial annual contribution to the solo 401(k) (a maximum of $49,000 in 2009, plus catch-up contributions for those over 50). If the business owner's spouse is the only full-time employee, the business still qualifies, and the spouse can also contribute a similar amount. A solo 401(k) participant has the freedom to select a custodian who will accommodate self-directed investments. *See Chapter 9 for more information on self-directed IRAs.*

The greatest benefit of 401(k) plans is that many employers match employees' contributions to up to 3 percent of their salaries. You can contribute to an IRA while contributing to a 401(k). When you leave the company or retire, you will be able to roll the 401(k) over into a new IRA or transfer the funds to an existing IRA.

IRC 403(b) and 457(b) plans

A 403(b) tax-sheltered annuity (TSA) plan is a retirement plan, similar to a 401(k) and offered by public schools and certain tax-exempt organizations. An individual 403(b) annuity can be obtained only under an employer's TSA plan. Typically, these annuities are funded by employer contributions and by employees voluntarily setting aside a percentage of their salaries.

IRC 457(b) Deferred Compensation Plans are available for certain state and local governments and nongovernmental entities that are tax-exempt under IRC 501. They can be either eligible plans under IRC 457(b) or ineligible plans under IRC 457(f). Eligible 457(b) plans allow employees of sponsoring organizations to defer income taxation on retirement savings, like 401(k) plans. Ineligible plans might trigger different tax treatment under IRC 457(f).

Stock bonus plans

A stock bonus plan is a defined-benefit plan in which distributions are made to employees in the form of company stock. Its structure and requirements are similar to a profit-sharing plan. A stock bonus plan rewards employees for their loyalty and their efforts on behalf of the company, as the value of the stock rises when the business is successful.

Money purchase pension plans

Under a money purchase pension plan, an employer makes a mandatory annual contribution to each employee's account. The contribution is typically a stated percentage of each employee's annual compensation. An employer cannot contribute more than 25 percent of the total combined compensation of all the employees. In making this calculation, the compensation for employees who receive high salaries is capped at $255,000. The maximum that can be contributed to each employee's account annually is $49,000 (for 2009), and the contribution cannot exceed the employee's annual salary. The contribution limits are adjusted from time to time to allow for inflation. The amount an employee receives as retirement income will depend on how much was contributed to his or her individual account and the performance of investments in the account.

Employee stock ownership plans (ESOPs)

An employee stock ownership plan (ESOP) is required by law to invest primarily in the employer's stock, effectively making employees into company shareholders. ESOPs are often used to buy out a retiring owner's interest in a company or as an additional employee incentive. Unlike other qualified employee benefit plans, ESOPs can borrow money to leverage their investing power. Depending on plan rules, an employee might be required to work for the company for several years before he or she is fully vested. Employees can receive cash distributions from an ESOP, as long as they have the right to receive company stock if they wish.

Defined benefit plans

Defined benefit plans promise employees a specific annual payment after they retire. The payment is typically based on the number of years the employee worked for the company and his or her level of compensation before retirement. Companies must determine each year how much they need to contribute to meet their obligations to employees. Defined benefit plans are the oldest type of retirement plan but have been dropped by many in favor of plans that make employees responsible for their own retirement accounts.

Target benefit plans

A target benefit plan is similar to a money purchase pension plan, except that instead of annually contributing a fixed percentage of an employee's income to an individual account, the company determines what annual contribution is needed to achieve an estimated target amount at retirement. Once the annual contribution has been determined for the first year, it does not change. Whether the account reaches its target, exceeds it, or falls short depends on the performance of the investments in the account.

Keogh plans

Sometimes called HR10 plans, Keogh plans are named for U.S. Representative Eugene James Keogh of New York, who authored the bill establishing them in 1962. They are qualified retirement plans for self-employed individuals that resemble the various company retirement plans described previously. Contribution limits are the same as for other qualified retirement plans, but in calculating the annual contribution, the individual's income is adjusted to account for the fact that a self-employed person must pay the individual and the employer's portion of the Federal Insurance Contributions Act (FICA) tax that pays for social security and Medicare.

IRAs and 401(k)s

IRAs, 401(k), 403(b), and 457(b) plans receive similar tax treatment, but there are some differences. An individual can set up an IRA with a bank, brokerage firm, or financial institution of his or her choice. Participants in an employer-sponsored plan, such as a 401(k), must select from the investments offered by the financial institution administering the plan. They must also pay the management fees of the 401(k) administrator. Critics claim that administrative costs and high management fees charged by the mutual funds sold by 401(k) custodians eat into earnings and cripple the growth of retirement savings. A few employer plans contribute to individual IRAs for each employee. Some companies contribute to IRAs that employees set up themselves, but many employers prefer to contribute to IRAs that are all held by the same custodian.

IRAs offer more flexibility than 401(k) plans, including the freedom to withdraw funds whenever you want (and pay the 10 percent penalty if you are younger than 59½). The penalty is not charged if the funds withdrawn are used for certain purposes. Company retirement plans have stricter rules regarding withdrawals and often require the participant to provide proof of financial hardship. Company retirement plans observe the same restrictions as IRAs, but they are not obligated to offer all the options available for individual IRAs. They might impose restrictions on how and when funds are paid out to your beneficiaries and might make it impossible for you to extend the tax benefits of your retirement account to your heirs after you die. They might also follow a protocol for designating your beneficiary if you have not named one. The annual contribution limits for company retirement plans are higher than for IRAs and are based on your annual salary. If you include an employer's matching contributions, you can set aside more in a tax-deferred company retirement plan than in an IRA. You may borrow from an employer-sponsored retirement account, subject to the retirement plan rules, and might be given as long as five years to pay back the loan, with interest. You cannot borrow from an IRA. Any withdrawal not rolled over into another IRA within 60 days is treated as a distribution and taxed.

Comparison of tax-advantaged retirement plans

Plan	Sponsor	Tax Treatment	Who Makes Contributions	Contribution Limits in 2009	Can Borrow From Account	RMD After Age 70½	Beneficiaries Can Extend Tax Deferral
Traditional IRA	Individual	Income tax is deferred on contributions and earnings until money is withdrawn	Individual	$5,000; $6,000 if you are over 50	No	Yes	Yes
Roth IRA	Individual	Income tax is paid on contributions; earnings are withdrawn tax-free	Individual	$5,000; $6,000 if you are over 50	No, but contributions can be withdrawn at any time	No	Yes
SIMPLE	Small business with fewer than 100 employees with $5,000 or more in compensation for the preceding year	Same as traditional IRA; employer contributions are tax-deductible	Company	Employee: 100% of compensation up to $11,500 in 2009. Employer: Additional $11,500 maximum per year based on a 100% matching contribution capped at 3%; if you are age 50 or older, you might be eligible for a catch-up contribution of $2,500	No	Yes	Yes
SEP IRA	Business or self-employed individual	Same as traditional IRA; employer contributions are tax-deductible	Company and/or individual	Employer: 0-25% of compensation up to $49,000 for each eligible employee in 2009	No	Yes	Yes
401(k)	Employer	Income tax is deferred on contributions and earnings until money is withdrawn	Company and/or individual	Employee: $16,500; $22,000 if you are over 50 Employer: Up to 6% of employee's salary	Yes	Yes	Depends on plan administrator
Roth 401(k)	Employer	Income tax is deferred on contributions and earnings until money is withdrawn	Company and/or individual	Employee: $16,500; $22,000 if you are over 50 Employer: Up to 6% of employee's salary	Yes	Yes	Depends on plan administrator

Plan	Who can establish	Tax treatment	Established by	Contribution limits			
Solo 401(k)	Self-employed	Income tax is deferred on contributions and earnings until money is withdrawn	Company and/or individual	**Employee/owner:** $16,500; $22,000 if you are over 50; **Employer:** Up to 6% of employee's salary	Yes	Yes	Depends on plan administrator
RC 457(b) Deferred Compensation Plan	State and local governments and non-governmental entities that are tax exempt under IRC 501	Income tax is deferred on contributions and earnings until money is withdrawn	Company and/or individual	$16,500; $22,000 if you are over 50, plus employer match	Yes	Yes	Depends on plan administrator
403(b) Tax-sheltered Annuity (TSA)	Public schools, certain tax-exempt organizations, and ministers	Income tax is deferred on contributions and earnings until money is withdrawn	Company and/or individual	**Employee:** 100% of includible compensation up to $16,500 in 2009. If you are age 50 or older, you might be eligible for a catch-up contribution of $5,500	Yes	Yes	Depends on plan administrator
Stock Bonus Plan	Employer	Depends on how the plan is set up	Company	The lesser of 25% of an employee's compensation or $49,000 in 2009	Depends on plan rules	Yes	Depends on plan administrator
Money Purchase Pension Plan	Employer	Income tax is deferred on contributions and earnings until money is withdrawn	Company	The lesser of 25% of an employee's compensation or $49,000 in 2009	Depends on plan rules	Yes	Depends on plan administrator
Employee Stock Ownership Plan (ESOP)	Employer	Income tax is deferred on contributions and earnings until money is withdrawn	Company	The lesser of 25% of an employee's compensation or $49,000 in 2009	Depends on plan rules	Yes	Depends on plan administrator
Defined Benefit Plan	Employer	Income tax is deferred on contributions and earnings until money is withdrawn.	Company	The lesser of 25% of an employee's compensation or $49,000 in 2009	Depends on plan rules	Yes	Depends on plan administrator
Target Benefit Plan (Defined Contribution Plan)	Employer	Income tax is deferred on contributions and earnings until money is withdrawn.	Company	The lesser of 25% of an employee's compensation or $49,000 in 2009	Depends on plan rules	Yes	Depends on plan administrator
Keogh Plan	Self-employed individuals	Income tax is deferred on contributions and earnings until money is withdrawn	Individual/business	Depends on the type of plan	Sometimes	Yes	Depends on plan administrator

Why Should You Have a Roth?

The idea of making a tax-deductible contribution to a retirement savings account is attractive. As the deadline for filing tax returns approaches, many people make a last-minute contribution to a traditional IRA to lower their taxable income. Unless you expect to be in a lower tax bracket when you retire, though, Roth IRAs offer several advantages over traditional IRAs.

Tax-free earnings

All earnings in a traditional IRA will eventually be taxed as income. Traditional IRAs and 401(k) plans have the effect of converting capital gains into income when you take the money out. If your tax bracket when you withdraw funds from an IRA account is higher than 15 percent, you could end up paying more tax on earnings in your traditional IRA than the capital gains tax on profits from the sale of assets in a taxable investment account. All earnings in a Roth IRA are tax-free. The longer investments in a Roth portfolio are allowed to grow and compound, the greater the tax-free benefit. A Roth is the only type of investment savings account that allows you to retain 100 percent of your earnings.

More time to grow and compound

As soon as you reach the age of 70½, you must stop making contributions and begin taking a required minimum distribution (RMD) every year from a traditional IRA. This means that you must take out earnings or sell assets each year, steadily depleting the account. There is no RMD for a Roth IRA. You can leave your money in a Roth to grow untouched until you need it. If you have other sources of retirement income, your Roth can become a vehicle for increasing your wealth. If you or your spouse is still working in your 70s, you can continue to contribute to a Roth IRA until you retire.

A Roth versus traditional IRA calculator such as the one on Banksite.com (**www.banksite.com/calc/rothira**) illustrates the consequences of rolling over a traditional IRA to a Roth, based on your age, annual contributions, and your ability to pay income tax on the rollover with outside funds.

Tax-free income

You do not pay income tax on amounts withdrawn from your Roth IRA account. When you make a withdrawal from a traditional IRA, it becomes taxable income, so you must subtract the income tax to determine the amount available for your use. Because you have already paid income tax on your Roth contributions, and its earnings are not taxed after you reach the age of 59½, your withdrawals are not part of your taxable income. You will not be bumped into a higher income tax bracket if you make a large withdrawal to pay for a retirement home or a car.

Your beneficiaries do not have to pay income tax

Beneficiaries must pay income tax on the distributions they receive from a traditional IRA, according to their own income tax brackets. Beneficiaries of a Roth IRA do not have to pay income tax on the money they receive. A surviving spouse, who receives less favorable tax treatment as a single individual than as married filing jointly, will not have any tax obligations from a Roth IRA.

A Roth account can be used as an emergency fund

Contributions (but not earnings) to a Roth account can be withdrawn at any time with paying income tax or early withdrawal penalties. Earnings are subject to early withdrawal penalties if they are taken out of the account before you reach the age of 59½. You should leave your retirement account to compound and grow untouched, but if you have an emergency, you can always have access to your Roth IRA contributions. A Roth can be used as a back-up savings plan for a home purchase or education expenses.

Roth 401(k)s and 403(b)s

In 1978, the U.S. government enacted legislation creating 401(k) plans that allowed employees to make tax-deductible contributions to individual retirement plans administered by their employers and defer paying income tax until after retirement. By 2006, approximately 58.4 million Americans participated in 466,000 401(k) plans. Public schools, tax-exempt organizations (section 501(c)(3) organizations) and certain ministers can establish similar plans called 403(b)s. The Economic Growth and Tax Relief Reconciliation Act of 2001 added a Roth option to 401(k) and 403(b) plans, beginning in 2006. It is up to the employer whether to include this option in its retirement savings plan, and the option must be included in the plan description. The employer deposits an employee's after-tax contributions into a designated Roth account (known as a "deemed account") and includes those amounts in the employee's gross income, subject to all applicable wage-withholding requirements. A 401(k) or 403(b) plan must offer traditional pre-tax elective contributions along with the Roth option. An employer can match contributions to a Roth 401(k) or 403(b), but these matching funds must be deposited in a pre-tax account because they are not part of the employee's gross income, and the employer is receiving a tax deduction for those amounts.

There are no income limits for making contributions to a Roth 401(k) or 403(b); all employees who participate in the company's retirement plan are eligible. Designated contributions to a Roth 401(k) or 403(b) are irrevocable. Employees must be given the opportunity to elect the Roth option at least once a year, and no contributions can be deposited in a designated Roth account until the election has been made. Employees can contribute to both a designated Roth account and a traditional, pre-tax account in the same year, in any proportion they choose. The law does not allow designated Roth contributions in SARSEP or SIMPLE IRA plans.

The combined amount that can be contributed to all designated Roth and traditional, pre-tax 401(k) or 403(b) accounts in any one year for any individual is limited under Code §402(g). If you were under 50 years of age at the end of 2010, the maximum contribution that you can make to a traditional or Roth IRA is the smaller of $5,000 or the amount of your taxable compensation for 2010. This limit can be split between a traditional and a Roth IRA but the combined limit is $5,000. The maximum contribution to a Roth IRA and the maximum deductible contribution to a traditional IRA may be reduced depending upon your modified adjusted gross income (modified AGI).

If you are 50 years of age or older before 2011, the maximum contribution that can be made to a traditional or Roth IRA is the smaller of $6,000 or the amount of your taxable compensation for 2010. This limit can be split between a traditional and a Roth IRA but the combined limit is $6,000. The maximum contribution to a Roth IRA and the maximum deductible contribution to a traditional IRA may be reduced depending upon your modified AGI.

When an employee leaves a company where he or she has a Roth 401(k) or 403(b) plan, the balance in the account can be rolled over directly into another Roth plan with a new employer, or it can be deposited in an individual Roth IRA within 60 days of distribution.

Roth Rules

The defining characteristic of IRAs is their tax status. The benefits of both traditional and Roth IRAs are derived from the way the IRS treats contributions, earnings from investments held in the accounts, and distributions. IRA rules have been carefully thought out to cover almost every eventuality, but they are complex and unfamiliar to many ordinary investors. However, some knowledge of IRS rules is essential if you want to gain the most from your Roth IRA. You might not understand the consequences of your actions until you are filling out your tax return at the end of the year or until you break one of the rules. The penalty for an early withdrawal or an excess contribution could impose a sudden and unexpected tax burden on a Roth IRA owner. A prohibited transaction might bring about the sudden end of your Roth IRA, causing the entire balance to be disbursed and all the earnings taxed. A simple mistake such as failing to name a beneficiary can derail the plans you made for your estate.

The rules governing IRAs can be found in IRS Publication 590: Individual Retirement Arrangements (**www.irs.gov/pub/irs-pdf/p590.pdf**) and its associated worksheets and schedules. The rest of this chapter contains a summary of these rules. In addition, there are numerous private letter rulings (PLRs), issued by the IRS in response to specific taxpayer queries, that set precedents for the treatment of complicated situations involving IRAs. Only an experienced tax accountant or IRA advisor will be aware of all the specialized IRS rulings on particular taxpayer situations. Most people have a straightforward and simple IRA administered by a financial institution or brokerage house that ensures compliance with IRS rules. If your IRA situation is complex, seek professional assistance.

See Chapters 10 and 11 for more information about the role of the Roth IRA in estate planning and your options when you inherit an IRA.

IRA tax rules change frequently.

The rules governing IRAs change frequently, sometimes from year to year. You will learn about these changes at tax time, but knowing about them in advance might affect other financial decisions you make during the year. Look for news and information on the IRS Web site, **www.irs.gov**.

Contributions

Who can contribute to a Roth IRA?

Under the current rules, only a person 18 or older who is working and whose annual earned income is under a certain amount, or the nonworking spouse of such a person, can contribute to a Roth IRA.

- You (or your spouse) must have earned income (taxable compensation) to contribute to a Roth IRA. Earned income includes wages, salaries and commissions, income earned from self-employment, nontaxable combat pay, alimony, and separate maintenance payments. Earned income does not include income from rental properties, interest and dividends from investments, income from pensions or annuities, deferred compensation earned in a previous year, foreign-earned income and housing subsidies, or income from a partnership in which you do not actively participate. There is no age limit; you can continue making contributions to a Roth IRA after you reach the age of 70½ as long as you or your spouse continue to have earned income. You cannot contribute more than your earned income for the year.

- You cannot contribute anything to a Roth IRA if your modified adjusted gross income (AGI) exceeds a certain limit. The following chart shows the income limits for 2009. Those in the lowest income brackets can make the full contribution each year; reduced contributions are allowed for those in intermediate income brackets.

In 2010, income limits were phased out for conversions from traditional IRAs, 401(k)s, and other qualified retirement plans to Roth IRAs.

Those in higher income brackets will be able to roll over high balances from traditional IRAs or retirement accounts into a Roth IRA. For 2010 only, income taxes on the rollover can be spread over two years, 2011 and 2012. After that, income tax must be paid in full the year the conversion is made. Once the conversion to a Roth IRA has been made, all future earnings can be withdrawn tax-free after a five-year holding period. Income restrictions will remain in place for contributions to Roth IRAs.

How much can you contribute?

The IRS limits how much you can contribute to an IRA in one year. The contribution limit is intended to prevent IRAs from being used as tax shelters to amass personal wealth. Contribution limits reflect what government economists consider to be a reasonable annual investment that will produce an adequate retirement nest egg for the average American. For years, the contribution limit for IRAs stayed at $3,000 per year. The Economic Growth and Tax Relief Reconciliation Act of 2001 (EGTRRA) changed the rules and, beginning in 2002, the maximum limit on contributions to all types of IRAs was raised to $5,000 per year.

An IRA is an individual account; the contribution limit for individual IRAs does not apply to contributions you make to a qualified retirement plan through your employer. You can contribute the maximum amounts to both an IRA and an employer plan in the same year, as long as you have enough earned income to cover your contributions.

The amount you can contribute to a Roth IRA might be limited by your annual income

Roth IRAs were created as incentives to encourage working-class families to save for retirement. Income limits were imposed to restrict high wage earners from participation. If your annual earned income exceeds a certain amount, you might not be able to make the full annual contribution to a Roth IRA.

Detailed instructions for figuring your modified AGI and calculating your contribution limit for a Roth IRA can be found in IRS Publication 590, Roth IRAs (**www.irs.gov/publications/p590/ch02. html#en_US_publink10006503**).

2009 contribution limits for Roth IRAs based on income

Income Tax Filing Status	Modified AGI in 2009	Contribution Limit in 2009
Married filing jointly or qualifying widow(er)	Less than $159,000	You can contribute up to $5,000 ($6,000 if you are age 50 or older).
	At least $159,000 but less than $169,000	The amount you can contribute to a Roth IRA is reduced. Use Worksheet 2-2 in IRS Publication 590 to determine your reduced Roth IRA contribution limit.
	$169,000 or more	You cannot contribute to a Roth IRA.
Married filing separately and you lived with your spouse at any time during the year	Zero (-0-)	You can contribute up to $5,000 ($6,000 if you are age 50 or older).
	More than zero (-0-) but less than $10,000	The amount you can contribute to a Roth IRA is reduced. Use Worksheet 2-2 in IRS Publication 590 to determine your reduced Roth IRA contribution limit.
	$10,000 or more	You cannot contribute to a Roth IRA.
Single, head of household, or married filing separately and you did not live with your spouse at any time during the year	Less than $101,000	You can contribute up to $5,000 ($6,000 if you are age 50 or older).
	At least $101,000 but less than $116,000	The amount you can contribute to a Roth IRA is reduced. Use Worksheet 2-2 in IRS Publication 590 to determine your reduced Roth IRA contribution limit.
	$116,000 or more	You cannot contribute to a Roth IRA.

Contribution and income limits might change from year to year.

Contribution and income limits are frequently adjusted for inflation, so it is important to review the IRS rules for retirement accounts every year.

Catch-up contributions

EGTRRA allowed workers over 50 to make an additional annual "catch-up" contribution of $1,000 because they are approaching retirement age and need to save as much as possible in a short time. Catch-up contributions are also permitted in special circumstances; for example, if you had a 401(k) with an employer who went into bankruptcy, and the employer had matched at least 50 percent of your contributions with company stock, you are allowed to contribute $3,000 extra to an IRA in a later year to compensate for your losses. Rules such as these might be changed if it is perceived that IRAs are not accumulating enough money to meet their owner's retirement needs.

Contributions cannot exceed your earned income

Combined annual contributions to all your IRAs cannot exceed your annual earned income. If your earned income is less than $5,000, you can only contribute an amount equal to your income for that year.

Contribution limit applies to all IRAs combined

If you have more than one IRA account, the contribution limit applies to the total amount contributed to all the accounts combined, not to each individual IRA. Total annual contributions by an individual to all types of IRAs, including Roth IRAs, cannot exceed the annual contribution limit ($5,000 in 2009). Workers older than 50 are allowed to make the additional catch-up contribution ($1,000 in 2009) every year.

Spouses cannot share a Roth IRA

Spouses cannot share an IRA. Each one is entitled to open an individual Roth IRA and contribute up to the maximum annual limit, even if only one spouse has earned income. In 2009, a married couple with an AGI of less than $159,000 was allowed to contribute a total of $10,000 to their Roth IRAs, or as much as $12,000 if both were 50 or older. The total contribution cannot exceed the couple's combined income.

Contribution deadlines

Contributions to an IRA can be made at any time before April 15 of the following year when income tax returns are due. Once the deadline has passed, you cannot contribute any more for that year.

Tell your IRA sponsor which year your contribution applies to.

If you make a contribution between January 1 and April 15 for the previous year, you must tell the IRA sponsor which year it is intended for; otherwise, it will be treated by the IRS as a contribution for the current year.

Income tax refunds

You can have your income tax refund, or a portion of it, deposited directly into your IRA as part of your annual contribution. If you want all your refund deposited directly into your Roth IRA, indicate this on the appropriate line of IRS Form 1040. On the IRS Form 8888: Direct Deposit of Refund to More Than One Account, you can divide your refund among up to three different accounts. Check Box 3, "Savings," for the IRA account.

Your tax refund must be deposited in your Roth IRA by April 15.

Your tax refund must be deposited into your Roth IRA by April 15 if you want to include it as part of the previous year's IRA contribution and claim it as an income tax deduction. There are no extensions. If the deposit is not made by that date, it will count as an IRA contribution for the next year. File your income taxes several weeks before the deadline so you can claim the deduction.

Penalty for exceeding contribution limits

If you contribute more than the annual limit to your Roth IRA and do not withdraw the excess amount from your account — plus any interest or earnings from that amount — before the date your tax return is due (including extensions) the following year, you must pay a 6 percent tax on the excess and earnings each year the excess amount remains in your IRA. You can apply the excess contribution to a later year as long as you do not go over the contribution limit for that year.

Repayments are allowed for certain withdrawals

You can withdraw contributions from a Roth IRA at any time if you need money for an emergency, but under ordinary circumstances you cannot return that money to the account. There are exceptions for reservist, qualified hurricane, qualified disaster recovery assistance, and qualified recovery assistance distributions. These can be repaid even if the repayments would cause your total contributions to the Roth IRA to be more than the general limit on contributions.

Reservist repayment is treated as part of the contributions to a Roth IRA.

Qualified reservist distributions that are repaid to a Roth IRA are treated as part of the contributions, which means they can be withdrawn without penalty at any time after the account is five years old. Repayments of qualified hurricane, qualified disaster recovery assistance, or qualified recovery assistance distributions to a Roth IRA are first considered to be a repayment of earnings, which cannot be withdrawn until after you reach the age of 59½. Only the amount of the repayment in excess of earnings is treated as a contribution.

If you contribute to a Roth 401(k) or 403(b) through your employer

If you make contributions to an employer-sponsored Roth 401(k) or 403(b) plan and you meet the income requirements, you can still contribute to an individual Roth IRA. If your income was less than $159,000 in 2009, you would have been able to contribute $5,000 to a Roth IRA ($6,000 if you were older than 50). If your income was more than $159,000, your contribution to a Roth would have been smaller, but you could have made an additional contribution to a traditional IRA to make up the $5,000.

Retirement savings contributions credit

You might be eligible for an additional tax credit, the retirement savings contributions credit, when you make contributions to an employer-sponsored retirement plan or an IRA. In 2009, if you were married filing jointly and your AGI was less than $55,000, you would have been eligible to take a tax credit equal to a percentage of your contribution to an IRA or retirement plan. The following chart shows how much you would have been able to deduct:

Retirement savings contribution tax credit for 2009

If your income is over	But under	And you are married, filing jointly	Head of house-hold	Single, married filing separately, or qualifying widower
$16,500	$18,000	50%	50%	20%
$18,000	$24,750	50%	50%	10%
$24,750	$27,000	50%	20%	10%
$27,000	$27,750	50%	10%	10%
$27,750	$33,000	50%	10%	0%
$33,000	$36,000	20%	10%	0%
$36,000	$14,625	10%	10%	0%
$41,625	$55,500	10%	0%	0%

The amount of the tax credit is calculated using IRS Form 8880, Credit for Qualified Retirement Savings Contributions, and entered on IRS Form 1040 or 1040A.

Withdrawals

Contributions can be withdrawn any time without penalty

A Roth IRA consists of two portions: the contributions you make to the account and the earnings from the stocks, bonds, funds, and other investments held in the account. Because income tax has already been paid on the contributions to a Roth IRA, they can be withdrawn at any time without penalty, even a few days after they were made. Earnings are not withdrawn from a Roth IRA until after all the contributions have been distributed.

No required minimum distribution

Owners of traditional IRAs must begin taking a RMD the year they turn 70½. There is no RMD for Roth IRAs. The IRS has no incentive to force withdrawals from a Roth IRA so that it can collect deferred taxes, as it does with traditional IRAs. Income tax has already been paid on contributions to a Roth IRA, and earnings can be withdrawn tax-free once all requirements are met. A Roth IRA owner who has other retirement income can leave the assets in the Roth untouched, continuing to increase until his or her death, when it passes to a beneficiary or an heir.

You cannot withdraw funds from a Roth IRA to satisfy the RMD for another traditional IRA that you own.

If you own multiple traditional IRAs, you can withdraw funds from one of them to satisfy the combined RMD for all of them. However, a distribution from a Roth IRA does not satisfy the RMD for a traditional IRA.

Earnings are subject to the 59½ rule

If you are younger than 59½ in the year you take a distribution of the earnings from your Roth IRA, you will be charged a 10 percent tax penalty in addition to ordinary income tax on the amount withdrawn. The 10 percent penalty on early withdrawals from an IRA is calculated and reported on IRS Form 5329. The penalty is intended to reverse the tax benefits of the IRA when it is not used for retirement savings.

The 10 percent penalty ensures a substantial loss.

The 10 percent penalty imposed on early withdrawals of earnings from a Roth IRA mirrors the penalty charged by banks for the early withdrawal of CDs or the closure of savings accounts. Unless the investments in your Roth IRA have been performing unusually well for a period of time, the 10 percent penalty effectively guarantees that you will lose all earnings and interest on your contribution and probably some of your principal as well.

Qualified distributions are not taxed

The earnings from investments in your Roth IRA will not be taxed when you withdraw them as long as they are qualified distributions. To take a qualified distribution, you must have held the Roth IRA for at least five years and have one of the qualifying characteristics: older than 59½, officially disabled, or withdrawing up to $10,000 for the purchase of a first home. The five-year holding period begins on January 1 of the first year for which you make a contribution to a Roth. If you make a contribution for the previous year just before the tax filing deadline on April 15, that previous year counts as the first year.

The earnings part of nonqualified distributions might be subject to taxation

A nonqualified distribution is a withdrawal from a Roth IRA made before you reach the age of 59½ or before the completion of the five-year holding period that begins on January 1 of the year you make your first contribution. Your contributions are never taxed when you take a distribution from the account, but any earnings that are part of a nonqualified withdrawal are taxed as regular income. A worksheet for calculating the taxable portion of a distribution from a Roth IRA can be found in IRS Publication 590, Roth IRAs, "How Do You Figure the Taxable Part?" (**www.irs.gov/publications/p590/ch02.html#en_US_publink10006526**).

Nonqualified withdrawals of contributions from a conversion or rollover might be subject to an additional 10 percent tax.

Portions of a nonqualified withdrawal that are part of a conversion from a traditional IRA or a rollover from a qualified retirement plan are subject to the same 10 percent additional tax as early distributions from these plans. The 59½ rule applies to any contributions that came from a tax-deferred plan.

Exceptions to the 59½ rule

There are several circumstances in which the 10 percent penalty for early withdrawal of earnings from a Roth IRA is waived. Amounts used for these purposes should be reported on line 2 of IRS Form 5329.

- **You have unreimbursed medical expenses that are more than 7.5 percent of your AGI.**

  You do not have to pay the 10 percent penalty on a withdrawal of earnings equal to the amount by which medical expenses — paid for yourself, your spouse, or a dependent out of your own pocket during that year — exceed 7.5 percent of your AGI. You can only count the medical expenses that are accepted as itemized deductions for medical expenses on Schedule A, Form 1040 when using money from your Roth IRA earnings. You do not have to itemize your deductions to take advantage of this exception to the 10 percent additional tax. Your AGI is the amount on Form 1040, line 38; Form 1040A, line 22; or Form 1040NR, line 36.

- **You are unemployed and paid for medical insurance for yourself, your spouse, and your dependents.**

If you lost your job and received unemployment compensation paid under any federal or state law for 12 consecutive weeks, you do not have to pay the 10 percent tax on an earnings withdrawal equal to the amount you paid for health insurance for yourself, your spouse, and your dependents that year. The withdrawal must be made either during the year you received the unemployment compensation or the following year, and no later than 60 days after you have been reemployed.

- **You are disabled.**

If you become disabled before you reach age 59½, any distributions of earnings from your Roth IRA are not subject to the 10 percent penalty. To be considered disabled, you must furnish proof that you cannot do any substantial gainful activity because of your physical or mental condition. You will need a statement from a physician confirming that your condition can be expected to result in death or to be of long, continued, and indefinite duration.

- **You are the beneficiary of a deceased IRA owner.**

If the owner of a Roth IRA dies before reaching the age of 59½, his or her beneficiary or estate does not have to pay the 10 percent penalty on distributions from the IRA. The spouse of a deceased Roth IRA owner who elects to take over the IRA as his or her own IRA will become subject to the 10 percent penalty for any earnings withdrawals made before he or she reaches the age of 59½.

- **You are receiving distributions from your Roth IRA as part of a series of equal annual payments (SEPP).**

If you retire early or are in financial need, you can make an arrangement with the IRS to take a series of equal annual distributions from your Roth IRA over your life expectancy or the joint life expectancy of you and your sole spouse beneficiary before you reach the age of 59½. The amount to be distributed is calculated using an IRS-approved distribution method and must be taken every year until your reach the age of 59½, or for five years, whichever occurs last. This arrangement is known as a series of substantially equal periodic payments (SEPP). Under a SEPP, you would avoid the 10 percent penalty on early withdrawals of earnings from your Roth IRA, but you would still pay income tax on them. Because you can withdraw contributions from a Roth at any time without penalty or tax, and because contributions are distributed before earnings, SEPPs are rarely used for Roth IRAs.

- **You paid for qualified higher education expenses during the year of the withdrawal.**

You do not have to pay the 10 percent penalty on an equivalent distribution of earnings from your Roth IRA if you paid for qualified higher education expenses during the year for you, your spouse, or the children or grandchildren of you or your spouse using funds earned from income, a gift, a loan, an inheritance given to you or the student, or money withdrawn from your personal savings, including qualified education savings accounts.

You cannot include expenses paid with Pell grants, tax-free portions of scholarships or fellowships, tuition benefits from your employer, veteran's education benefits, tax-free distributions from a Coverdell education savings, or any other tax-free payment.

Qualified higher education expenses are defined by the IRS in Section 72(t)(7) of the Tax Code as "tuition, fees, books, supplies, and equipment required for the enrollment or attendance of a student at an eligible educational institution." Room and board are also qualified higher education expenses for students enrolled in classes at least part-time; that amount is determined by the school and is the cost of living in on-campus housing at that school. Books, supplies, and equipment include only those required for all the students in a particular class, such as a set of dental implements, and not those purchased for individual needs, such as stationery, reference books, and art supplies.

- **You used up to $10,000 from your Roth IRA earnings to buy, build, or rebuild a first home for yourself or an immediate family member.**

You can withdraw up to $10,000 of your Roth IRA earnings free of the 10 percent penalty to pay for the costs of buying, building, or rebuilding a home, and any usual or reasonable settlement, financing, or other closing costs. The home can be for you; your spouse; or the parents, other ancestors, children, or grandchildren of you or your spouse. The funds must be used to pay qualified acquisition costs before the close of the 120th day after the day you received the distribution.

The total amount of your qualified first-time home distributions from your IRA cannot exceed $10,000. If both you and your spouse are first-time home buyers, you are each entitled to withdraw up to $10,000.

IRS Publication 590 defines a first-time home buyer as "a person who has had no present interest in a main home during the two-year period ending on the date of acquisition of the home which the distribution is being used to buy, build, or rebuild." If you are married, your spouse must also meet this no-ownership requirement.

The date of acquisition is "the date on which you enter a binding contract to buy a home or the date on which building or rebuilding of the home begins."

- **The distribution is due to an IRS levy of the qualified plan.**

If the IRS taps your IRA to collect unpaid taxes, the withdrawal is not subject to the 10 percent penalty.

- **You were a qualified reservist between 2001 and 2008.**

The IRS recognizes that people called to active duty in the reserve forces might need to tap into their retirement savings to cover certain expenses such as mortgage or loan payments because they have temporarily left their usual employment. The qualified reservist exception allows people called to active duty in the reserve forces to withdraw funds from their IRAs or 401(k)s without the 10 percent penalty.

You are a qualified reservist if you were in the Army National Guard of the United States, Army Reserve, Naval Reserve, Marine Corps Reserve, Air National Guard of the United States, Air Force Reserve, Coast Guard Reserve, or Reserve Corps of the Public Health Service, and you were called to active duty after September 11, 2001, for a period of 180 days or more. The distribution must have been made no earlier than the date of the order or call to active duty and no later than the close of the active duty period. After the end of the active duty period, qualified reservists are allowed to make a catch-up contribution to an IRA equal to the amount that they withdrew during active duty.

- **You transferred funds out of your Roth IRA as part of a divorce settlement.**

You do not have to pay the 10 percent penalty on earnings transferred out of your IRA as a result of a court-ordered divorce settlement.

- **You withdrew excess contributions to your Roth IRA before the tax deadline.**

You do not have to pay the 10 percent penalty on excess contributions and associated earnings withdrawn from your Roth IRA before the date your tax return is due (including extensions) the following year.

- **You rolled a distribution from your IRA over to another IRA.**

When you withdraw money from your Roth IRA, you have 60 days to roll over that money into another Roth IRA. If you are younger than 59½, then once the 60 days have passed, you will be required to pay the 10 percent penalty, and you cannot put the money you took out into another Roth IRA.

> *There is no personal hardship exception to the 10 percent penalty.*
>
> Though there are several situations in which the 10 percent penalty on early withdrawals of earnings will be waived, personal or economic hardship is not one of them. If you withdraw the funds because you need money during a period of economic hardship and you are younger than 59½ years old, you must pay the penalty.

Early withdrawals from Roth IRAs

The attraction of a Roth IRA is that earnings can accumulate and be withdrawn tax-free. However, this tax benefit applies only to qualified distributions. A qualified distribution is one made on or after the date you become age 59½, made to your beneficiary or your estate after you die, made to you after you become disabled according to IRS definitions, or subject to one of the exceptions previously listed. In addition, it must pass the five-tax-year rule. *See the following section to learn more on this rule.*

Your annual contributions to a Roth IRA; amounts contributed through a conversion from a traditional IRA or rollover from a qualified retirement plan; and earnings in a Roth IRA are all treated differently if you withdraw them before you reach the age of 59½. Regular contributions to a Roth IRA can be withdrawn at any time, tax-free and penalty-free, because income tax has already been paid on them. Earnings and amounts converted from another retirement account are subject to a five-year holding period before they can be withdrawn without penalty. Earnings in a Roth IRA might be subject to the 10 percent early withdrawal penalty.

Calculating taxes and penalties for an early withdrawal from a Roth IRA can become complicated, so you should consider the consequences carefully before you decide to take money out.

Five-tax-year rule

Even if you are older than 59½, you cannot withdraw earnings tax-free from a Roth IRA until five tax years after you have made your first contribution to a Roth IRA. Tax years are not determined in the same way as calendar years. The five-tax-year period begins on January 1 of the first year that you make a contribution to a Roth IRA. Whether you convert to a Roth IRA in January or in December, or even by April 15 of the following year, the first tax year begins on January 1 of the year for which you made the contribution.

The five-year holding period is known as the "non-exclusion period." The Tax Technical Corrections Act of 1998 (TTCA-98) defines the Roth IRA non-exclusion period as "the five-taxable-year period beginning with the first taxable year for which the individual made a contribution of any kind to a Roth IRA."

Earnings

After the five-tax-year holding period, earnings in a Roth IRA can be withdrawn tax-free, if you are older than 59½. If you are younger, earnings from contributions to a Roth IRA are subject to the 10 percent early withdrawal penalty — unless they qualify for one of the exceptions to the 59½ rule listed earlier — and will be taxed as income.

Conversions to Roth IRAs

Amounts contributed to a Roth IRA through a conversion from a traditional IRA or a qualified retirement plan such as a 401(k) or 403(b) are treated differently from other contributions. Each conversion has its own five-tax-year holding period beginning with the tax year in which the conversion was made. The amount converted and any earnings from it are subject to the 10 percent early withdrawal penalty if withdrawn within five tax years of the conversion. Converted amounts do not have to be physically segregated from regular contributions in separate Roth IRAs, but taxes and penalties are assessed separately for contributions and conversions.

Non-deductible amounts converted from traditional IRAs are subject to the same five-tax-year rule as tax-deferred amounts.

If you are contemplating an early withdrawal and have non-deductible contributions in a traditional IRA, it might be better to take the withdrawal directly from the traditional IRA.

Will you need the money before the five-tax-year holding period has expired? If you wait five years, converted funds can be taken out of a Roth IRA without paying the early withdrawal penalty, even if you are not yet 59½. If you cannot wait five years, the 10 percent penalty will be imposed on the entire converted amount when it is withdrawn from the Roth IRA. When you take an early distribution directly from a traditional IRA, the portion representing your non-deductible contributions will not be subject to the 10 percent penalty.

Order of withdrawal

The IRS imposes strict rules on the order in which contributions are taken out of a Roth IRA. Amounts from regular contributions come out first; these are followed by amounts contributed by conversions on a first-in, first-out basis (FIFO); and, finally, earnings. You can withdraw your regular contributions without taxes or penalties at any time. Amounts converted to Roth IRAs from traditional IRAs or retirement plans can be withdrawn without taxes or penalties when five tax years have elapsed after the conversion, regardless of your age. Earnings will be subject to income tax and early withdrawal penalties if you withdraw them before you reach the age of 59½, unless they are qualified distributions under one of the exceptions to the 59½ rule.

Withdrawals from an employer Roth 401(k) plan are treated differently. If contributions make up 80 percent of a Roth 401(k) and earnings make up 20 percent, 80 percent of any non-qualified withdrawal will be tax-free, but 20 percent of it must be reported as income on your tax return and might be subject to the 10 percent early withdrawal penalty.

Multiple Roth IRAs are treated as one

Multiple Roth IRAs are treated as a single account when contributions, conversions, and earnings amounts are calculated for withdrawals. The calculation can be complicated if you have several conversions made in different years. You might have a Roth to which you have contributed for many years, and another Roth created when you converted a 401(k) two years ago. According to the "aggregation rule," you must add both Roths together when calculating a withdrawal. The aggregation rule allows you to withdraw money from either of the Roth accounts. The total amount you contributed to your Roths can be withdrawn without penalty. For any amount over that, you will pay income tax plus the 10 percent early withdrawal penalty on earnings if you are less than 59 ½ years old, and an early withdrawal penalty on the amount converted from your 401(k) if fewer than five years have passed since the conversion.

The aggregation rule does not apply to inherited Roth 401(k)s or to inherited Roth IRAs unless you inherited a Roth IRA from your spouse and elected to take it over as your own.

Roth IRA rollovers

The special tax status of Roth IRAs means that assets from one Roth IRA can be rolled over to another Roth IRA, but not to any other type of retirement plan. If you take a distribution from one Roth IRA with the intention of rolling it over to another Roth IRA, you have 60 days in which to complete the transaction. You are permitted one Roth-to-Roth rollover per year. Rollovers between Roth IRAs are not subject to income tax withholding.

There are several reasons why you might want to roll over assets from one Roth IRA to another. You might want to transfer your Roth IRA to a financial institution that offers specific investment opportunities that were not available at the old institution, or that offers lower fees and management costs. You can use a rollover to combine two Roth IRAs into one, or to move assets from an inherited Roth IRA into one that you own, if you are a spouse beneficiary.

If you do not complete the transfer of assets withdrawn from one Roth IRA to another Roth within 60 days, the withdrawal will be treated as a distribution, and you will lose the opportunity to maintain those assets in a tax-free account. If you have not held the Roth for more than five years, or if you are younger than 59½ years old, you will have to pay income tax and a 10 percent penalty on the earnings.

Types of Investments

A Roth IRA can hold many types of investments, including stocks, bonds, mutual funds, exchange-traded funds (ETFs), precious metals, commodity futures, real estate, and annuities. It can also be used to invest in a business. An IRA must be administered by a custodian, such as a bank, brokerage, credit union, or a financial institution approved by the IRS. Most banks and brokerages offer IRAs with a selection of stocks, bonds, mutual funds, and money market accounts, but some custodians offer specialized IRAs and self-directed IRAs that allow you to manage your own investments.

IRAs have one purpose: to help you save for retirement. Every investment made by an IRA is intended to benefit the IRA, not the IRA owner. Certain types of transactions that would allow an IRA owner to take personal advantage of the tax-deferred status of an IRA are prohibited. For example, you cannot purchase collectibles or life insurance with a Roth IRA, or use a house owned through your IRA as your residence.

Reporting a Loss on a Roth IRA

What if, after you have paid income tax on your contributions to a Roth IRA, the investments in it drop in value and, instead of accumulating tax-free earnings, you find yourself losing money? You can report investment losses on a Roth IRA only after you have withdrawn everything from all your Roth IRAs and the total amount of the withdrawal is less than your total contributions. You can claim the loss as a miscellaneous itemized deduction on IRS Schedule A, Form 1040.

You cannot claim an itemized deduction for an amount that is less than 2 percent of your AGI.

Itemized deductions are subject to a 2 percent rule; if the loss on your Roth IRA is less than 2 percent of your AGI for that year, you cannot claim the itemized deduction. This is unfortunate because if your loss were on a taxable account, you would be able to claim it as a capital loss. If your income is too high in the year that you empty your Roth IRA, you will not be able to claim the deduction.

Most tax professionals would advise against withdrawing everything from your Roth IRA just to get a deduction from your taxable income. You cannot replace the funds in a tax-deferred account once you have taken them out, except by making your annual contribution while you have earned income. There is always a possibility that the delinquent stocks might recover some of their value. Instead of withdrawing the money from your Roth IRA, you can sell the poorly performing stocks and reinvest the money in more favorable investments, keeping the tax-free status for your future earnings.

There might be some circumstances in which you could benefit by withdrawing all the funds and taking the loss; for example, if most of the IRA is invested in the stock of a failed company with no hope of recovery or if the amount of the loss would be enough to significantly lower your taxes for that year. Before taking such a step, talk to a professional tax advisor or financial consultant who can help you determine if there is really any financial benefit to withdrawing everything from your Roth.

A loss on earnings in a Roth IRA cannot be deducted.

If you incur a loss in your Roth IRA when the balance consists only of earnings because you have previously withdrawn all your contributions, you no longer have basis in the account, and the loss cannot be deducted.

Inheriting a Roth IRA

After the death of its owner, a Roth IRA is subject to the same rules as a traditional IRA whose owner dies before his or her required beginning date (RBD). The required beginning date (RBD) is the year in which the owner of a traditional IRA turns 70½ and begins taking RMDs. The entire Roth IRA must either be distributed by December 31 of the fifth year after the year of the owner's death or paid out as RMDs based on the life expectancy of the beneficiary. Extending RMDs over the life expectancy of a beneficiary is known as "stretching" an IRA because it allows assets to remain in the IRA and accumulate tax-free earnings for as long as possible. These RMDs must begin in the calendar year following the year in which the IRA owner died. A spouse who is a sole beneficiary can delay the RMDs until the year after the IRA owner would have reached the age of 70½, or take over the Roth IRA as his or her own.

Distributions from a Roth IRA to a beneficiary are tax-free because income tax was already paid on the distribution. *This topic is discussed in more depth in Chapter 11.*

Your beneficiary cannot withdraw earnings from your Roth IRA tax-free until the five-year holding period has been completed.

If you die within five years of making a first contribution to a Roth IRA, converting a traditional IRA to a Roth IRA, or rolling over a qualified retirement plan to a Roth IRA, your beneficiary must wait until your five-year holding period has ended before he or she can withdraw earnings tax-free. If your beneficiary opts to receive a distribution of the entire IRA within five years of your death, he or she will have to wait to withdraw earnings after the five-year holding period has ended.

Prohibited Transactions

The IRS defines a prohibited transaction as "any improper use of your traditional IRA account or annuity by you, your beneficiary, or any disqualified person." Disqualified persons include your IRA custodian or administrator and members of your family (spouse, ancestor, lineal descendant, and any spouse of a lineal descendant). The same rules regarding prohibited transactions apply to traditional IRAs and Roth IRAs. According to the IRS, prohibited transactions include:

- **Selling your own property to your Roth IRA.** For example, your Roth IRA cannot buy your home as a real estate investment.

- **Receiving unreasonable compensation for managing your own IRA.** IRA administrators, custodians, and trustees typically charge management fees. You may not pay yourself excessive compensation for managing your own self-directed IRA. *See Chapter 9 for more information on this topic.*

- **Using your IRA as security for a loan.** If you use a part of your Roth IRA account as security for a loan, that part is treated as a distribution and is included in your gross income. If you borrow money against a Roth IRA annuity contract, you must include the fair market value of the annuity contract in your gross income for that tax year. You will have to pay the 10 percent additional tax on early distributions of earnings.

- **Buying property for personal use (present or future) with IRA funds.** You are allowed the one-time use of $10,000 of the earnings in a Roth IRA toward buying a first-time home for yourself, your children, or your parents without paying the early withdrawal penalty.

Penalty for engaging in a prohibited transaction

If you or your beneficiary engages in a prohibited transaction in connection with your Roth IRA, then as a rule, the account stops being an IRA. The account is treated as though all its assets had been distributed to you at their fair market values on the first day of that year. If you are younger than 59½ or have not held the account for five years, the earnings will be included in your taxable income for that year, and you will be subject to the early withdrawal tax and other penalties. Your Roth IRA then becomes an ordinary investment account and all earnings are taxable.

You do not lose your IRA tax treatment if your employer or the employee association administering your Roth IRA engage in a prohibited transaction, unless you participated in the transaction yourself. For example, an employer might break the rules by using funds from the IRAs it administers to purchase a company property as an "investment." Anyone other than the owner or beneficiary of a Roth IRA who engages in a prohibited transaction could be liable for a 15 percent tax on the amount of the prohibited transaction, and a 100 percent additional tax on that amount if the transaction is not reversed or corrected.

Investing in collectibles

You cannot use your IRA to buy works of art, rugs, antiques, gems, stamps, coins, metals, alcoholic beverages such as wines, or certain other tangible personal property like sports memorabilia, Beanie Babies, or baseball cards. The purchase of such items with a Roth IRA is treated as an immediate distribution. The earnings are taxed as regular income, and you will be charged a 10 percent penalty on the earnings if you are under the age of 59½.

You are allowed to invest in 1-, ½-, ¼-, or 1/10-ounce U.S. gold coins, or 1-ounce silver coins minted by the U.S. Treasury Department, and in certain platinum coins and certain gold, silver, palladium, and platinum bullion because their value is represented by the precious metals they contain and not by their historical context.

Strategies: Making the Most of Your Roth IRA

CHAPTER
03
T H R E E

Financial advisors promote the Roth IRA as a powerful vehicle not only for growing retirement savings, but also for increasing personal wealth. The most important characteristic of a Roth is tax-free earnings. In its early stages, the money in a Roth IRA is made up mostly of the owner's contributions. Over time, as the balance of the account grows, the percentage made up of earnings increases. If the investments do reasonably well, the owner of a Roth IRA will be able to harvest a substantial amount of tax-free income. The second important characteristic of a Roth is the fact that the owner can leave assets in a Roth IRA for accumulating wealth untouched for as long as he or she lives. Owners of traditional IRAs are required to gradually deplete their accounts by taking annual RMDs, so that the accounts earn less and less each year.

These benefits sound appealing, but contribution and income limits restrict the use of Roth IRAs. A married couple earning more than $170,000 in 2009, or a single person earning more than $110,000, could not contribute to a Roth IRA. The most anyone could contribute to a Roth IRA in 2009 was $6,000. The fastest way to get a substantial balance in a Roth IRA is to convert a 401(k) or a traditional IRA that has already been growing for several years to a Roth. This entails paying income tax on the tax-deductible contributions and all the earnings in the 401(k) or traditional IRA. Until 2010, income limits prevented many people with large traditional IRAs or 401(k)s from converting to a Roth; now, anyone can make the conversion, regardless of their annual earned income. *See Chapter 4 for more information on converting to a Roth IRA.*

The challenge, then, is to work within the restrictions to get the most out of your Roth IRA. This chapter will discuss how to maximize your contributions, achieve earnings growth by implementing sound investment strategies, use your Roth to help manage your personal finances, and leave as much as possible for your heirs.

Roth IRA versus Traditional IRA

When dealing with personal finances, people tend to be preoccupied with their present circumstances, particularly if their income is low and their resources are stretched. The primary concern for many young workers is how to pay the month's bills and perhaps find a little extra to pay for a new or used car, or a short vacation. Saving for retirement requires an entirely different approach: thinking of financial transactions in terms of what the result will be two, three, or four decades from now, instead of looking at immediate, short-term gains.

If all your circumstances remain absolutely unchanged from now until your retirement, a traditional IRA and a Roth IRA will give you the same amount of retirement income. The following chart is a hypothetical example. You decide that you have $5,000 to contribute to a retirement account. The entire $5,000 will go into a traditional IRA because income tax is deferred. Or, if you are in a 15 percent income tax bracket, you will pay $750 in taxes on the $5,000 and deposit $4,250 into a Roth IRA. Now leave that money untouched in the account for 20 years, growing steadily at an annual rate of 7 percent. After 20 years, the traditional IRA has accumulated $19,348.42, but when you withdraw the money, you have to pay $2,902.63 in income taxes (you are still in the 15 percent tax bracket), giving you $16,446.16 to spend. During the same 20 years, the Roth IRA has accumulated $16,446.16, all of which is yours to spend because the money is tax-free.

	Traditional IRA	Roth IRA
Income tax bracket at time contribution is made	15%	15%
Contribution	$5,000	$4,250
Years to grow	20	20
Rate of growth	7%	7%
Income tax bracket at retirement	15%	15%
Balance in IRA account	$19,348.42	$16,446.16
Amount available to spend after taxes	**$16,446.15**	**$16,446.16**

In real life, your circumstances will not remain exactly the same during your entire working career. In deciding whether to contribute to a traditional IRA and take the tax deduction that year, or to contribute to a Roth and pay income tax, you have to consider how your circumstances might change as time passes. For example, if your income is high enough to put you in a 28 percent tax bracket now, but you expect to be in a 15 percent tax bracket at retirement, the outcome would be quite different. If nothing else in the scenario is changed, the Roth will give you $2,515.29 less to spend than the traditional IRA.

If your tax bracket is lower when you retire, and all other circumstances are the same, the traditional IRA yields more spending money than the Roth

	Traditional IRA	Roth IRA
Income tax bracket at time contribution is made	28%	28%
Contribution	$5,000	$3,600
Years to grow	20	20
Rate of growth	7%	7%
Income tax bracket at retirement	15%	15%
Balance in IRA account	$19,348.42	$13,930.86
Amount available to spend after taxes	**$16,446.15**	**$13,930.86**

Suppose that your tax bracket remains unchanged, but you go ahead and contribute the maximum contribution of $5,000 to the Roth IRA and pay your income taxes with additional funds. Now the Roth IRA will give you $2,902.27 more to spend than the traditional IRA, because no income tax is paid on the withdrawal from the Roth.

An equal contribution results in a higher yield from the Roth

	Traditional IRA	Roth IRA
Income tax bracket at time contribution is made	15%	15%
Contribution	$5,000	$5,000
Years to grow	20	20
Rate of growth	7%	7%
Income tax bracket at retirement	15%	15%
Balance in IRA account	$19,348.42	$19,348.42
Amount available to spend after taxes	**$16,446.15**	**$19,348.42**

If your income tax bracket was 15 percent when you contributed the $5,000 to the Roth, you paid $750 in income tax, so the Roth would really be giving you only $2,152.77 more than the traditional IRA. If you were in the 28 percent tax bracket when you contributed, you would have paid $1,400 in income taxes. By waiting to pay income taxes on the traditional IRA when the money is withdrawn, you are paying $2,902 in taxes, giving the Roth an edge of $1,502.27. That amount represents 30 percent of the original investment of $5,000.

This example does not consider state income taxes.

Income from a traditional IRA is subject to state income taxes as well as federal taxes. Remember to include state income taxes in your calculations. You can find links to tax information for individual states on Taxsites.com (**www.taxsites.com/State-Links.html**).

Planning for the future requires you to think about all the things that might change between now and then. The U.S. government might increase taxes to pay for universal health care and economic bailouts. You could have a successful career and be in a higher tax bracket when you retire, or you might be laid off at age 55 and be earning less than you are now. You might inherit a fortune and not need the money in your IRA for retirement. Once your income rises above a certain level, you will no longer be eligible to make contributions to a Roth IRA.

Everything you can do to tip the balance in favor of a Roth IRA, such as making the full allowable contribution every year, will ultimately result in more money for your retirement. Suppose you purchase a business with your self-directed Roth IRA and achieve 15 percent growth instead of 7 percent. Your $5,000 could become $58,919.

Roth IRA achieves higher earnings
through purchasing a business

	Traditional IRA	Roth IRA
Income tax bracket at time contribution is made	15%	15%
Contribution	$5,000	$5,000
Years to grow	20	20
Rate of growth	7%	15%
Income tax bracket at retirement	15%	15%
Balance in IRA account	$19,348.42	$58,919.53
Amount available to spend after taxes	**$16,446.15**	**$58,919.53**

If you achieved the same growth in a traditional IRA, you would only be able to withdraw $50,081.60. As the earnings in a traditional IRA increase, so does the amount of income tax that has to be paid when the money is withdrawn.

Income Tax Brackets

It is important to have a clear understanding of income tax brackets when you are planning your financial future or deciding when to convert a traditional IRA or 401(k) to a Roth.

Your federal income tax bracket is the highest percentage tax rate that you are taxed on any of your annual adjusted income. If you are in the 35 percent tax bracket, you do not pay 35 percent of your entire income in taxes. In 2007, if you were married filing jointly, you would have been taxed 10 percent on the first $15,650 of your AGI; 15 percent on the next $48,050 ($63,700 minus the first $15,650); and so on. You would have paid 35 percent only on the amount exceeding $349,700.

U.S. federal income tax brackets for 2007-2009

Tax Rate	Married Filing Jointly			Single Filers		
	2007 Taxable Income	2008 Taxable Income	2009 Taxable Income	2007 Taxable Income	2008 Taxable Income	2009 Taxable Income
10%	Not over $15,650	Not over $16,050	Not over $16,700	Not over $7,825	Not over $8,025	Not over $8,350
15%	15,650 – 63,700	16,050 – 67,100	16,700 – 67,900	7,825 – 31,850	8,025 – 32,550	8,350 – 33,950
25%	63,700 – 128,500	67,100 – 131,450	67,900 – 137,050	31,850 – 77,100	32,550 – 78,850	33,950 – 82,250
28%	128,500 – 195,850	131,450 – 200,300	137,050 – 208,850	77,100 – 160,850	78,850 – 164,550	82,250 – 171,550
33%	195,850 – 349,700	200,300 – 375,000	208,850 – 372,950	160,850 – 349,700	164,500 – 357,700	171,550 – 372,950
35%	Over 349,700	Over 372,500	Over 372,950	Over 349,700	Over 357,700	Over 372,950

Federal income tax brackets are adjusted every year for inflation. You can find an updated federal tax bracket calculator on MoneyChimp.com (**www.moneychimp.com/features/tax_brackets.htm**). By looking at the preceding chart, you can see that any amount of income that raises you into a higher tax bracket will be taxed at the higher rate. For example, in 2007, if you had income from other sources such as wages, social security, interest on savings bonds, or self-employment amounting to $15,000, and you had to take an RMD of $4,500 from your traditional IRA, you would end up paying taxes of 15 percent on $3,900 of that distribution because your total income would exceed $15,650 by that amount.

Your tax bracket is based on your taxable income, which is your actual income reduced by a number of deductions. These deductions include:

- Personal exemptions for each person filing and each dependent ($3,650 in 2009)

- Standard deductions ($11,400 for married couples filing jointly in 2009)

- Itemized deductions for:

    o   Mortgage interest

    o   Medical expenses

    o   Local and state income taxes

- Self-employed individuals and couples might be able to deduct business expenses

- Deductions for children:

    o   Deduction for each dependent

- o   Earned income tax credit (EITC) ($5,028 in 2009) for moderate and low-income working parents with two or more children

- o   Deductions for child care or dependent care expenses

- Contributions to a traditional IRA

- Retirement savings contributions credit

Retired individuals who no longer have earned income or dependent children living with them are not able to take many tax deductions, but their younger beneficiaries who are still raising families will probably be in the lower tax brackets.

How Much Do You Need for Retirement?

How old will you be when you retire? How will your lifestyle change? Will you need more or less than your current income? Are you moving to a smaller house, or to a state like Florida that does not have a state income tax? How much do you need to cover medical expenses and long-term care insurance? Many retirees spend more during their early retirement than in their later years. Experts calculate you can withdraw approximately 4 percent of your retirement funds every year and still maintain enough growth in your retirement account to supply income for the rest of your life. If that is true, you would need $1 million in your retirement account to supply you with an annual retirement income of $40,000. You might not need to rely entirely on your savings for retirement income if you have other sources of income such as social security, royalties, or part-time employment. You might expect to benefit from a windfall such as an inheritance or the sale of a large home. When you reach your mid-80s or 90s, you can begin to deplete your retirement savings because you will not need to depend on them for longer than another 10 or 15 years. Taking all these things into account, you can estimate how much you need to accumulate in retirement savings.

Below are some helpful resources that will guide you in estimating your retirement expenses.

- The American Association of Retired Persons (AARP) Web site has a worksheet to help you estimate your expenses during retirement. You can find this online at **www.aarp.org/money/financial_planning/sessionseven/retirement_planning_calculator.html**.

- **http://vanguard.com** and **http://fireseeker.com** have calculators that show the expected long-term results from your portfolio.

Start Early and Save as Much as You Can

Young people are strongly encouraged to start saving for retirement as soon as they start working. The ideal time to open a Roth IRA is early in your career because income limits might make it impossible for you to contribute when you start earning a higher salary. Even if your initial contributions are small, over the years, earnings will accumulate and the account will grow substantially. The Roth IRA you opened when you were young can provide welcome tax-free income later in life.

The power of compounding

Two factors drive the growth of a retirement savings account: time and compounding. Compounding is what happens when you put your money in an investment with an annual return, then continually reinvest those returns. At first, the amount in your investment account grows slowly, but as time passes and the earnings mount, the balance in your account mushrooms. Even a modest investment can become a substantial amount over one or two decades.

The following chart illustrates the power of compounding and the importance of starting to save as early as possible. In this example, a young person who invested $2,000 every year for eight years starting at age 19, and then did not invest anything more, ended up with $307,270 at the age of 65. In contrast, someone who started 8 years later and invested almost five times more earned only an additional $28,000 during the same time period. The third person, who started at age 19 and continued to invest $2,000 every year until age 65, earned almost double what was earned by the person who delayed 8 years before starting to save. If you are young, time is on your side.

Power of compounding: $2,000 invested annually with a return of 7 percent

Age	Saved $2,000 per year for 8 years beginning at age 19		Saved $2,000 per year for 39 years beginning at age 27		Saved $2,000 per year for 47 years beginning at age 19		$2,000 saved annually at 10% growth rate	
19	$2,000	$2,140	$0	$0	$2,000	$2,140	$2,000	$2,200
20	$2,000	$4,430	$0	$0	$2,000	$4,430	$2,000	$4,620
21	$2,000	$6,880	$0	$0	$2,000	$6,880	$2,000	$7,282
22	$2,000	$9,501	$0	$0	$2,000	$9,501	$2,000	$10,210
23	$2,000	$12,307	$0	$0	$2,000	$12,307	$2,000	$13,431
24	$2,000	$15,308	$0	$0	$2,000	$15,308	$2,000	$16,974
25	$2,000	$18,520	$0	$0	$2,000	$18,520	$2,000	$20,872
26	$2,000	$21,956	$0	$0	$2,000	$21,956	$2,000	$25,159
27	$0	$23,493	$2,000	$2,140	$2,000	$25,633	$2,000	$29,875
28	$0	$25,137	$2,000	$4,430	$2,000	$29,567	$2,000	$35,062
29	$0	$26,897	$2,000	$6,880	$2,000	$33,777	$2,000	$40,769
30	$0	$28,780	$2,000	$9,501	$2,000	$38,281	$2,000	$47,045
31	$0	$30,794	$2,000	$12,307	$2,000	$43,101	$2,000	$53,950

32	$0	$32,950	$2,000	$15,308	$2,000	$48,258	$2,000	$61,545
33	$0	$35,257	$2,000	$18,520	$2,000	$53,776	$2,000	$69,899
34	$0	$37,724	$2,000	$21,956	$2,000	$59,680	$2,000	$79,089
35	$0	$40,365	$2,000	$25,633	$2,000	$65,998	$2,000	$89,198
36	$0	$43,191	$2,000	$29,567	$2,000	$72,758	$2,000	$100,318
37	$0	$46,214	$2,000	$33,777	$2,000	$79,991	$2,000	$112,550
38	$0	$49,449	$2,000	$38,281	$2,000	$87,730	$2,000	$126,005
39	$0	$52,911	$2,000	$43,101	$2,000	$96,011	$2,000	$140,805
40	$0	$56,614	$2,000	$48,258	$2,000	$104,872	$2,000	$157,086
41	$0	$60,577	$2,000	$53,776	$2,000	$114,353	$2,000	$174,995
42	$0	$64,818	$2,000	$59,680	$2,000	$124,498	$2,000	$194,694
43	$0	$69,355	$2,000	$65,998	$2,000	$135,353	$2,000	$216,364
44	$0	$74,210	$2,000	$72,758	$2,000	$146,968	$2,000	$240,200
45	$0	$79,404	$2,000	$79,991	$2,000	$159,395	$2,000	$266,420
46	$0	$84,963	$2,000	$87,730	$2,000	$172,693	$2,000	$295,262
47	$0	$90,910	$2,000	$96,011	$2,000	$186,922	$2,000	$326,988
48	$0	$97,274	$2,000	$104,872	$2,000	$202,146	$2,000	$361,887
49	$0	$104,083	$2,000	$114,353	$2,000	$218,436	$2,000	$400,276
50	$0	$111,369	$2,000	$124,498	$2,000	$235,867	$2,000	$442,503
51	$0	$119,165	$2,000	$135,353	$2,000	$254,518	$2,000	$488,953
52	$0	$127,506	$2,000	$146,968	$2,000	$274,474	$2,000	$540,049
53	$0	$136,432	$2,000	$159,395	$2,000	$295,827	$2,000	$596,254
54	$0	$145,982	$2,000	$172,693	$2,000	$318,675	$2,000	$658,079
55	$0	$156,200	$2,000	$186,922	$2,000	$343,122	$2,000	$726,087
56	$0	$167,135	$2,000	$202,146	$2,000	$369,281	$2,000	$800,896
57	$0	$178,834	$2,000	$218,436	$2,000	$397,270	$2,000	$883,185
58	$0	$191,352	$2,000	$235,867	$2,000	$427,219	$2,000	$973,704
59	$0	$204,747	$2,000	$254,518	$2,000	$459,264	$2,000	$1,073,274
60	$0	$219,079	$2,000	$274,474	$2,000	$493,553	$2,000	$1,182,801
61	$0	$234,415	$2,000	$295,827	$2,000	$530,242	$2,000	$1,303,282
62	$0	$250,824	$2,000	$318,675	$2,000	$569,499	$2,000	$1,435,810
63	$0	$268,381	$2,000	$343,122	$2,000	$611,504	$2,000	$1,581,591
64	$0	$287,168	$2,000	$369,281	$2,000	$656,449	$2,000	$1,741,950
65	$0	$307,270	$2,000	$397,270	$2,000	$704,540	$2,000	$1,918,345
Total Amount Invested	$16,000		$78,000		$94,000			$94,000
Earnings	$291,270		$319,270		$610,540			$1,824,345

The preceding chart assumes an annual return on investment of 7 percent, which has been the average inflation-adjusted historical return of the stock market. The last column in this chart illustrates the impact of an increased annual rate of return. With an annual return of 10 percent, $2,000 invested annually could grow to almost $2 million during a working career.

Seven percent is only a historical average; the stock market's real annual rate of return has fluctuated between almost 60 percent for some few years and almost minus 50 percent in 1931 and 2008.

This chart is only an illustration of how retirement savings can grow. You cannot depend on a steady rate of return; the stock market will do well during some periods and poorly during others. Financial analysts can only speculate on how quickly the stock market can rebound from the crisis of 2008, and whether millions of Americans will be able to recover the losses in their retirement savings accounts.

Young Workers Pay Less Income Tax

Young workers who are just starting their careers typically pay less income tax because they earn less and because young families receive tax credits for dependent children, child care, and education expenses. Including a Roth IRA contribution in taxable income is less likely to bump a young worker into a higher tax bracket. It makes sense to pay income tax now at a lower rate and benefit from tax-free earnings instead of paying taxes on those contributions and the earnings later at a higher rate.

Contribution Strategies

Regular investment of capital is essential for the accumulation of retirement savings. The average couple needs to set aside an estimated 15 percent of their annual income to generate a retirement income that will support the lifestyle enjoyed during their working years. Deciding how much priority to assign to retirement savings is a personal matter, and one that often does not receive enough attention. According to a study by the Investment Company Institute, "The Role of IRAs in U.S. Households' Saving for Retirement, 2008," only four of ten U.S. households — or 47.3 million households — held some type of IRA account in 2008, up from 46.2 million in 2007 and 38 million in 2000. Most of these accounts were either employer-sponsored IRAs or rollovers from 401(k) plans. It is alarming that only 14 percent of eligible households made a contribution to any type of IRA in the 2007 tax year. This indicates that, unless they are participating in some kind of employer-sponsored plan, most families are not inclined to put aside savings for retirement. Yet experienced investors will assure you that there are substantial benefits to holding assets in a tax-deferred account. Even a small regular contribution will grow into a sizable sum after two decades. You will not regret having set aside money for your future use.

Contributions to a Roth IRA can always be accessed for emergency funds, and even earnings can be withdrawn without penalty for certain types of expenses such as higher education, a home purchase, or health insurance for your family when you become unemployed.

You can use several strategies for making regular contributions:

- **Payroll deductions:** If your IRA is part of an employer-sponsored plan, you will be able to direct a percentage of each paycheck to be deposited directly into your IRA. Some employers will match your contribution up to 3 percent of your salary; this is free money and you should take full advantage of it. Under an SEP or a SIMPLE IRA, your employer makes contributions on your behalf.

- **Automatic contributions from your bank account:** Most financial institutions offer incentives to sign up for a regular monthly contribution to be automatically transferred from your bank account into your IRA. Once you have set up an automatic transfer you will be more inclined to include it in your monthly budget.

- **Accumulate money in a savings account:** Put money aside for emergencies in a savings account whenever you can and make a contribution when the account balance surpasses the amount you need for three months' living expenses. If your bank charges a fee for a savings account, open a free online savings account with a direct bank such as Capital One (**www.capitalone.com/ directbanking/online-savings-account/index.php**), ING Direct (**http://home.ingdirect.com/open/open.asp**), or HSBC Direct (**www.hsbcdirect.com/1/2/1/mkt/savings**). Your money will earn interest while it is in the savings account. Many banks now encourage their customers to save with "keep the change" programs that round up the amounts paid for purchase to the nearest dollar and channel the extra cents into a savings account. Use such a program to gradually put money aside.

- **Dedicate income from a specific source to your IRA:** If you receive lump-sum payments such as royalties, income from freelancing, or a small inheritance, make a contribution to your IRA instead of spending the money on inconsequential things.

The earlier in the year you make your annual contribution, the better.

Many people wait until just before the tax filing deadline to make a contribution to their IRA. If you know how much you are going to contribute for the year, it is better to make that contribution as early in the year as you can. The value of the stock market typically rises during the year. Also, your money will be earning interest and dividends for several months longer than if you had waited until the last minute to contribute.

If You Have a 401(k) or 403(b) at Work

If you are contributing to a 401(k) or a 403(b) at work, you can still contribute to an individual Roth IRA, as long as your income does not exceed the limit. Your contributions to a 401(k) might even help you meet the income requirements for a Roth by decreasing your taxable income. Several factors can help you decide where to put your retirement savings, including whether your employer matches your contributions, the types of investments offered by the company plan, expenses, and the rules governing the 401(k) plan.

Contributions

The contributions you make to an employer-sponsored 401(k) or 403(b) do not affect your contribution limits for individual IRAs. In 2009, you were allowed to contribute a maximum of $16,500 to an employer-sponsored plan ($22,000 if you were older than 50). In addition, if you were married filing jointly and your AGI was less than $159,000, you could have contributed $5,000 to a Roth IRA ($6,000 if you were over 50) for a maximum combined contribution of $28,000 if you were older than 50. If your AGI was more than $159,000, your contribution to a Roth would have been smaller, but you could have made an additional contribution to a traditional IRA to make up the $5,000.

Make the Most of Employer Matching

Employers are allowed to make matching contributions to a 401(k) or a 403(b) of up to 6 percent of your salary. Many employers offer matching contributions as an incentive to inspire employee loyalty. There might be a waiting period of several months or years before you become fully "vested" and are allowed to claim all the matching funds as your own. The employer match is free money; your contribution is automatically and immediately doubled. You are not likely to double your investment in a Roth IRA within one year, no matter how successful your investments are. You should contribute enough to your 401(k) plan to take full advantage of matching funds before you begin contributing to a Roth IRA.

Investment Choices and Expenses

Critics of 401(k) plans point out that they frequently do not perform as well as predicted because too much money is siphoned off by administrative fees and management fees, and because many of the investment offerings in 401(k)s are lackluster mutual funds that underperform the stock market. Fees and expenses are often disguised in quarterly statements so that owners of 401(k) plans are not able to decipher what they are paying for. Look carefully at the investment choices in your 401(k). Some employer plans offer a wide variety of attractive investment choices or a selection of choice mutual funds while others are mediocre. A 401(k) might give you access to institutional mutual funds with lower expenses than the mutual funds available in an individual Roth IRA. You might also be able to invest in stable value funds, typically composed of bonds and insurance contracts, that are guaranteed to produce a specific, if low, rate of return.

If you can earn greater returns from the investments in your Roth IRA, you should contribute as much as you can to the Roth after you have taken advantage of employer matching in your 401(k).

Keep your portfolio balanced.

When you are contributing to both a 401(k) or 403(b) and a Roth IRA, remember that all your retirement accounts combined make up your portfolio. Do not duplicate investments in your Roth that you already hold in your 401(k) and spread your asset allocations across all your retirement accounts. See Chapter 7 for more information on building and maintaining your portfolio.

Access to Your Money

Contributions to a 401(k) are typically locked away until you retire or leave the company, although many plan rules do allow a withdrawal for qualified education expenses or a "hardship" distribution if, for example, you are in danger of foreclosure or have heavy medical expenses. Ideally your retirement funds should be left untouched, but if you anticipate needing some of that cash sooner, put it in a Roth IRA so that you can take it out whenever you need it. Some 401(k) plans allow you to take a loan from your retirement savings, which must then be paid back within five years. You cannot borrow money from an IRA; if you take money out and do not deposit it in another IRA within 60 days, you can never replace it.

Funds withdrawn early from a 401(k) are subject to income tax and the early withdrawal penalty (if you are younger than 59½). If you are younger than 59½ or have not held the account for five years, earnings in a Roth IRA are taxable as income, and you might be subject to the 10 percent withdrawal penalty, depending on how the money is used.

Employers eliminated matching contributions to 401(k) and 403(b) retirement accounts to cut costs during the 2008-2009 recession.

According to a study by Spectrem Group, a retirement benefits consulting firm, in response to the economic crisis of 2008, one-third of U.S. employers reduced or eliminated their matching contributions to retirement accounts in 2008, and another 29 percent planned to do so in 2009. These cost-cutting measures might have saved jobs, but they have removed the strongest incentive for contributing to a 401(k). Without the extra money coming in from matching contributions, 401(k)s do not perform better than IRAs. To get an idea of how much employer-matching contributes to a 401(k) balance over the years, you can use a calculator such as the 401(k) Calculator at Calcnexus.com (**http://calcnexus.com/401k-calculator.php**). For some employers, the cut may only be temporary; after past cuts, many employers restored matching contributions to 401(k)s when the economy improved.

If your employer has eliminated matching contributions to your 401(k), it might be time to redirect your retirement savings contributions to a Roth IRA. Make the maximum allowable contribution to a Roth IRA ($5,000 in 2009; $6,000 if you were over 50), and contribute additional amounts to your 401(k) plan at work. An analysis by T. Rowe Price suggested that most investors younger than 50 will have more income in retirement if they shift unmatched contributions to a Roth IRA.

Roth IRA as a Back-up Emergency Fund

Because income tax has already been paid on contributions to a Roth IRA, you can withdraw your contributions (but not your earnings) at any time without penalty. It is never advisable to take money out of your retirement account, but if you need cash for an emergency, you will have access to it.

Funds taken out of your retirement account for other purposes cannot be replaced.

The purpose of a retirement savings account is to allow investments to grow untouched for several decades. Except for certain special circumstances, money withdrawn from a retirement account cannot be replaced; you can only make the allowable annual contribution of $5,000 ($6,000 if you are over 50). You should always try to find emergency funds from another source and only use your IRA as a last resort.

Paying for an Education

Young parents might have difficulty deciding whether to save for their children's education or for retirement. A Roth IRA can serve both purposes. Contribution limits for an IRA in 2009 were $5,000. If one parent contributes that amount to a Roth IRA every year for 17 years, at an average annual return of 7 percent, the account will hold $165,000 by the time the child is ready to go to college. Of this amount, the $85,000 in contributions can be withdrawn tax-free and penalty-free, and another $10,000 can be withdrawn penalty-free for qualified education expenses. Each parent can open a Roth IRA and save for education. If the child is a good student or an athlete and receives a scholarship, the money can stay in the Roth as retirement savings.

A Roth IRA offers several advantages over Coverdell education savings accounts (CESAs), including the opportunity to make larger contributions and the ability to use the money for any kind of education expense. Qualified education expenses only account for part of the actual cost of attending a college or university. Money will still need to be found for a student's unqualified expenses, such as transportation, a car, supplies that are not specifically required by a course syllabus, recreation, travel, clothing, a computer, and room and board beyond what is stipulated by the school.

Education IRAs: Coverdell education savings accounts (CESAs)

An educational savings account (ESA), like a Roth IRA, allows you to make an annual non-deductible contribution to a specially designated investment trust account where the earnings grow tax-free. The beneficiary can withdraw funds from the ESA in any year and use them tax-free for qualified higher education expenses (QHEE), and even for some elementary and high school expenses. If the beneficiary withdraws more than the amount of qualified expenses, the earnings portion of that excess amount is subject to income tax and an additional 10 percent penalty tax.

Anyone can open an ESA account, and the beneficiary does not have to be a relative or family member. You can open an ESA account with any bank, mutual fund company, or financial institution that can serve as custodian of traditional IRAs. A parent or guardian of the beneficiary will be made responsible for the account. Your cash contribution can be invested in any qualifying investments available through the sponsoring institution.

Unused funds in an ESA can go to another family member.

Unused funds in an ESA can be rolled over into a Coverdell ESA for another family member, including a spouse, sibling, stepsibling, niece, nephew, first cousin, parent, aunt, uncle, child, or grandchild who is under the age of 30. The age limit does not apply to a special-needs beneficiary.

Several rules limit the effectiveness of ESAs:

- You cannot make any further contributions to an ESA after the beneficiary's 18th birthday.

- A beneficiary can receive only $2,000 in total contributions per year from all sources, even if he or she is the beneficiary of more than one ESA.

- Joint tax return filers with adjusted gross incomes (AGIs) above $220,000 and single filers with AGIs above $110,000 cannot contribute to an ESA. This requirement can be circumvented by gifting the $2,000 to a child and having the child contribute to the ESA account.

- The ESA must be fully withdrawn by the time the beneficiary reaches age 30. If it is not, the remaining amount will be paid out within 30 days, subject to tax on the earnings and the additional 10 percent penalty tax. If not used for education, the money in an ESA cannot be reclaimed by the person who contributed it; it will eventually be disbursed to the student.

- Scholarships do not affect the tax benefit of an ESA. If a student earns a scholarship, you can make a withdrawal equal to the amount of scholarship money spent on qualified education expenses from an ESA without paying taxes or penalties.

- ESA withdrawals are tax-free only when used for qualified education expenses.

Some ESA benefits expired after 2010.

Unless Congress changes the legislation governing ESAs, certain benefits expired after 2010: K-12 expenses will no longer qualify, the annual contribution limit will be reduced to $500, and withdrawals from an ESA will be taxed in any year in which a Hope credit or Lifetime credit is claimed for the beneficiary.

Budgeting for Retirement Savings

Review your monthly expenses and take control of your finances by adopting a budget plan. Treat your IRA as a serious financial obligation. Look for places where you can shave a few dollars off your discretionary spending to add to your monthly contribution. If you are not already using online banking, sign up for it. Most banks offer online money management tools that categorize your payments, show you where your money is going, and keep track of all your accounts — including your IRAs and investment accounts — in one place.

A number of software programs help you set up a budget and track your finances, including the following:

Mint.com

Mint.com (**www.mint.com**) is a free online budget management tool. It allows you to set up an anonymous account online, automatically imports data from your bank, credit card, home loan, and finance accounts, and categorizes your expenses. The information is updated automatically through secure connections to 7,000 banks and financial institutions. Mint's budgeting tools show your average expenditure in each category, help you set goals, and track your spending. You can view your balances using an iPhone application and set up text message or e-mail messages to alert you when you exceed your budget. Mint.com is funded through targeted advertising; the site identifies credit card offers and other products appropriate for each user.

Quicken

Quicken offers a variety of money-management products. Quicken Online (**http://quicken.intuit.com/online-banking-finances.jsp**) is a free money management tool that gathers information from all your online accounts and organizes it into an overview of your finances. It helps you set budget goals and tracks your spending to help you meet those goals.

Tools for Money

(**www.toolsformoney.com/personal_budget_software.htm**)   sells   an inexpensive budget tool that uses Excel spreadsheets. It includes a financial planning tool that projects your family finances far into the future and shows how various circumstances, such as a disability or loss of income, might influence your finances.

Converting to a Roth

C hapter 2 discussed the IRS rules for contributing to a Roth IRA: Your AGI in 2009 could not exceed $159,000, and you could contribute a maximum of $5,000 ($6,000 if you were older than 50). The contribution limits mean that when you first open a Roth IRA, you will not have enough capital to invest in stocks or bonds and will have to buy mutual funds or ETFs, or put your money in money market accounts. When you accumulate enough capital you can add other investments such as individual stocks, bonds, or real estate to your portfolio. If you contributed the maximum of $5,000 every year and your account grew at an average annual rate of 7 percent (the growth rate during 2008 was negative), at the end of five years you would have a balance of $30,766. After 30 years, you would have accumulated about $550,000 — not enough to fund a comfortable retirement. You would need to work another ten years to achieve a target of $1 million in your retirement account.

If you want to retire wealthy by using your Roth IRA to generate tax-free earnings, it is clear that you need to get more money into that Roth account. Contributions alone will not achieve your goals. There is a way to deposit a substantial sum of money into your Roth IRA account — by converting a traditional IRA or 401(k) to a Roth. You must pay income tax on all earnings and tax-deductible contributions in the account, but if you are able to pay this income tax with outside funds, you can transfer the entire balance from a traditional IRA or 401(k) into a Roth, and all future earnings will be tax-free.

Until 2010, you were not eligible to convert to a Roth IRA if your modified AGI exceeded $100,000, or if you were married filing a separate return. If you did not live together with your spouse during the entire year and were filing separately, your filing status was treated as single, and you were eligible for conversion. The Tax Increase Prevention and Reconciliation Act, which was signed into law in May 2006, lifted income restrictions for conversion to Roth IRAs starting in 2010 and included a special provision allowing income tax payments for conversions made in 2010 to be spread over two years, 2011 and 2012. Congress was hoping to collect a large amount of revenue by motivating owners of large traditional IRAs to convert to Roth IRAs and pay the deferred income tax. Owners of traditional IRA accounts who convert to Roth IRAs are able to withdraw future earnings from these accounts tax-free, subject to the 59½ rule and the five-year rule. For those prepared to take advantage of it, this presents an unprecedented opportunity.

Converting a traditional IRA or retirement account to a Roth IRA is a relatively simple process, but IRS rules must be carefully followed. The rules regarding the withdrawal of earnings from a converted Roth IRA can be complex depending on the source of the conversion. For most people this will not present a problem, because the funds will be left untouched over a long period of time until retirement. If cash is needed before that, it is possible to withdraw contributions and leave the earnings untouched. This chapter explains how to convert to a Roth IRA, the rules governing withdrawals, and how the conversion might affect beneficiaries.

Why Convert?

There are a number of reasons for converting traditional IRAs to Roth IRAs.

- **Tax-free earnings**: Traditional IRAs were established in 1974 and have been in existence 23 years longer than Roth IRAs, which were created in 1997. Some traditional IRAs have accumulated a large balance; converting them to Roths now assures the owner of substantial tax-free earnings in the future.

- **More flexibility**: Roth IRAs have more flexibility than traditional IRAs, including freedom to withdraw contributions at any time without a penalty and continue making contributions if you are working after you reach the age of 70½.

- **Pay income tax at a lower rate**: The same contribution limit applies to both traditional and Roth IRAs, but contributions to a Roth IRA are taxed now at your current income tax rate. After two or three decades, income tax rates might go up, or you might have been so successful that you will be in a higher tax bracket after you retire.

- **Tax-free inheritance for beneficiaries**: Your beneficiaries will not have to pay income taxes on distributions from your IRA after you die.

Do not convert if your income tax bracket is higher than your beneficiaries'.

If your primary goal is to leave your IRA to your children, and they are in a lower tax bracket than you are, you will end up paying more in taxes if you convert to a Roth than they will pay if they pay income tax on distributions from the traditional IRA when they inherit it.

- **No required minimum withdrawals:** If you are older than 70½ and are already taking RMDs from a traditional IRA but have other retirement income, you can convert to a Roth. Once you have converted your traditional IRA to a Roth IRA, you will no longer have to take RMDs and can leave your assets to grow untouched in the Roth IRA.

You have to take RMDs from a Roth 403(b) or a Roth 401(k).

Although you do not have to take RMDs from a Roth IRA, you must take them from a Roth 401(k) or 403(b) after you reach the age of 70 ½. If you convert a Roth 403(b) or 401(k) to a Roth IRA after you leave employment with the company, you will not pay income tax on the amount converted, and you will be able to hold your assets untouched in your Roth IRA for as long as you want.

Conversions from Retirement Plans

Starting in 2008, it became possible to convert 401(k) plans, tax-deferred annuities (403(b) plans), and government plans (457 plans), as well as traditional IRAs including SEP-IRAs and SIMPLE IRAs, directly into Roth IRAs. Prior to that, it was necessary to convert a retirement plan first to a traditional IRA and then to a Roth IRA, if the owner met income requirements.

A SIMPLE IRA cannot be converted to a Roth IRA for two years.

A SIMPLE IRA only becomes eligible for conversion to a Roth IRA after two years from the date that the SIMPLE IRA was first established.

Most 401(k) and 403(b) plans do not allow you to withdraw funds from your account until you leave employment with the company. You must be eligible to convert from a traditional IRA or qualified retirement plan to a Roth IRA, and you must pay income tax on the amount being distributed.

In addition to increased flexibility, tax-free earnings, and the opportunity to pay income tax at a lower rate on contributions, Roths typically offer more, less-costly investment options than retirement plans. Retirement plan rules governing withdrawals and treatment of beneficiaries might be more restrictive than IRAs.

How to Convert to a Roth IRA

You can convert to a Roth IRA in three ways:

Rollover: Take a distribution from your traditional IRA or retirement plan and contribute it to a Roth IRA within 60 days. Notify your plan administrator that you wish to take a distribution. You will typically be provided with a form, on which you can specify whether you want all or part of your account disbursed, and give your bank account information or a physical address where the disbursement check should be sent.

The rollover to the Roth IRA must be the same assets that you withdrew from your traditional IRA or retirement plan; for example, if you withdrew stocks, you must contribute those stocks to the Roth IRA. You cannot take out cash, buy stocks, and then contribute the stocks to a Roth IRA. Contributions to Roth IRAs are typically made in cash; only conversions allow you to deposit property in an IRA.

If you open a new Roth IRA and deposit the disbursement in it or deposit it in a Roth that you already own within 60 days, there will be no 10 percent early withdrawal penalty. If you decide to keep some of the money instead of reinvesting it, you might be subject to the 10 percent penalty on that amount. Administrators of traditional IRAs and retirement plans are required to withhold income tax and penalties when making a disbursement; if you want to deposit the full balance of your traditional IRA or 401(k) in a Roth IRA, you might have to make up the difference from other funds. You will receive a refund or tax credit for the amount that was withheld when you file that year's taxes.

An IRS rule prohibits doing more than one IRA rollover during a 12-month period. Using the rollover method to convert from a traditional to a Roth IRA is excepted from this rule, but if you do a rollover and a conversion in the same 12-month period, the rule could prevent you from reversing the conversion. *See the section in this chapter regarding recharacterizing for more information.*

Trustee-to-trustee transfer: Open a Roth IRA with a bank, stock brokerage, or financial institution, and direct the trustee of your traditional IRA or retirement plan to transfer an amount to the trustee of the Roth IRA. Many Roth IRA trustees will make the request for you by having you sign the appropriate forms and submitting them on your behalf.

Same-trustee transfer: Direct the trustee of your traditional IRA to transfer an amount to a Roth IRA held by the same trustee. This allows you to keep the same investments you had in your traditional IRA. Conversions between accounts held by the same trustee can be carried out by redesignating the traditional IRA as a Roth IRA, rather than by opening a new account.

Find out about fees and charges before you do a rollover or a transfer.

There might be exit fees, brokerage fees, and other costs involved in cashing out or transferring assets from an IRA. Before you decide whether to transfer your assets or sell them and transfer cash, find out what fees are involved. Some IRA and 401(k) custodians charge a hefty fee for transferring assets such as stocks, but nothing for cashing out an account. Mutual funds might have exit fees when you cash them out, or load fees when you purchase them with your new IRA. Trustees might charge fees for transferring stocks.

Determining the Value of a Conversion

The amount to be converted is the value of everything that is converted to the Roth IRA on the date of the transfer. If you cash out your traditional IRA or retirement plan, that is the amount of cash that can be deposited in the Roth IRA and taxed. If you are transferring stocks, bonds, or other assets, their market value on the date of the transfer must be determined. It does not matter if these assets have increased in value since you acquired them, or if they are now worth less than what you paid for them.

Profit will be taxed as income, not as capital gain.

When an asset in an IRA or a tax-advantaged retirement account sells for more than you paid for it, the profit is taxed as income. In a taxable investment account, this profit would be taxed at a lower rate as a long-term capital gain. Financial instruments such as certificates of deposit (CDs) might incur penalties if you cash them out early.

Treatment of a Conversion

For tax purposes, you must report the distribution from your retirement plan or traditional IRA as gross income on your tax return just as you would if you had not rolled it over into a Roth IRA. You must first enter the entire amount of the distribution on the tax form, then subtract any non-deductible contributions that you made to the Roth. If your AGI was above a certain amount, you might have had to pay income tax on some of your contributions to your traditional IRA. Non-deductible contributions to a retirement account or traditional IRA are known as your "basis." You have already paid taxes on them, so those amounts are not taxed again.

Tax withholding and estimated tax.

If you are including a distribution from a traditional IRA or other retirement plan in your gross income for the year in which you roll over to a Roth IRA, you might have to increase the amount of income tax withheld from your paycheck for that year, or make estimated payments. More information is available in IRS Publication 505, Tax Withholding and Estimated Tax (**www.irs.gov/publications/p505/index.html**).

Calculating the income tax on your conversion is relatively simple if you own a single traditional IRA and convert it to a Roth. If you own more than one IRA, the calculation becomes more complicated. For purposes of calculating income tax on a conversion, you must treat all your IRAs as a single IRA, even if they are held at different banks and the money came from different sources. IRAs held under your employer's SEP or SIMPLE plans are included. The taxable amount of your conversion is calculated according to the amount of non-deductible contributions (basis) in your combined IRAs. If basis makes up 20 percent of the combined balances of all your IRAs, you will not pay taxes on 20 percent of the conversion, no matter which IRA account you convert. You can calculate basis using IRS Form 8606.

Convert Early in the Year

Under most circumstances, the value of the stock market rises during the year. If you plan to convert a traditional IRA or a retirement plan to a Roth, try to do it early in the year. When you convert, you will pay income tax on the total value of your account. By converting early in the year, you are likely to pay less in taxes because the value of your account will be lower in January than it will be at the end of the year. If the value of the stock market declines after you make your conversion, or if you find you do not have enough cash on hand to pay the income tax on the conversion, you will have until October 15 of the following year to reverse it by recharacterizing.

Converting early also gives you many months of tax-free earnings before you have to pay the income tax on the conversion, though you might have to pay an estimated withholding tax. If you convert in January but do not pay taxes until the filing deadline in April of the next year, that makes 15 months of tax-free earnings. If you wait to convert in December, you will have only four months of tax-free earnings. Converting early also gives you almost two years to watch the market and evaluate the tax benefits of the conversion. You have until October 15 of the following year to recharacterize (and convert again) if you discover you are going to be in a lower tax bracket in the subsequent year.

Conversion that Covers More than One Tax Year

A conversion that was started in December might not be completed until the next tax year. When you do a rollover, you have 60 days from the day you withdraw assets from your traditional IRA or retirement plan to deposit them in a Roth IRA. If you take the disbursement in December and deposit it in the Roth IRA in January, the deposit is technically occurring in the next tax year. In such cases, the income tax on the conversion is applied to year that the conversion was begun, not the year in which it was completed.

> *The five-year rule applies to the year the transaction was completed.*
>
> Even if the transaction was started in the previous year, the five-year rule counts the year in which the transaction was completed as the first year. This is important to remember when you are considering making a withdrawal from your Roth IRA.

Taking Money Out of a Roth IRA After a Conversion

Five-year rule

As explained in Chapter 2, you must be older than 59½ and have held a Roth IRA for five years before you can withdraw earnings tax- and penalty-free. Contributions can be withdrawn at any time without tax or penalty. Amounts converted from a traditional IRA or a tax-advantaged retirement plan to a Roth IRA are treated differently from contributions to a Roth IRA. Congress wanted to prevent people from avoiding the 10 percent early withdrawal penalty by converting a traditional IRA to a Roth and then withdrawing the funds.

Amounts converted from a traditional IRA to a Roth IRA are subject to the five-year rule: If withdrawn within five years of the conversion, a 10 percent early withdrawal penalty will be assessed even if you are older than 59½. The year in which the money is deposited in the Roth IRA is counted as the first year, even if it was taken out of the old IRA late in the previous year. If you make several conversions in different years, the five-year waiting period is calculated separately for each conversion.

Direct transfers from a Roth 403(b) or a Roth 401(k) with one employer to another Roth retirement plan with a new employer are exempted; the new account will be treated as though it was established on the same day as the old account. Most employer plans have rules prohibiting withdrawals until you retire or leave employment with the company.

Converting After You Have Begun Taking Substantially Equal Payments

One way to avoid the early withdrawal penalty on distributions from a traditional IRA is to set up a substantially equal payments program (SEPP), an arrangement under which someone younger than 59½ can begin to receive annual distributions from an IRA based on his or her life expectancy. The payments must continue for a minimum of five years or until the IRA owner reaches the age of 59½ or becomes disabled, whichever occurs last.

If you have already started taking substantially equal payments from your traditional IRA under a SEPP program, you can convert to a Roth IRA, but you must continue taking the SEPP payments. You will no longer be paying income tax on the payments. If you are younger than 59½, you will not be charged the 10 percent early withdrawal penalty on earnings as long as the payments are part of a series of substantially equal payments.

Converting After You Have Begun Taking RMDs

You can convert to a Roth after you have already begun taking RMDs from a traditional IRA. You will have to take the RMD for the year in which you make the conversion. The RMD must be taken before you make the conversion, because the IRS does not consider the money eligible for a conversion. If you convert in the year you turn 70½, you must take your first RMD before making the conversion, even though you would have been allowed to defer that first RMD until April 1 of the following year if you kept your traditional IRA.

An RMD taken after a partial conversion to a Roth IRA reverses the conversion.

Your RMD for the year of conversion is based on the total amount in the account on December 31 of the previous year. If you fail to take your RMD before converting part of the account to a Roth, the conversion will be treated as a failed conversion.

Recharacterization: Undoing the Conversion

Until 2010, if you converted a traditional IRA or retirement plan to a Roth IRA and then discovered that you were not eligible for a Roth IRA because your AGI exceeded the income limit, you could correct the error by performing a recharacterization. In 2010, income limits for converting to a Roth were eliminated, and recharacterization to correct a mistake will no longer be necessary.

You can recharacterize if, after converting to a Roth IRA, you decide that you no longer want to pay income tax on the converted amount. You might earn unexpected income near the end of the year and suddenly find yourself in a higher tax bracket. If the value of the assets converted to a Roth IRA decreases dramatically after the conversion, and you realize that you are going to be paying income tax on money that no longer exists, you can recharacterize.

In a recharacterization, the funds are transferred back into a traditional IRA before the due date (and any extensions) for your tax return, and it is treated as though the conversion never took place. The deadline for recharacterization is October 15 of the year after the conversion, even if you have already filed your tax return. If you have already filed your tax return, you will have to file an amended return reporting the recharacterization.

To recharacterize, ask the custodian of the Roth IRA to transfer the funds and any investment earnings from them back to the custodian of the traditional IRA. Funds disbursed from a retirement account such as a 401(k) or 403(b) cannot be returned to that account, so you will have to open a traditional IRA account to receive them, or deposit them in a traditional IRA you already own.

You can recharacterize only once during a tax year. After you have recharacterized, you must wait until the next tax year before you can convert to a Roth IRA again. You could recharacterize in December of one year and again in January of the next tax year, but each recharacterization would have to be applied to a different tax year.

You can recharacterize only part of a converted IRA. For example, you might find that converting the entire balance of your traditional IRA has pushed you into a higher tax bracket, causing you to pay income tax at a higher rate on part of that balance. You could recharacterize just enough of the balance to drop you back into the lower income tax bracket and leave the rest in the Roth IRA.

Reconversion

Once you have used recharacterization to undo a conversion, you are not allowed to re-convert to a Roth right away. The new conversion cannot be in the same tax year as the old conversion, and it cannot occur until 30 days after the recharacterization. Because the deadline for recharacterization is October 15 of the year following a conversion, you could wait 30 days and then reconvert, but the new conversion would belong to the current, and not the previous, year.

You must wait 30 days after a recharacterization before you can reconvert to a Roth IRA. This rule does not apply to the conversion of different money. You could convert money from a different traditional IRA, or even money from the same traditional IRA that was not included in the first conversion, without waiting. One way to make it clear that you are not converting money that has been recharacterized is to perform the new conversion before you recharacterize the old one.

For example, you might have converted an investment worth $30,000 from a traditional to a Roth IRA. During the year, that investment does poorly, and by tax time it is worth only $20,000. You do not want to pay income tax on $30,000 when the Roth IRA balance has dropped to $20,000, so you decide to recharacterize that investment and convert a different investment from your traditional IRA to a Roth. By converting the different investment before you recharacterize the one that has dropped in value, you make it clear that you are not reconverting the same money. When you do the recharacterization, make sure your IRA custodian understands that only the first conversion and not the second is being recharacterized.

Converting to a Roth IRA in Several Stages

The benefits of conversion are diminished and might even disappear if you have to use some of the funds in a traditional IRA to pay the income taxes when you convert to a Roth IRA. Your goal is to put as much money as possible in the Roth IRA by paying the income tax with outside funds. If you do not have funds available to pay income tax on the entire balance of your traditional IRA at once, convert portions of it over a period of several years.

If your traditional IRA contains non-deductible contributions (basis), you are not allowed to convert only the nontaxable part to a Roth. Any conversion you make will be composed of taxable and nontaxable amounts in proportion to the basis in your traditional IRA. For example, if $4,000 of a $10,000 IRA is non-deductible, 40 percent of the amount you convert will be nontaxable and you will pay taxes on the other 60 percent.

For 2010 conversions only, income tax can be spread over two years.

Owners of traditional IRAs who convert to Roths in 2010 are given the option of spreading the income tax payments over two years, 2011 and 2012. Those who convert in subsequent years will be required to pay the entire amount of income tax in the year the conversion was made.

Converting an Inherited IRA

When you inherit a traditional IRA from your spouse, you have the option of treating it as your own IRA. Once the IRA is your own, it can be converted according to the usual rules: Income tax must be paid on the amount converted, minus any non-deductible contributions, and you cannot make withdrawals until five years from the first day of the year of conversion. If you have elected to treat a traditional IRA inherited from your spouse as your own, you are not required to begin taking RMDs until the year after you reach the age of 70½. Select a year when you are in a low income tax bracket to make the conversion.

Have You Been Laid Off?

The economic crisis of 2008-'09 hit retirement savings hard: Not only did the investments in many 401(k)s lose as much as 40 percent of their value, but hundreds of thousands of workers lost their jobs. If you have lost your job at a company where you had a 401(k), you now have an opportunity to convert to a Roth IRA while your retirement plan balance is relatively low. Many 401(k) custodians offer traditional and Roth IRAs for ex-employees, allowing you to transfer many of your investments directly into the new IRA. If you choose to do a trustee-to-trustee transfer or a rollover, look for investments with potential for strong growth as the economy revives. *Later sections of this book discuss how to select investments for your portfolio.*

The challenge is finding the money to pay the income tax on the conversion. If you have become unemployed, your AGI for the year will be lower and might put you in a lower tax bracket. Ordinarily you should not use funds from the 401(k) to pay income taxes on the conversion for two reasons: The balance in your retirement savings account will be lowered, and you might have to pay a 10 percent early withdrawal penalty on those funds. You might be able to avoid the penalty if you have certain types of expenses, such as buying health insurance while you are unemployed or paying for qualified higher education expenses for a family member.

If you cannot find a way to pay the income tax on a conversion right away, convert your 401(k) to a traditional IRA now and do the Roth conversion later, or in increments. You will still be able to select investments with lower fees and expenses than those in your 401(k) and to position yourself for growth as the economy recovers. IRAs place fewer restrictions on beneficiaries than qualified retirement plans, so your heirs will have more options.

One-time Conversion Opportunity in 2010

The Tax Increase Prevention and Reconciliation Act of 2005 (TIPRA) lifted income limits for converting a traditional IRA or qualified retirement plan to a Roth IRA, which began in 2010. To encourage conversion, IRA owners who converted in 2010 were given a one-time option of spreading the income tax payments over two years, 2011 and 2012. The conversion will automatically be reported as income over 2011 and 2012 unless you chose to report all of it as income on your 2010 tax return. You must decide before the tax filing deadline for 2010, which is October 17, 2011. You can change your mind any time before that deadline, even if you have already filed your 2010 tax return. For example, if you choose to report the income in 2011 and 2012, then realize that you will be in a higher tax bracket in those years than in 2010, you might decide you want to report all the income in 2010 and pay taxes on it at a lower rate. If your return has already been filed, you will have to file an amended tax return to notify the IRS of the change.

The option to report the income over the two subsequent years is a one-time opportunity. Beginning in 2011, anyone can convert to a Roth, but all the income must be reported in the year of conversion. If an IRA owner converted a traditional IRA to a Roth in 2010 and dies before 2012, all untaxed conversion money must be reported in the deceased owner's final tax return. There is an exception for a spouse beneficiary, who can choose to report the income over 2011 and 2012, just as the owner would have. The spouse must choose this option before October 15 of the year following the IRA owner's death. An IRA owner who converted to a Roth in 2010 and then withdraws some of the conversion money before 2012 will be required to pay income tax on that amount in the year it is withdrawn. If the Roth contains money contributed before the conversion, any distribution will come from that older money first, and then from the conversion money. The IRA owner is not allowed to include basis (non-deductible contributions) from the conversion as part of the withdrawal — the entire amount withdrawn will be taxable.

The prospect of being able to convert a traditional IRA or 401(k) with a large balance to a Roth is exciting to financial planners and attracts plenty of attention from financial commentators and journalists. Before rushing into conversion, you should consider the tax consequences:

- **Do you have enough funds outside your IRA to pay the income tax on the conversion?** The greatest benefit of conversion is being able to transfer assets into an account where all future earnings will be tax-free. If you have to dip into the IRA to pay income taxes on a large conversion, you will be losing assets from the account that cannot be replaced and reducing future earnings. Consider making a partial conversion and converting only the amount you can afford to pay taxes on.

- **Will you be in a lower tax bracket when you retire?** The opportunity to spread income taxes on a conversion over two years is attractive, but if your income puts you in a high income tax bracket in 2011 and 2012, and you expect to be in a lower tax bracket later on, you might have more money in retirement if you wait until then and convert to a Roth over a period of several years.

A conversion calculator such as the one on Statefarm.com (**www.statefarm. com/learning/calc/conversion.asp**) or Morningstar.com (**http://screen. morningstar.com/IRA/IRACalculator.html**) will help you estimate the impact of converting when you are in a lower tax bracket and determine whether a conversion makes sense for you.

CASE STUDY: EXCERPT FROM "AMERICANS UNDERWHELMED BY ROTH IRA CONVERSION OPPORTUNITY, FIRST COMMAND REPORTS."

Business Wire, November 19, 2009:

First Command Financial Services and its subsidiaries, including First Command Bank and First Command Financial Planning, assist American families in their efforts to build wealth, reduce debt, and pursue their lifetime financial goals and dreams — focusing on consumer behavior as the first and most powerful determinant of results. Through personalized financial plans that emphasize accumulating wealth while reducing risk, First Command Financial Advisors have established lasting relationships with hundreds of thousands of client families since 1958. Find more information on Roth IRAs at **www.firstcommand.com/rothnow**.

The October survey of the First Command Financial Behaviors Index™ reveals that 84 percent of middle-class consumers are not aware that a new law goes into effect on January 1, lifting the $100,000 income limit on Roth IRA conversions and allowing investors to pay the resulting tax bill over a two-year period. Even after learning of the new law, only 6 percent of survey respondents indicated they plan to pursue a Roth IRA conversion.

Twenty-three percent of respondents said they do not plan on converting their traditional retirement accounts because they expect to be in a lower income tax bracket in retirement. Terri Kallsen, CFP® and executive vice president of strategic development at First Command, says, "We are troubled by the prevalence of this particular response, which was the one most often cited in the survey. Consumers need to be concerned about future tax rates. Many people think rates will rise in the future. By converting traditional IRA dollars now, your tax burden may be less in the future. The tax benefits may be particularly appealing if you think you will be in the same or higher tax bracket in retirement."

Americans also say they will not convert because they do not have money to pay the conversion taxes (12 percent), and because it would bump them into a higher tax bracket (11 percent).

Kallsen says, "We expect the level of interest and commitment to rise appreciably during the coming weeks as financial professionals continue to reach out to their clients. Notably, 22 percent of survey respondents with a financial plan are already aware of the new law, and 10 percent of those working with a financial planner expect to convert their traditional accounts into Roth IRAs. Clearly, financial advisors are busy educating Americans about this unique but admittedly complex opportunity and helping them determine the best course of action for their own situation. Americans may never have a better reason to seek the assistance of a financial advisor. This is an ideal time to create tax-free income for retirement. While this is a special opportunity, it may not make sense for everybody. That's why it is important to consult with a professional. Financial advisors have the tools and training to help consumers explore this unique opportunity and decide on the best strategy for their personal financial situation."

Roth IRA Investments

Shopping for a Roth IRA

You can open a Roth IRA at almost any bank, credit union, or stock brokerage firm. Go to a search engine online and type in "Roth IRA"; pages of ads and listings will appear. Many financial institutions offer the same investments for traditional and Roth IRAs — the only difference is the tax treatment of your contributions and withdrawals. Many IRAs market themselves with highly charged investment language, promising low costs and higher-than-average rates of return. Do not take these claims at face value. Find out if they are true by comparing similar IRAs to see what benefits each one offers.

If you are satisfied with the investments in your traditional IRA portfolio, consider converting to a Roth with the same IRA custodian.

The IRS does not "approve" IRA investments.

Some of the literature marketing IRA investments fraudulently implies that the IRS has reviewed and approved the plans. The IRS does not endorse nor approve any IRA investment. The IRS only certifies that IRA sponsors, trustees, and custodians are complying with regulations concerning account administration and tax deductions.

Before making any important purchase, you should compare prices, the quality and features of different brands and models, and the financing options available from different stores and dealerships. You probably should ask your friends and coworkers for recommendations, and you might even go online to read the reviews and comments posted by people who have already used the product. An IRA is no different. Banks and financial institutions have a variety of investment choices, and the fees they charge for their services vary widely. Take some time to compare several IRAs and read recommendations and reviews in business magazines and on investment Web sites. Most IRA trustees charge a fee to open an account and/or transfer out of an account; save money by doing research and finding the most appropriate Roth IRA the first time.

The first place to look for a Roth IRA is the bank where you have your checking and savings accounts or the brokerage that manages your investments. Many waive fees or offer premium accounts with lower transaction costs for existing customers, especially for those who maintain a high balance. Some credit unions offer no-fee IRAs for their members. Another option is discount online brokerages that offer low fees and incentives to attract new investors. Your broker or financial advisor might recommend an IRA to you and offer to help you set one up; be sure to compare the fees and investment offerings before committing yourself. When you feel you have a good understanding of services, investment options, and fees, you are ready to proceed.

You can open a Roth IRA with a financial institution, a bank, or a stock brokerage firm, and select any of the investments they offer. A brokerage is likely to offer more investment options than a bank. Many brokerages and banks allow you to open an IRA account online in just a few minutes, but transferring money into the account might take several days. You might be asked to sign and mail in printed documents, or you might be able to sign electronically online.

Comparing IRA plans

The selection of an IRA is a very personal matter. A feature that is important for one person might mean very little to someone else. Do you want easy access to a customer service representative who will answer all your questions over the phone, or do you just want simple, inexpensive trading? Are you planning to make regular monthly contributions, or a single yearly contribution? Do you want to read economic news and investment advice, or do you simply want to set up your portfolio and maintain it automatically? Are you interested in a structured investment plan, or do you want to plan and manage your own portfolio? When deciding where to open your IRA, look for:

- A good selection of investment options, including mutual funds, ETFs, common stocks, and bonds. If you want to invest in real estate, commodities, foreign funds, or precious metals, look for an IRA that offers those types of investments.

- Low commissions and account fees. Some IRAs currently charge an annual custodial fee of $25 or $30, and $50 or $60 for closing an account or transferring funds to another IRA. Some charge a small fee for sending you paper statements. In addition, the investments you select for your IRA might have management fees and/or "load fees," and buying and selling stocks will incur trading fees.

- Easy access to your account information.

- The ability to make automated fund transfers from your bank account.

- Good customer service.

- Additional services such as investment counseling, newsletters and information, e-mail alerts, and tax advice.

- The minimum balance required to open an account or purchase a fund.

- The way in which an IRA manages reinvestments of earnings and dividends.

- The ease with which you can withdraw cash from the account.

Purchases of stocks and ETFs involve trading fees. If you plan to make small, regular contributions, a low-cost mutual fund is the best choice. Some IRAs allow you to invest regular contributions and reinvest earnings by purchasing fractional shares of stocks. You can also accumulate your contributions in a money market account and make one or two larger investments in stocks or ETFs during the year.

Comparison of IRAs at Some Major Financial Institutions*
(All Web sites accessed November 23, 2009.)

Company	URL	Benefits	Minimum Balance	Custodial Fee	Transfer-Out Fee	Rollover Fee	Termina-tion Fee	Trading Fees, Expenses
AARP Financial Inc.	www.aarpfinancial.com	Objective financial advisors, simplicity (only 5 funds), automatic contributions of as little as $25 per month	$100	No	No	No	No	Funds are no-load; management fees and other expenses may be associated with the individual funds and investments in your account
Bank of America	www.bankofamerica.com	Bank of America customers can open an IRA by signing up for automatic contributions of $100 per month	$1,000, which is waived if you sign up for automatic monthly contributions of $100	No	Yes	No	$75	Management fees and other expenses may be associated with the individual funds and investments in your account; trading fees depend on the type of account held with Bank of America or Banc of America
E*Trade Financial	https://us.etrade.com/e/t/home	Offers 100 commission-free trades with new account	No minimum investment if you sign up for electronic statements	$25 annual custodial fee, which is waived if you sign up for electronic statements and have a $25,000 balance	$60	Yes	Yes	Management fees, trading fees, and other expenses may be associated with the individual funds and investments in your account
Fidelity Investments	www.fidelity.com	$2,500 minimum is waived if you sign up for automatic contributions of at least $200 per month; low-balance fee		No	Possibly	No	Yes	Management fees, trading fees, and other expenses may be associated with the individual funds and investments in your account; fidelity funds are no-load
Scottrade	www.scottrade.com	Online stock trading platform, real-time balance updates available online; direct access to cash in your account		No	No	No – will reimburse you for up to $100 in account transfer fees charged by another broker when you transfer to Scottrade	No	Management fees, trading fees and other expenses may be associated with the individual funds and investments in your account

Share-builder (ING Direct)	http://content.sharebuilder.com/mgdcon/jump/Web/welcome/proseasy/index.htm		No minimum	$25 per year, waived for certain types of accounts				$4 for each pre-scheduled trade; $9.95 for each real-time trade
T. Rowe Price	http://individual.troweprice.com/public/Retail/IRA/	Free automatic rebalancing of asset allocations in your portfolio every quarter	$1,000					Management fees, trading fees, and other expenses may be associated with the individual funds and investments in your account
TIAA-CREF	www.tiaa-cref.org	Non-profit, available only to employees of not-for-profit or government organizations	No minimum investment	No	No	No	No	Management fees, trading fees, and other expenses may be associated with the individual funds and investments in your account
Trade King	www.tradeking.com	Sign up to have cash balances automatically transferred to money market sweep accounts that pay higher interest rates than ordinary money market accounts; good customer service.	No minimum	No	$50	No; will reimburse you for up to $150 in account transfer fees charged by another broker when you transfer	$50	$4.95 per trade
Vanguard	https://personal.vanguard.com/us/home?fromPage=portal_image	Low-cost funds	$1,000 - $3,000	Waived with electronic statements				
Wachovia	www.wachovia.com	Free personal retirement consultation		$40, waived for certain types of accounts	$95	Yes	$95	
Zecco Trading	www.zecco.com/trading/signin.aspx	Ten free trades every month with $25,000 balance or 25 trades per month	No minimum	$30 per year	$50			$4.50 for each additional trade after the first 10 each month

* Fees and other information are subject to change. This chart is intended only to give an idea of the options available.

> *Use outside funds to pay custodial fees.*
>
> If you open a Roth IRA that charges an annual custodial fee or transfer out of an IRA, then pay the fees from your checking account to avoid having that $30 or $50 deducted from the tax-deferred earnings in your IRA.

Financial advisors

Consult a fee-only financial planner if you need professional assistance to define your financial objectives, determine your optimum portfolio asset allocations, and select bonds. A fee-only Certified Financial Planner® (CFP®) will charge only an hourly or one-time consultation fee and does not receive commissions from the sale of financial products. To check the accreditation and legal status of brokers or financial advisors, look them up on the SEC Web site at **www.sec.gov/investor/brokers.htm** or the FINRA Web site at **www.finra.org/Investors/ToolsCalculators/BrokerCheck/ index.htm**. The SEC site also has information on the regulatory compliance of brokerages.

> *Do not rely only on the advice of your IRA custodian.*
>
> Many banks and brokerages offer personalized financial advice as part of their services. While their advisors might offer sound suggestions, do your own research and confirm that the investments they are recommending are really your best choice. Ask whether the advisor receives a commission on your purchase. See if your IRA custodian offers investment options other than its own products and compare expense ratios, management costs, and fees.

Introduction to IRA investment options

When you open a Roth IRA, your IRA custodian will ask you to select from a menu of investment options, many of which will be mutual funds. If you plan to make regular contributions, you will probably allocate a percentage of each contribution to each of your selected investments. The names of the various mutual fund offerings often indicate the type of investments in the fund, such as "Classic International Equity," "Value Income Stock," or "Investment Grade Bond," but not all the names are easy to decipher. *The different types of investments in these mutual funds will be described in greater detail later in this chapter.* IRA custodians typically categorize each fund by its investment style to help clients with portfolio allocation. *See Chapter 7 for more information on asset allocation.* You might see the following, or similar, categories:

- **Aggressive growth**: Funds containing stocks and investments with potential for rapid growth, but associated with greater risk.

- **Growth**: Funds containing investments that are more stable and offer a promise of steady but slower growth, with less risk.

- **Income**: Bond funds that almost guarantee a steady, but lower, rate of return with little risk.

- **Capital preservation**: Stable asset funds that contain a mixture of bonds and insurance contracts, and are guaranteed to produce a specific rate of return. These funds are often "wrapped" with insurance that will make up the difference if the fund performs below the guaranteed rate of return.

Your IRA custodian might offer other products that allow you to diversify your portfolio, such as commodities funds and individual stocks and bonds. A self-directed Roth IRA allows you to invest in precious metals, real estate, or a business or partnership.

Structured investment plans

Some IRA custodians offer ready-made portfolios known as structured investment plans that combine fixed-income products such as bonds with stocks and derivatives. The fixed-income securities protect the investors' capital, while equity, options, futures, and derivatives are used to achieve growth. The plan's rate of return is based on the performance of its underlying assets. Some of these plans do not guarantee capital protection and therefore involve greater risk. A structured investment plan is a fixed-term investment, meaning that the promised rate of return is achieved only when the investment is held for a specific period of time. If you withdraw your money before the underlying assets reach maturity, you could lose part of the principal and the promised returns.

Managed and special strategy Roth IRAs

You can pay professional managers to manage your IRA investments and carry out special investment strategies, such as active trading of stocks or investing in foreign currency, for you. You will pay for the services of a manager, and you will also pay trading fees and other costs when investments are bought and sold.

Self-directed Roth IRAs

A self-directed Roth IRA is structured so that you manage the investments in your IRA yourself. Instead of selling you mutual funds or stocks, the custodian of a self-directed IRA administers your IRA according to your directions. Self-directed IRAs permit you to use your knowledge and experience to invest in a wide variety of assets with potential for more growth than mutual funds, stocks, and fixed-income investments. *See Chapter 9 for information on how to set up and manage a self-directed IRA.*

Types of Investments

Stocks

Stocks are typically regarded as the engine that drives the growth of an IRA portfolio because throughout the past 80 years, the stock market has grown at a rate of 10 percent. While the stock market is growing, inflation is decreasing the buying power of the dollar at a rate of 3 percent, resulting in an overall average growth rate of 7 percent — a much higher rate of return than the interest realized from bonds. Brokerage firms make a point of stating that "past performance does not guarantee future results," a warning that buying stock is always a gamble and that a stock might perform differently after you have made your investment from how it has in the past.

When you buy a stock, you are essentially purchasing a share in a business. There are two ways to make money directly from stocks: by selling them after their value has gone up, and by receiving dividends paid out from company profits. Money can also be made indirectly by selling contracts (stock options) to buy or sell your stock at a specific price by a specific date, and by borrowing from a brokerage to purchase additional stock for a period of time before selling at a profit and returning the money (leverage).

The overall growth rate of the stock market incorporates all the fluctuations that occur as certain companies fail and others flourish, and some industries flounder while others experience explosive growth. Conventional wisdom states that in order to achieve a similar rate of growth, your portfolio should hold a variety of stocks that reflect the stock market as a whole. If all your money is invested in a single company and that company goes bankrupt, you will lose everything. In the beginning, most IRAs are too small to purchase a variety of stocks, so diversity is achieved by purchasing mutual funds or ETFs constructed to reflect the whole market. These are known as broad market funds.

Stocks are classified by styles or industry sectors. Style refers either to the size of a company measured by the value of its outstanding shares (capitalization) or whether a company's stock is considered to be a "growth" or a "value" investment. The dividing line for classifying by capitalization is arbitrary, but a common classification is:

- **Large cap** — $5 billion or more
- **Mid cap** — $1 billion to $5 billion
- **Small cap** — $250 million to $1 billion
- **Micro cap** — Less than $250 million

A growth stock is a company that has the potential to grow substantially in the near future. A value stock is one that is selling at a price lower than a company is actually worth and is likely to increase in value or produce a healthy dividend. Each major provider of stock market indexes has its own method for determining whether a stock is "growth" or "value." Russell uses two factors to separate value from growth; Dow Jones uses six; S&P and S&P/Citigroup uses seven; MSCI uses eight; and Morningstar uses ten. These factors include price-to-earnings ratio (PE), debt, cash flow, assets owned by the company, and even the quality of the management.

Ten or eleven major industry groups are widely recognized. As new technologies are developed, new types of businesses are listed on the stock exchange, creating new industry sectors and subsectors, while old established industries disappear.

The eleven major industry sectors are:

- Computer technology
- Financial services
- Health care
- Industrial materials
- Energy

- Utilities
- Media
- Telecommunications
- Consumer services
- Business services
- Consumer goods

If you are diversifying a portfolio by industry sectors, it is important to include representatives of all the sectors so your portfolio can benefit from growth and development in any of them.

In addition, it is important to include international stocks in your portfolio to achieve diversity. During the 2000s, U.S. stocks made up between 38 and 43 percent of the global stock market; some experts suggest that this proportion should be reflected in the international holdings of a portfolio.

Though stocks have the potential to drive growth in a portfolio, they involve greater risk than fixed-income investments because their performance is not guaranteed. The volatility of the stock market means the value of your IRA could ebb just at the time when you need to begin taking withdrawals. If you make poor choices or fail to diversify your portfolio, you could suffer substantial losses and not reach your savings goals. To mitigate these risks, most portfolios include bonds and other fixed-income investments.

Bonds

The fixed-income portion of an IRA portfolio might contain dividend-producing stocks, but it is mainly composed of bonds and money market funds. Buying a bond essentially involves loaning your money to a government entity or a corporation for a specified time, then receiving interest and the return of your principal when the bond matures. Though the bond market does not experience the volatility and related growth potential of the stock market, the average private investor invests approximately 50 percent of long-term savings in fixed-income assets. The public U.S. fixed-income market ($28.25 trillion at the end of 2008) is much larger than the public U.S. equity market.

The lower volatility of bonds offers a safety net in difficult times, but adjusted for inflation, the real return on bonds has averaged 2.4 percent over the past 80 years. You can make money on bonds in two ways: from their regular interest payments, and by selling them when they are in demand. The demand for bonds increases when the economy is weak because they are considered a safer investment than stocks. During periods of economic decline, the interest rate is often lowered, making older bonds with higher interest rates more valuable and causing the prices of these older bonds to escalate.

Bonds carry different kinds of risk from stocks, including the risk that the agency or company issuing the bonds will not be able to pay you back, and the risk that you will lose the opportunity to make money when interest rates go up because you have already bought a bond with a lower interest rate. If the rate of inflation exceeds the rate of interest on your bonds, in terms of actual value, then they will be worth less when they mature than they were worth when you bought them. Bonds that are insured against default or protected against inflation offer lower interest rates.

The length of time for which the bond is issued is called its maturity. The longer the maturity of a bond, the greater the likelihood that interest rates will rise before it matures (interest-rate risk). A three-year bond will have a far lower interest-rate risk than a 20-year bond. Bonds must be redeemed when they reach maturity, which means that you have to seek new investments to keep your money growing. A bond fund continually redeems mature bonds and purchases new ones, but because the rate of return is lower on bonds, expenses charged by the fund are likely to consume a greater portion of your earnings.

Bonds are classified by type, maturity, and credit rating.

Type

Fixed-income assets include T-notes, government agency issues, mortgages, corporate bonds, municipal bonds, asset-backed securities, and inflation-protected securities.

U.S. Treasury securities, used to finance the federal government debt, are considered to have the bond market's lowest risk because they are guaranteed by the U.S. government's "full faith and credit" — in other words, its authority to tax the citizens of the United States.

Government agencies, such as the Government National Mortgage Association (Ginnie Mae), issue debt to support their role in financing mortgages. As divisions of the government, their securities are also backed by the full faith and credit of the United States.

Government-sponsored enterprises (GSEs) are financing entities created by Congress to fund loans to certain groups of borrowers, such as homeowners, farmers, and students. Though GSEs are sometimes referred to as federal agencies or federally sponsored agencies, their debt is sponsored but not guaranteed by the federal government. They are considered a greater credit risk than agencies of the federal government, and their bonds often offer a higher yield than U.S. Treasury bonds with the same maturity. Student Loan Marketing Association (Sallie Mae), Federal National Mortgage Association (Fannie Mae), and Federal Home Loan Mortgage Corporation (Freddie Mac) are privately owned corporations established with a public purpose, and the Federal Home Loan Banks and the Federal Farm Credit Banks are systems comprising regional banks.

Treasury inflation protected securities (TIPS) are issued by the U.S. government and carry its full-faith-and-credit backing. TIPS have a fixed interest rate, indexed to inflation through adjustments to their principal amount made on the basis of changes in the Consumer Price Index-U (CPI-U). The CPI-U is a monthly measurement of the price for a fixed basket of goods and services that U.S. urban consumers, including professional and self-employed people, buy regularly. At maturity, investors receive the greater of the inflation-adjusted principal or the par amount. To compensate for the guaranteed protection against inflation, the interest rate on these bonds is lower.

Corporate bonds are debts issued by industrial, financial, and service companies to finance capital investment and operating cash flow. The corporate bond market is bigger than each of the markets for municipal bonds, U.S. Treasury securities, and government agencies securities. Corporate bonds have a wide range of bond structures, coupon rates, maturity dates, credit quality, and industry exposure.

Mortgage-backed securities (MBS) represent an interest in pools of loans, typically first mortgages on residential properties. They are primarily issued by a government agency, such as Ginnie Mae, or a government-sponsored enterprise, such as Fannie Mae or Freddie Mac, which typically guarantee the interest and principal payments on their securities. The MBS market also includes "private-label" mortgage securities that subsidiaries of investment banks, financial institutions, and home builders issue.

Asset-backed securities (ABS) also represent an interest in a pool of asset-backed loans, such as credit card receivables, auto loans and leases, or home-equity loans. ABS carries some form of credit enhancement, such as bond insurance, to make them attractive to investors.

Maturity

Bond maturities are typically classified into three ranges:

- **Short-term:** Bonds that have an average maturity of three years or less.
- **Intermediate:** Bonds that have an average maturity of four to nine years.
- **Long-term:** Bonds that have an average maturity of ten years or longer.

Bond mutual funds typically purchase bonds that emulate a particular market index. When a bond index has an average maturity of five years, all the bonds in that index do not necessarily mature in five years. The maturity of individual bonds in the index might range from one year to ten years, with the total average maturity being five years.

The average maturity of a bond index is a measure of interest rate risk. When interest rates rise, bond funds and ETFs benchmarked to indexes with longer durations will decrease in value more than those benchmarked to indexes with shorter durations. Because of the higher risk associated with long-duration bonds, they are expected to generate a higher total return.

Credit rating

Credit risk is a reflection of the financial strength of the government, agency, or company issuing a bond. The greater the chance of a default, the higher the interest rate must be to compensate for the risk. The U.S government and its agencies are low credit risks; investment-grade corporate bonds are higher. Companies whose financial future is uncertain issue the highest-yield bonds, called junk bonds. The greater the credit risk and the longer the duration of the bonds in an index, the higher the expected long-term rate of return.

Bonds are rated by rating agencies, private companies that evaluate a bond issuer's financial health and assess its ability to repay its obligations in a timely manner. A rating is an evaluation of the likelihood that an issuer will repay the principal and interest of a particular bond on time and in full. In the United States, the major rating agencies are Moody's Investors Service, Standard and Poor's Ratings Services, and Fitch IBCA.

Investors in the marketplace determine bond prices and credit ratings influence investor confidence. When bond ratings are lowered, their price often goes down, and when ratings are raised, prices go up. Investors do not rely wholly on credit ratings; price changes often precede ratings changes because investors' assessment of risk has been altered based on other factors, such as economic news.

Mutual funds

A mutual fund is company that pools money and invests in a selection of stocks, bonds, and other investments that follows a stated set of objectives. Investors who purchase a share of a mutual fund own a share in all the underlying investments the fund holds. The share price of a mutual fund fluctuates according to the value of its underlying assets (net asset value, or NAV). Mutual funds must calculate their NAV at least once every business day, typically after the major U.S. exchanges close. Investors can sell their shares back to the fund at any time, but might not know the exact selling price until the transaction is complete. Typically, a fund will create new shares to accommodate new investors by buying more assets.

There are three ways to make money with mutual funds. If the underlying value of the assets in a fund increases, you can sell shares of the fund for a higher price than you paid for them. You can receive dividends and interest payments from securities the funds hold, and you might receive distributions of capital gains when the fund sells securities for more than it paid for them. Earnings in an IRA account will be reinvested.

There are more than 10,000 mutual funds in the United States, representing a wide variety of investment strategies. A mutual fund might hold stocks, bonds, notes, commodities, real estate, precious metals, or any combination of these assets. The most popular mutual funds are broad market funds that simulate the stock market as a whole, or those that hold a balanced portfolio of stocks and fixed-income investments.

Mutual fund investment strategies attempt to track the performance of an index. There are two basic types of indexes: market indexes and custom indexes. Market indexes follow the broad price levels and value of a specific financial market. Two of the most famous market indexes are the Dow Jones Industrial Average and the Standard & Poor's 500. A custom index is more like an investment strategy, a method for managing a portfolio that is used as the basis of a mutual fund. Fund sponsors who design their own indexes are required by the SEC to designate a third party to monitor the fund's compliance with its stated investment objectives. Every mutual fund issues a prospectus setting out its investment objectives and containing important information about the fund.

Contribution limits restrict the amount of investment capital in a newly opened Roth IRA. Mutual funds are well-suited to IRAs because a relatively small investment gives access to a diverse array of assets. An investor can create a diverse portfolio with just one or two mutual funds. Additional shares of a mutual fund can be purchased easily as contributions are made to the IRA. Mutual funds offer the expertise of professional managers, and earnings can be automatically reinvested. All mutual funds will redeem (buy back) your shares on any business day and must send you the payment within seven days. Mutual funds are easy to buy and sell; their liquidity makes it convenient to sell shares when cash is needed for distributions. In addition to broad market funds and bond funds, mutual funds exist for every type and style of investment, and every market and industry sector. Growth funds invest in assets that have the potential to gain in value. Income funds contain stocks that pay dividends.

Many mutual funds charge a load fee to enter the fund or an exit fee, as well as management charges, transaction fees, and marketing costs. A fund's annual operating expenses divided by the average annual value of its assets, expressed as a percentage, is known as the fund's expense ratio. Expense ratios vary widely. It is important to compare expense ratios and load fees when shopping for a mutual fund because high expenses eat into earnings. Financial experts consider these expenses a major obstacle to the growth of an IRA.

Excerpt from Invest Wisely: An Introduction to Mutual Funds, a publication of the U.S. Securities and Exchange Commission .

Key points to remember:

- Mutual funds are not guaranteed or insured by the FDIC or any other government agency — even if you buy through a bank and the fund carries the bank's name. You can lose money investing in mutual funds.

- Past performance is not a reliable indicator of future performance, so do not be dazzled by last year's high returns. But past performance can help you assess a fund's volatility over time.

- All mutual funds have costs that lower your investment returns. Shop around and use a mutual fund cost calculator at **www.sec.gov/investor/tools.shtml** to compare many of the costs of owning different funds before you buy.

ETFs

An IRA with a small balance can achieve instant diversity with the purchase of one or two exchange-traded funds (ETFs). They can also be used to add specific industries and market sectors to a portfolio. ETFs resemble mutual funds, except that their shares are traded on stock exchanges like shares of stock. Shares of an ETF represent ownership of a basket of stocks, bonds, and other assets. ETF shares can either be sold in a secondary market or redeemed for the underlying securities.

There are more than 700 ETFs following indexes and investment strategies similar to those of mutual funds. ETFs are also suited to IRAs because of their liquidity and because you can achieve a diverse portfolio by purchasing shares of one or two broad market ETFs.

ETFs typically have a lower expense ratio than similar mutual funds, and there are no load or exit fees. You will pay only a trading fee when you buy or sell shares. ETFs are more transparent than mutual funds because they are required to make their holdings public. The net asset value (NAV) of an ETF is calculated throughout every business day, and its current market price can be seen on the stock exchanges.

Money market funds

A money market fund is a type of mutual fund that makes highly liquid investments and pays dividends reflecting short-term interest rates. Money market funds are required by law to invest in low-risk securities. Money market funds typically invest in government securities, certificates of deposit, commercial paper of companies, or other highly liquid and low-risk securities. They attempt to keep the value of their underlying assets (NAV) at a constant $1 per share; only the yield fluctuates with interest rate changes. A money market fund's per share NAV can sometimes fall below $1 if the investments perform poorly.

A money market account in an IRA can temporarily hold earnings until enough cash has accumulated to purchase a new investment, until the cash is needed for a RMD, or to pay expenses for IRA investments. Many IRAs have an "automatic sweep" that regularly deposits earnings and excess cash into a money market account, where it can earn interest until it is needed. A money market fund earns approximately twice as much as a savings account. Though they offer a low rate of return, during the economic instability of 2008-'09, money market funds became popular as an alternative to losing money in the stock market.

Real estate

Real estate has little correlation with bonds and limited correlation with the stock market. Adding real estate to your portfolio helps to lower its volatility and ensure steady returns. There are two ways to invest in real estate with your IRA: by buying shares of funds or ETFs that invest in real estate or purchasing real estate with a self-directed IRA. *See Chapter 9 for more information on self-directed IRAs.*

Real estate investment trusts (REITs) are companies that hold portfolios of properties, such as office buildings, shopping malls, hotels, and timberland; or assets related to real estate, such as commercial mortgages. They use shareholders' investments to purchase, build, and maintain properties; manage tenants and collect rents; and return the profit to investors as dividends. Shares of an REIT represent ownership of actual property. There are approximately 200 publicly held REITs in the United States, and their stocks trade on the stock market. Because REITs make up only a small segment of the economy, the best way to gain exposure to them is to purchase an REIT fund. A number of mutual funds and several ETFs have ownership of groups of REITs.

REITs are good investments for a long-term portfolio because of their low correlation with broad market indexes and because the annual dividend rate of a typical REIT is between 5 and 7 percent — two to three times higher than the highest dividends non-REIT stocks pay. Whether the share price of an REIT rises or falls, dividends continue to be paid as long as the

REIT is bringing in money. REITs are required by law to pay out 90 percent of their income as dividends to shareholders.

Commodities

Commodities are products that are required every day, including food, such as livestock, grain, and sugar; and basic materials, such as steel and aluminum. Energy is traded as crude oil, natural gas, and electricity. Commodities are produced, bought, and sold all over the world, all of the time. When a shortage results in increased demand and higher prices, new producers gradually enter the market, and existing producers increase their output.

Investment in commodities is usually in the form of futures, or forwards. Futures are contracts to buy a commodity in the future at an agreed price. Only a small amount of money is required to secure the contract, with the remainder to be paid when the commodity is delivered. This amount is usually placed in a money market account or other short-term investment until the contract fulfillment date.

If you are knowledgeable about trading in commodities, you can use a self-directed IRA to buy and sell futures contracts. Commodity mutual funds and ETFs allow you to add commodities to your portfolio without becoming involved in day-to-day trading.

Precious metals

Precious metals do not generate income until they are sold for a profit. Certain gold, silver, and platinum coins and gold, silver, palladium, and platinum bullion can be purchased and held in a secure storage facility until you are ready to sell them. *See Chapter 9 for more information on how you can use an IRA to invest in precious metals.*

Best investments for tax-advantaged accounts:

All types of investments do not benefit in the same way from the tax-free status of a Roth IRA. To make the most of your contributions to your Roth IRA, you need to select investments that maximize the benefits of tax-free earnings. Some investments, such as tax-exempt municipal bonds, do not belong in a Roth at all because they are not subject to income tax. Traditional IRAs, Roth IRAs, 401(k)s, 403(b)s, and other qualified retirement accounts are commonly referred to as "nontaxable" because earnings from the investments in them are reinvested, rather than being taxed immediately. All other investment accounts are known as "taxable accounts" because earnings and dividends from investments in those accounts are taxed in the year they are received, even if they are reinvested.

Once you have reached the annual limit for your 401(k) and IRA contributions, any additional savings will have to be invested in nontaxable accounts. If you have both nontaxable and taxable investment accounts, it is important to distribute your investments so you pay the minimum amount of tax on your earnings from them and maximize the amount you can reinvest. Tax-efficient investments should be held in a nontaxable account.

Best investments to hold in a traditional IRA, 401(k), or 403(b):

- High-yield bonds
- Taxable bonds
- REITs
- Stocks and stock funds that pay dividends
- Balanced mutual funds

Best investments to hold in a Roth IRA or Roth 401(k):

- Balanced mutual funds
- Small cap stocks
- Small value stocks
- Large value stocks
- International stocks
- Large growth stocks
- Most index funds
- Real estate
- Investments that you expect to sell before you reach the age of 59½

Best investments to hold in a taxable account:

- U.S. savings bonds

- Tax-exempt municipal bonds (these are not taxed anyway)

- Tax-managed mutual funds (these funds are managed to minimize the taxes you pay on earnings and dividends)

- Investments that you expect to cash out within a short time

Profit made from selling stocks and other assets in a taxable account is taxed as capital gains and not as income.

All withdrawals, except for non-deductible contributions, from a traditional IRA — whether they come from earnings or the sale of stocks and assets — are taxed as income. Profits made from selling stocks in a taxable account are taxed at the lower capital gains rate. When possible, it makes sense to hold stocks in a Roth IRA.

Principles of Investing

Y ou are putting your hard-earned savings into a Roth IRA because you want to provide an income for yourself in retirement by letting your money grow over a period of several decades. The first key to success is to save more of your money and spend less. You cannot rely on the stock market alone to fuel the growth of your retirement savings. A few years of aggressive risk-taking will probably not compensate for failing to save enough and could result in financial disaster. Contribute early and contribute as much as you can to keep your Roth IRA growing strongly.

Making regular contributions to your Roth IRA is the first and most important step, but your responsibility does not stop there. The "I" in IRA stands for "individual." The burden rests on you, as an individual, to make the choices and decisions that will result in your eventual success. No one else is looking out for you. However much your IRA custodian, employer, or financial advisor might profess to be concerned about your financial well-being, you are the one who will bear the consequences of any mistakes. Whether you invest in a few well-chosen mutual funds or choose to actively manage your own portfolio, it is important to have a good understanding of basic investing principles. You cannot arrive at your goal without knowing how you are going to get there and how to make adjustments when things go wrong along the way. No one can predict exactly how the stock market is going to behave, but by knowing the warning signs, you can anticipate what might happen and make plans to avert disaster.

Just as familiarity with tax laws and IRA rules will prevent you from making costly mistakes with your Roth IRA, familiarity with the principles of investing will help you avoid mistakes with your investment decisions that could hamper the growth of your portfolio. This chapter discusses some of the basic concepts of investing and how you can put them to work to make yourself wealthy.

Modern Portfolio Theory

Modern portfolio theory assesses the growth potential and the risk associated with investment by looking at all the holdings in a portfolio rather than at the investments individually. It was developed by Harry Markowitz and first presented to the public in an article entitled "Portfolio Selection" in the 1952 *Journal of Finance*. Markowitz suggested that risk should be calculated not by looking at the risk and return of a single investment, but by evaluating that risk in relation to all the other securities in a diversified portfolio. The risk of owning one investment could be offset by purchasing the stock of companies in other sectors whose risk was not directly related. A portfolio containing a number of high-risk investments could actually carry a moderate risk as a whole if those investments were selected from sectors or styles that historically move up and down under different economic conditions. In other words, the likelihood of achieving successful growth is highest if your portfolio is balanced across a wide variety of investments.

Your portfolio is not limited to your IRA. It includes all your wealth-producing assets: taxable investment accounts, savings bonds, businesses, CDs and savings accounts, real estate, and even valuables such as gold, precious stones, and collectibles. Your home should not be considered part of your portfolio. When you are selecting investments for your Roth IRA or balancing your IRA portfolio, avoid duplicating investments that you hold outside of your IRA. For example, if you hold stock options in the telecommunications company where you work, you should not include telecommunications stocks or mutual funds in your Roth IRA. If the telecommunications sector experiences a slump in the stock market, the steady performance of other types of investments in your IRA will help to compensate for the drop in value of your stock options.

If you are participating in an employer retirement plan, look at its holdings before you select your Roth IRA investments. When the employer plan includes company stock or has a heavy emphasis on a particular investment style or market sector, select IRA investments from other styles or sectors. You can complement an employer plan holding well-diversified mutual funds with a similar selection of investments in your Roth IRA, or use your IRA to explore investments that have a higher rate of return and higher risk. Your IRA portfolio should be fully diversified if your only investment account is your IRA and you do not hold other wealth-building assets.

Correlation

Correlation is the degree to which two investments move together in the market. The correlation coefficient is a measure of how closely the standard deviations of two stocks or indexes follow each other. *See the following section for more on this.* A correlation coefficient can range between 1 and -1, with 1 indicating that the standard deviations of the two investments are perfectly synchronized, and -1 indicating that they always move in opposite directions from each other. Including two investments with a correlation of -1 in your portfolio would constitute ideal diversity and provide optimum protection against risk. Unfortunately, negative correlations between two investments that both bring in positive returns are hard to find.

An online correlation tracker at Select Sector SPDRs (**www.sectorspdr. com/correlation**) allows you to enter up to four stocks, funds, or ETFs and see how they correlate with each other. When you already hold a particular stock or fund in your IRA, you can use a correlation tracker to search for additional investments that will behave differently when the stock market declines. A well-balanced portfolio holds funds, bonds, and stocks that do not correlate closely with each other.

Efficient frontier

The historical returns from a specified period are used to calculate and assign an expected value — the value it is expected to achieve after a certain amount of time — to each investment in the portfolio. Each investment's standard deviation (a measure of an individual stock's volatility), correlation, and expected value are then used to calculate the expected return and volatility of the entire portfolio. Certain portfolios, which optimally balance risk and reward, make up what Markowitz called an "efficient frontier." Ideally, an investor should select a portfolio from the efficient frontier.

Negative correlation among market sectors appears to be decreasing.

Recent analysis shows different market sectors and types of investments no longer experience the same degree of negative correlation as they did a few decades ago. It appears historical data does not accurately predict expected value because the nature of the national and global economy is changing. For example, globalization has closely linked the economies of countries that once operated in separate economic spheres. Other factors that do not have a historical precedent are the rapid growth of technology, speed of communication and delivery of information through the Internet, and the emergence of mega-corporations that dominate whole market sectors and stifle competition.

Volatility

Volatility is the tendency of an investment to fluctuate in value. It is an indicator of the likelihood that you will be able to realize a reasonable return on your investment at the time you begin withdrawing funds from your IRA.

Volatility is often measured in terms of standard deviation, the degree to which the returns from a security have fluctuated from its mean return over a given period. Standard deviation can be used to compare the relative volatility of two or more securities. If a security has a three-year standard deviation of six, it would be considered twice as volatile and, therefore, twice as risky as another security with a three-year standard deviation of three. The standard deviation for most short-term bond funds, considered to be the most secure investment, is around 0.7, while the standard deviation for most precious metal funds is around 26. The standard deviation of a Standard & Poor's 500 index fund that represents a broad sampling of the stock market is about 15 percent. An investment with a standard deviation of 0 would have an unvarying rate of return, such as a bank account paying compound interest at a guaranteed rate.

A highly volatile investment represents an opportunity to make higher-than-average returns by buying when the price is low and selling when it is high, but it also represents the possibility of big losses if its price drops after you purchase it. A Roth IRA comes with built-in time restraints; if the value of your investments has ebbed when you need to take money out, you will not be able to recoup those losses. Before undertaking a highly volatile investment, you should plan what you will do when it threatens to lose value.

Defensive stocks

Defensive stocks are stocks that tend to remain stable and provide a constant dividend through every phase of the economic cycle. Even during a recession, people continue to buy energy, food, medicine, fuel, shelter, tobacco, and alcohol. Stocks of companies that provide basic needs are also called "noncyclical" because they have little correlation with the business cycle. These stocks have a low P/E and a Beta of less than one. During a recession they tend to perform better than the stock market, but during an economic expansion they lag behind because the demand for the goods and services provided by these companies does not increase as dramatically as the demand for other types of goods. Examples of defensive stocks are Kraft Foods (KFT), Pepsico, Inc. (PEP), Coca-Cola Co. (KO), Procter & Gamble (PG), ConAgra Foods Inc. (CAG), Costco (COST), Wal-Mart Stores (WMT), and Hormel Foods Corp. (HRL).

Defensive stocks offer higher returns than bonds, but lower returns than more volatile stocks. During economic downturns, these stocks remain stable not only because they represent industries that supply basic needs, but because the demand for them increases as investors turn to safer investments. Defensive stocks in your portfolio provide a buffer against market downturns, similar to that provided by fixed-income investments.

Risk management

Risk is the possibility that things will not go as you plan — that, due to circumstances beyond your control, something will go wrong, and you will experience some kind of detrimental effect. Your long-term goal is to provide for your financial needs during retirement by investing your capital in the stock market, but there is always some risk that your capital will be lost or diminished. You can protect your capital and reduce risk by choosing safe investments, such as U.S. Treasury bills, CDs, and Federal Deposit Insurance Corporation (FDIC)-insured savings accounts, which offer lower returns. You can also protect yourself against risk by selecting investments that have a demonstrated rate of return, keeping expenses low, and maintaining a diversified portfolio. You can go further and buy some investments in one sector that might compensate for possible losses in another. You might deliberately choose to take on additional risk in hopes of accelerating the rate of return and watch closely for signs the value of your investment is about to drop so you can sell before it is too late. But no matter how much research you do to protect yourself against risk, there are some circumstances, such as an economic downturn or a natural disaster, over which you have little or no control. A successful investor is always aware of risk and has a good understanding of what it involves.

The following chart illustrates what volatility means to your wallet. It shows the annual percentage rate at which the market value of the S&P 500 (or its equivalent) rose or fell each year from 1825 until 2008. The S&P 500 is an index of 500 large-cap companies traded on U.S. stock exchanges. Each column represents a range of ten percentage points. From the chart you can see that the stock market rarely continues to increase steadily in value from one year to the next. Instead, the annual rate of growth fluctuates, sometimes increasing or decreasing by as much as 50 percent. The value of the stock market experienced positive growth in 129 years, but negative growth in 55 years.

You can see that if you retired in 2007, your IRA would have been increasing in value by up to 20 percent over the four previous years. If you retired in 2008, though, the value of your IRA would have dropped by 43 percent from the previous year. Fortunately, you are not required to take money out of your Roth IRA until you need it. Congress waived the RMD for traditional IRAs for 2009 because IRA owners would have been forced to sell at such a loss.

Percentage change in the S&P Market Index (or a similar equivalent) by year from 1852-2008

-50	-40	-30	-20	-10	0	10	20	30	40	50	60
						2007					
						2005					
						1994					
						1993					
						1992					
						1987					
						1984					
						1978					
						1970					
						1960	2006				
						1956	2004				
						1948	1988				
						1947	1986				
						1923	1979				
						1916	1972				
						1912	1971				
				2000		1911	1968				
				1990		1906	1965				
				1981		1902	1964				
				1977		1899	1959				
				1969		1896	1962				
				1962		1895	1949				
				1953		1894	1944	2003			
				1946		1891	1926	1999			
				1940		1889	1921	1998			
				1939		1887	1919	1996			
				1934		1881	1918	1983			
				1932		1877	1905	1982			
			2001	1929		1875	1904	1976			
			1973	1914		1874	1898	1967			
			1966	1913		1872	1897	1963	1997		
			1957	1903		1871	1892	1961	1995		
			1941	1890		1870	1886	1951	1991		
			1920	1887		1869	1878	1943	1989		
			1917	1883		1868	1864	1942	1985		
			1910	1882		1867	1858	1925	1980		
			1893	1876		1866	1855	1924	1975		
			1884	1861		1865	1850	1922	1955		
			1873	1860		1859	1849	1915	1950		
		2002	1854	1853		1856	1848	1909	1945		
		1974	1841	1851		1844	1847	1901	1938	1958	1954
		1930	1837	1845		1842	1838	1900	1936	1936	1933
		1907	1831	1835		1840	1834	1880	1927	1928	1885
2008		1857	1828	1833		1836	1832	1852	1908	1863	1879
1931	1937	1839	1825	1827		1826	1829	186	1830	1843	1862

Two Kinds of Investment Risk

There are two types of risk involved in investing: systemic and non-systemic. Non-systemic risk is associated with investing all your capital in a single company or market sector. Your financial future is tied to the fortunes of that company or the economic growth of that market sector; if the business fails, or if public uncertainty causes the price of its stock to fall, your capital is lost. A mutual fund that is highly concentrated in a particular sector or that contains only a few stocks might be subject to some non-systemic risk.

Systemic risk is the risk associated with the stock market and the economy as a whole. Systemic risk affects the entire stock market and includes:

- **Market fluctuations**: As the stock market rises and falls, the value of most (though not all) stocks will follow.

- **Rising interest rates**: When interest rates increase, the value of bonds and bond funds will fall.

- **Inflation**: Rising inflation decreases the value of fixed-income investments and cash.

- **Recession**: As the economy contracts, businesses become less profitable, and every market sector is affected.

- **War and political unrest**: If you are holding stocks, bonds, or currency of a country where political unrest occurs, their value will fall.

Non-systemic risk can be mitigated by diversifying the investments in your portfolio or by investing in a mutual fund that holds shares in a basket of diversified securities. Systemic risk can be managed by observing the economy and responding appropriately when there are signs of inflation, recession, and changes in interest rates. No one can accurately predict the exact moment when changes will occur, but there are indicators and trends that provide warnings.

Measuring risk

A correct assessment of the risk associated with an investment is crucial to successful investing. Economists and mathematicians have developed measurements that can be used to compare the relative risks of two or more investments. The development of computer technology during the last three decades has helped to refine these measurements by enabling mathematical analysis of large amounts of data and making information on stock trades immediately available.

Beta

A popular indicator of risk is a statistical measure called beta. Beta measures the volatility of a stock or a fund in relation to the volatility of the market as a whole, represented by the Standard & Poor's 500 Index. The market is assigned a beta of 1, and individual stocks are ranked according to how much they deviate from the market. If a beta is above 1, the stock has fluctuated more than the market as a whole over time. A stock with a beta of less than 1 fluctuates less than the market as a whole. A stock with a high beta involves more risk but has the potential for higher returns; a stock with a low beta is less risky but promises lower returns.

You can often find the beta for a particular fund or security in the information supplied by a stock brokerage or fund provider. Morningstar.com gives the beta for each fund under "Modern Portfolio Statistics" on the "Ratings and Risk" tab of the fund's page. The New York Stock Exchange (**www.nyse.com**) includes the beta on the "Data" tab of each company's page.

Sharpe and Treynor ratios

It is possible for two investments with very different investment risks, such as pharmaceuticals and ten-year Treasury notes, to produce the same rate of return over time. In 1966, Bill Sharpe, a professor at Stanford, developed a ratio that provided an objective measurement of the risk inherent in an investment. The formula for the Sharpe ratio is:

$$\frac{\text{(Average monthly returns of the asset)} - \text{(Risk-free rate of return)}}{\text{(Standard deviation of the asset)}}$$

The risk-free rate of return is represented by the return on short-term Treasury bills. The average monthly returns are multiplied by 12, and the standard deviation is multiplied by the square root of 12. The Sortino ratio, a variation of the Sharpe ratio, measures return only against downward price volatility and ignores rises in stock prices.

A good investment is one that offers high returns with a minimum of risk. The higher the Sharpe ratio, the higher the return of the investment in relation to its risk will be. A stock or a fund with a high rate of return and a high Sharpe ratio is considered a sound investment. A low Sharpe ratio means the high returns were achieved by taking excessive risk. Throughout the past ten years, the Sharpe ratio for the whole cash Standard & Poor's Index was 0.29; for the New York Stock Exchange, it has ranged between 0.30 and 0.40. An asset or fund with a Sharpe ratio greater than 0.50 would have a better-than-average ratio of reward to risk.

The Sharpe ratio measures the total risk of an investment. Another ratio, created by Jack Treynor and popularized in 1965, measures the systemic risk using beta, instead of the standard deviation of the stock, as the denominator. The Treynor ratio can be used to compare the risk of a particular investment to the risk inherent in the stock market as a whole:

$$\frac{\text{(Average monthly returns of the asset)} - \text{(Risk-free rate of return)}}{\text{(Beta of the asset)}}$$

Sharpe and Treynor ratios for stocks and funds are available on several financial Web sites and are often included in investment research reports. You can find a Sharpe Ratio calculator on the A Financial Revolution Web site at **www.afinancialrevolution.com/2007/01/06/sharpe-ratio-calculator**.

Evaluating performance in relation to risk

The performance of an investment can be measured according to its nominal return or its risk-adjusted return. Nominal return is the average return from an investment or a portfolio return compared to the return for the whole U.S. stock market over the same period. Risk-adjusted return measures the return on an investment relative to the volatility of its price. Most ordinary investors look only at nominal return of an investment; if it is higher than the stock market, they consider it successful.

An ordinary investor might think that a higher nominal return is better, but it does not necessarily mean more cash in your wallet. A nominal return is calculated by averaging the daily returns on an investment over time. On the specific day that an investor wants to sell an investment, it will sell for an amount higher or lower than the averaged nominal return. How much higher or lower? The price of a highly volatile stock could be significantly higher or lower than the average price. If the price is much higher, the investor can consider himself or herself lucky and pocket a substantial profit. If the price is much lower, the investor will realize lower-than-expected returns and possibly even take a loss, making the investment meaningless and even harmful. A risk-adjusted return incorporates the probability that the investment will realistically achieve the expected return.

A Roth IRA is a temporary investment account intended to grow untouched for several decades during the working career of a single owner, after which it is disbursed over the remaining two or three decades of the owner's life, or in some cases over the life of a beneficiary. If the price of an investment has dropped at the time the owner is obliged to sell it, he or she will suffer an irrecoverable loss. These time restrictions make a risk-adjusted return especially significant for an IRA. Large institutional investors, foundations, trusts, and insurance companies manage their portfolios using risk-adjusted returns because they offer a realistic projection of how much money will be in an account when they have to withdraw it.

Investments are often advertised using their nominal returns.

Brokerages often advertise the expected nominal return of an investment and hope the investor will not look at the risk-adjusted return. Consider the volatility of an investment when deciding whether to buy it.

Rules for Success

The following guidelines will help to keep your Roth IRA well-oiled and running smoothly:

- **Keep your eye on the target.** Calculate how much you will need to provide you with a comfortable retirement income and make a clear plan for achieving your goal. Always keep this plan in mind when you are making financial decisions, and review your portfolio at least once a year to see if you are saving enough and staying on track. Keeping your goal in mind will remind you of the importance of saving. Everything will not always run smoothly. You will encounter setbacks: bad years in the stock market, periods of unemployment when you are unable to save, family emergencies, unexpected education expenses. The important thing is not to lose sight of your target and to make the necessary adjustments when your circumstances change.

> ### *Make realistic savings goals.*
>
> If you own multiple traditional IRAs, you can withdraw funds from one of them to satisfy the combined RMD for all of them. However, a distribution from a Roth IRA does not satisfy the RMD for a traditional IRA.

- **Diversify your portfolio**. After making regular contributions, diversification is the second most important factor in achieving success with your Roth IRA. Do not concentrate all of your capital in a single investment. Own a little bit of everything: stocks, bonds, cash, international securities, stocks in different industries and market sectors. See Chapter 7 for more information on building and maintaining your portfolio. You will gain from whichever area is doing well and you will not lose everything when one stock or market sector goes bad.

- **Stay in for the long haul**. Success depends on keeping your money in the Roth IRA for several decades. Avoid temptation to withdraw money from your Roth, and find other ways to finance large purchases.

- **Decide your asset allocation and stick with it**. Based on your goals and your tolerance for risk, determine the asset allocation for your portfolio and stick to it, even in years where you experience a loss in a down market. Do not attempt to "beat the market" by buying and selling stocks when the price is right. Studies have shown that investors who make regular contributions at the same time every month do almost as well as they would if they had picked the most ideal day to enter the stock market each month.

- **Try to keep expenses under 2 percent**. When selecting your investments, keep trading fees, management costs, and other expenses under 2 percent. Expenses higher than 2 percent represent a serious inroad into your earnings and could inhibit the growth of your IRA.

- **Rebalance your portfolio at regular intervals.** Evaluate your portfolio regularly to confirm that your asset allocations are still in place. Always take a look at your investments after a major market fluctuation and after important changes in your life, such as the death of a spouse, an inheritance from a family member, or retirement. *See Chapter 7 for more information on rebalancing a portfolio.*

Building and Maintaining Your Portfolio

CHAPTER 07 SEVEN

You are technically allowed to own almost any type of investment in a Roth IRA, with a few exceptions, but your IRA balance and the size and the frequency of your contributions determine what types of investments are practical. If you are opening a new Roth with a contribution of $5,000, you will not have enough money to invest in a well-diversified portfolio of individual stocks and bonds. IRA custodians offer a range of special investment products, mostly mutual funds and ETFs, which provide instant diversity and can accommodate small, regular contributions. As your balance grows, you can move some of that money into individual investments or even transfer it into a new Roth devoted to a particular type of investing. When you convert a traditional IRA or 401(k) to a Roth, you might have a large accumulated balance that allows you more latitude in choosing investments for your portfolio.

What is Your Investing Style?

The various styles of investment are characterized by the degree to which the investor manipulates the investments in a portfolio and tries to profit from market changes. The majority of IRAs are "buy-and-hold" portfolios: The investor purchases certain investments and keeps them untouched for long periods. Contribution limits restrict the amount of investment capital that can go into the account each year, and you can only contribute to an IRA when you are earning income.

Most working people are preoccupied with jobs and family and have little time to do the extensive research required to "play the market." They just want to put money aside in a retirement account and let it grow. Active investors, on the other hand, attempt to increase returns by implementing investment strategies within an IRA account and integrating its tax benefits into a larger investment plan. Most investors combine investment styles; even a "buy-and-hold" investor will need to make some changes as he or she approaches retirement.

Many IRA custodians offer ready-made portfolios with various investment styles, and you can also purchase mutual funds or ETFs designed to carry out specific investment strategies. There are two major types of mutual funds and ETFs: index funds and managed funds. Index funds contain a selection of investments that reflect a market index, such as the Standard & Poor's 500, and strive to follow the performance of that index. Actively managed funds attempt to outperform the stock market by carrying out a specific investment strategy. Their names often contain words like "growth" and "strategic." Actively managed funds and ETFs are typically more expensive than index funds because they incur trading costs and charge management fees. The name of a fund or portfolio typically incorporates information about its investment style or objective. For example, AARP Moderate and Vantagepoint Long-term Growth are both funds with broad holdings that aim for long-term growth. The T. Rowe Price SmartChoice IRASM is a ready-made diversified portfolio of T. Rowe Price mutual funds based on an investor's target retirement date.

Whether you choose to create and manage your own portfolio or invest in a ready-made portfolio, it is important to understand the various investment styles and strategies.

Passive and active management

Passive investing, a popular strategy implemented by millions of investors, is often called "buy and hold." The goal of passive management is to achieve the same return as the stock markets by creating a well-balanced portfolio that mirrors the markets as a whole. The only trading in a passively managed portfolio is done when it is necessary to rebalance asset classes or when cash is added or withdrawn.

The historical return of the stock market has been about 7 percent, adjusted for inflation.

Historically, the return from the stock market has been about 10 percent, and 7 percent when adjusted for inflation. Stock brokerages often warn that "past returns do not guarantee future performance." During the economic crisis of 2008-'09, stocks lost nearly half of their value, and no one knows whether the stock market will behave as it has in the past — or whether we are entering a new type of economic cycle.

The concept of buy and hold implies that an investor must hold on to a particular stock or fund indefinitely, no matter how it performs in the market. In reality, a successful passive investment strategy requires regular review of the investments in a portfolio, the removal of assets that have lost potential to gain in value, and the addition of new and expanding market sectors. The business world is evolving so rapidly that in just a few years, some technologies become obsolete, and the nature and character of well-established companies can change completely.

Active investing is an attempt to achieve returns greater than those of the financial markets by identifying and buying stocks, funds, and other investments that are about to increase in value and selling those that are about to decline. An active investor spends time researching the market on a daily basis, looking for opportunities such as price and value discrepancies, studying economic forecasts, and keeping an eye on price momentum.

Active management involves the risk of misjudging the market and losing money. It might also encourage you to become too involved with your investments. Frequent buying and selling incurs trading costs that eat away at earnings and ultimately results in lower returns, unless a successful strategy produces enough gains to compensate. Historical comparisons show that over the long run, active management strategies produce the same average results as passive management. The gains achieved by successfully beating the market part of the time are offset by trading costs and the losses incurred the rest of the time.

Buy and hold

Buy and hold is a passive investment strategy in which an investor selects a portfolio of "plain vanilla" investments that mirror the financial markets as a whole, and leaves them untouched for as long as possible. Earnings and interest are reinvested, and compounding helps the portfolio increase in value. A buy-and-hold portfolio is intended to achieve the same rate of growth as the stock market in general.

The key to the success of a buy-and-hold portfolio is the allocation of assets between equity (stocks) and fixed income (bonds and cash accounts). Asset allocation is discussed later in this chapter. A buy-and-hold strategy requires a portfolio be rebalanced from time to time to maintain the targeted asset allocations.

A buy-and-hold strategy does not entirely exclude speculation. A portion of a buy-and-hold portfolio can be devoted to riskier investments that have the potential to bring in higher returns, as long as the risk is balanced with more conservative investments. This approach is often referred to as "core and explore."

Life-cycle investing

Life-cycle investing is a form of buy-and-hold strategy in which the allocation of assets in a portfolio is adjusted as the investor moves through different stages of life. During each stage, the asset allocations remain constant. Investment strategies change as the investor moves from youth to middle age to retirement.

Life-cycle investing assumes that a person passes through four general stages during his or her financial life:

- An aggressive stage during youth, with few financial obligations and time to make up for financial losses;

- A more conservative stage during middle age, when an investor considers the need to prepare for old age and retirement;

- Retirement, when the investor relies on investment to provide a steady stream of income; and

- Late retirement, when an investor begins to consider the needs of his heirs as well as his own requirements.

A different percentage of the investor's portfolio is allocated to fixed income during each stage, with the goal of preserving capital as the investor grows older.

Example of life-cycle asset allocations in a portfolio

	Early Savers Portfolio	Mid-life Accumulators Portfolio	New Retiree	Mature Retiree
U.S. Stocks and REITs	45%	30%	10%	5%
Real Estate	10%	10%	0%	0%
International Stocks	25%	20%	0%	0%
Fixed Income	20%	40%	45%	55%
Cash	0%	0%	45%	40%

Some financial institutions offer life-cycle funds among their investment choices. A life-cycle fund is designed to take over an investor's entire portfolio and alter the asset allocations as the investor arrives at different ages. A life-cycle fund is not a good choice if you hold investments in other IRAs or taxable accounts. Unless the asset allocations in your other accounts mirror the allocations in the lifestyle fund, you will be defeating the purpose of a life-cycle strategy by throwing its asset allocations out of balance.

> ### A life-cycle fund is intended to be your whole portfolio.
>
> Many investors mistakenly decide to "sample" a life-cycle fund in combination with other investments in a portfolio. This results in an unbalanced portfolio and the risk that investment objectives will not be met.

Overview of investing styles

	Passive Management	Active Management	Buy and Hold	Life-cycle Investing
Strategy	Attempt to achieve the same return as the stock markets by creating a well-balanced portfolio.	Attempt to achieve returns greater than those of the financial markets by actively buying investments when the price is low and selling them when the price is high.	Buy good-quality investments and leave them untouched for as long as possible.	Adjust allocation of assets in a portfolio as the investor moves through different stages of life.
Benefits	A well-balanced portfolio minimizes risk. Does not require constant attention.	An experienced and knowledgeable investor might be able to achieve greater growth.	As the overall value of the stock market increases over the years, the value of stocks will increase with it.	Younger investors will take more risk to achieve more growth; assets will be protected in safer investments as retirement age approaches.
Risks	Losses can occur if the investor does not review the portfolio regularly and adjust for changes in market sectors. Loss of opportunity to earn more in certain types of investments. A downturn in the stock market can wipe out assets if an investor does not respond quickly.	Bad investments can result in big losses. Money is lost when frequent trades incur trading fees and brokerage expenses. Requires a great deal of research and constant surveillance of the market. Stress and anxiety can take a physical and emotional toll.	Even good-quality stocks can lose their value after a few years as the economy changes and technology advances. Investor should review their portfolio regularly.	There is no guarantee that this strategy will produce a better outcome. Younger workers might not be able to recover losses from volatile investments, especially if they experience periods of unemployment. Older workers might need to invest more aggressively to save enough for retirement.

Asset Allocation

Allocation of investment capital among stocks, bonds, and other assets has been identified as the single most important factor in the growth of a buy-and-hold portfolio. Asset allocation is said to be responsible for almost 90 percent of a portfolio's growth. Selecting a good allocation of asset classes from the beginning is the key to success. The long-term mix between growth and value stock funds and fixed-income funds will determine the ultimate return and risk of a portfolio. Over the past century, stocks have performed well, but when the stock market falls, bonds retain their value and act as a safety net. On the other hand, if the rate of inflation rises near or above the interest the bonds return, a portfolio too heavily invested in fixed income will barely retain its value and will not produce any real gains.

A mixture of stocks, bonds, and cash is a stable foundation for an IRA portfolio. This can be achieved by investing your initial contribution in two or three diversified mutual funds or ETFs. As the balance of your IRA grows, you can add individual bonds and stocks, Treasury securities, international funds, ETFs, real estate investment trusts (REITs), precious metals, commodities, private equity, and other financial instruments.

Asset allocation is a very personal matter and is based on two main factors: time and risk tolerance. You have more of both if you start contributing to your IRA early in your career. If you have only a decade to grow your retirement savings, it might seem that you should invest in aggressive growth stocks, but with so little time you cannot afford to lose any of your capital. Instead, you should choose conservative investments, such as quality bonds and stocks that protect your capital and promise steady growth. If you lose your capital in the stock market during a slow economic cycle, there will not be enough time for your stocks to recover their value.

Risk tolerance is how willing or able you are to lose everything in a bid for higher returns. Someone close to retirement cannot afford to lose everything, while someone with several decades of a career ahead will have time to recover from loss. An investor with other sources of wealth or income can tolerate more risk because he or she will still have something to live on if the investments in a portfolio lose most of their value.

Risk tolerance is a matter of common sense.

Risk tolerance is often portrayed as an emotional quality: If you have nerves of steel, you have a "high tolerance" for risk. Whether you are a nervous wreck or cool, calm, and collected when you lose your investment capital, you will be without retirement income unless you have something else to live on. Real risk tolerance means having additional sources of retirement income or enough time for your portfolio to recover from a loss.

Investing too heavily in volatile stocks might result in loss of capital, but putting too much into safe investments with lower returns, like bonds and money market accounts, might inhibit the growth of your IRA, expose you to the risk of inflation, and leave you short of retirement income. Choosing the right balance of risk in your portfolio is a delicate process. The Iowa Public Employees Retirement System has an online asset allocator (**www.ipers.org/calcs/AssetAllocator.html**) that shows, according to conventional investment wisdom, the percentages of your portfolio that should be invested in different classes of assets on an evolving pie chart that alters as you change your age, degree of risk tolerance, and annual contribution amount.

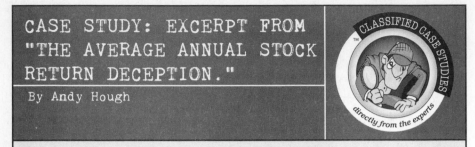

CASE STUDY: EXCERPT FROM "THE AVERAGE ANNUAL STOCK RETURN DECEPTION."

By Andy Hough

Andy Hough is a law school graduate who makes his living as a writer. You can read his blog at TightFistedMiser.com.

There are a couple of reasons why the average annual stock return figures can be deceptive. The first is in regard to how the average is calculated. If a simple average is used, it can be quite different than your actual return. Here is an example: If you invested in a stock and it went up 100 percent one year and down 50 percent the next, you would have an average return of 25 percent, but your actual return would be zero because you would just have the same amount of money that you initially invested.

The 10 percent annual return figure is also deceptive. It takes a long time period before stock returns average out to around 10 percent. Over the 40-year period from February 1969 to February 2009, stocks had an annual return of 5.3 percent. That is a pretty long period for stocks to not return the average 10 percent. This figure comes from an article on The Motley Fool about a study by Rob Arnott showing that bonds outperformed stocks over 40 years. This data may have been cherry-picked to show bonds in the best possible light, but it still shows that it is possible for bonds to beat stocks over the long term.

One other complaint I have about the average 10 percent stock return figure is that after writers have gone to great lengths to show how stocks average 10 percent over the long term, they will state that past performance is no guarantee of future results. My point is that stocks are not quite as great an investment as they are made out to be, and that keeping a portion of your portfolio in a fixed-rate investment does not guarantee lesser returns.

Determining your asset allocations

Historically, bonds have manifested a low correlation to stocks. Most investors allocate between 40 and 50 percent of their portfolios to less-volatile bonds and other fixed-income investments, and the remainder to stocks. This can be achieved in a simple portfolio by investing in two or three broadly diversified mutual funds.

There is not one single asset allocation formula that is ideal for every buy-and-hold portfolio because every investor has unique economic circumstances and financial goals, as well as different levels of risk tolerance. One person might be willing to take extra risk to grow his or her savings more rapidly, while another might be primarily concerned with preserving capital. An investor could already hold securities from one or more asset classes in another account. Another factor affecting asset allocation is the investor's need to access cash on short notice.

Typical stock/bond allocations for different styles of buy-and-hold portfolios

Portfolio Style	Global Equity (stocks)	Fixed-income (bonds)	Expected Long-term Return
Income-oriented	20%	80%	5.80%
Conservative	40 %	60 %	6.40 %
Moderate	50 %	50 %	6.70 %
Moderate Growth	60 %	40 %	7 %
Aggressive	80 %	20 %	7.70 %

As you approach retirement age, when you will begin taking distributions from your IRA, some of the stocks should be converted to cash and cash equivalents, and most of the assets should be moved into fixed income to ensure they are intact when you need them. If you have other sources of retirement income and want to use your Roth primarily as a vehicle to accumulate wealth for your heirs, you can leave the asset allocations in your Roth IRA untouched.

Expanding Your Portfolio

As the balance of your Roth IRA grows, each asset category can be expanded by the addition of more specialized funds, ETFs, individual stocks and bonds, and financial instruments. Maintain the same asset allocations, but diversify within each asset category. Instead of continuing to invest more into the same mutual funds and ETFs, purchase some solid individual stocks of the same styles or buy shares of more specialized ETFs.

Many IRA custodians restrict their offerings to a selection of mutual funds and are not prepared to handle stock market transactions or bond purchases. You might need to open another Roth IRA with a stock brokerage firm or a financial institution that accommodates the type of investment you want to add to your portfolio. There is no limit to the number of IRAs you can own, but you cannot contribute more than the annual limit to all the IRAs combined. When calculating the taxable portion of an early withdrawal and early withdrawal penalties, all your IRAs must be treated as a single IRA. You can also transfer your existing Roth IRA to another custodian, but if the transfer involves cashing out mutual funds, you could lose money on exit fees. If you cash out of mutual funds on a day when the market has fallen, you risk locking in a loss that cannot be recovered.

The following is a sample asset allocation for a portfolio from *Active Investing: Maximizing Portfolio Performance and Minimizing Risk Through Global Index Strategies*, by Steven Schoenfeld. In a small, simple portfolio, each major asset class can be represented with a single, broad-market index mutual fund or ETF. Larger portfolios can be allocated among funds from each of the asset subclasses.

Asset Class	Conservative Portfolio	Moderate Portfolio	Aggressive Portfolio
U.S. Equities	25%	45%	55%
Large Cap	15%	30%	35%
Mid/Small Cap	10%	15%	20%
International Equities	5 %	10%	20%
Developed	5 %	8%	15%
Emerging	—	2%	5%
Fixed Income	55%	30%	10%
Short Term	15%	5%	—
Long Term	15%	10%	5%
High Yield	10%	5%	5%
TIPS	15%	10%	—
Alternatives	15%	15%	15%
REITS	10%	10%	5%
Commodities	5%	5%	5%
Hedge Funds	—	—	5%

International stocks

International investments are essential to any diversified portfolio. Today, more than two-thirds of the world stock market is outside the United States. Historically, American investors have been underinvested in foreign assets, but during the past few years they have been hurrying to correct the imbalance. During 2005, 70 percent of money invested by U.S. citizens went to funds that invest overseas.

Experts' opinions differ over what percentage of the equity in a portfolio should be devoted to foreign investments, ranging from a conservative estimate of 15 to 25 percent to an aggressive 50 percent. In the past, investing in foreign countries meant opening a foreign brokerage account, paying sizable commissions, and assuming substantial currency risk. Mutual funds and ETFs that hold foreign stocks and bonds have now made international investing as easy as a few clicks on an online brokerage Web site. ETFs are a good tool for adding foreign investments to a portfolio because they give instant access to a broad range of stocks and allow you to move your investment capital easily from one style or market sector to another.

There are several good reasons for including international equity in your Roth IRA portfolio.

Advantages of international investments

- **Diversification:** Adding foreign ETFs to your portfolio increases the number of securities in which you are investing and gives you exposure to more companies and industry sectors that could potentially expand and grow. Returns from foreign investments are in foreign currencies. At times when the U.S. dollar weakens, their relative value increases for investors living in the United States. This might help to compensate for declines in the returns from domestic securities.

- **Lower correlation:** The prices of stocks in different markets tend to go up and down at different times. Since 1975, dominance of the world stock market has regularly alternated between U.S. stocks and non-U.S. stocks in cycles of approximately three years. When these fluctuations occur, a globally diversified portfolio naturally hedges one market against another. In the past, regularly rebalancing a portfolio between U.S. and international stocks has lowered overall risk and slightly increased returns.

- **Recent returns of foreign stocks have been greater than returns from U.S. stocks:** Economists and financial analysts are grappling with a rapidly changing global economy and with market trends that might turn out to be irreversible. New economic developments over the last two decades — such as the rapid industrialization of China and India, the establishment of the European Union and success of the euro, the movement of U.S. manufacturing overseas, and innovations in telecommunications — might have permanently altered the landscape of the investing world.

Throughout the past few years, returns from foreign stocks have been greater than returns from U.S. stocks. There is no way to predict exactly when the performance of U.S. stocks will improve relative to foreign stocks, but it is clear that foreign stocks would have been wise investments during the U.S. downturn of the mid-2000s.

Disadvantages of international investments

International funds and stocks have some disadvantages that domestic investments do not. If you are buying a broad-market fund with international investments, the fund managers have probably taken these disadvantages into account, and you can rely on the information in the fund prospectus. If you are diversifying with more specialized international funds and ETFs, or investing directly in foreign stocks, you should be aware of the following considerations:

- **You cannot claim a foreign tax credit for dividends from investments held in an IRA:** When a company in a foreign country issues dividends to foreign investors, that country often removes taxes before the cash is paid out overseas. U.S. investors with taxable accounts can claim a U.S. tax credit for the amount of foreign tax withheld. However, if the investments are held in a nontaxable account, such as an IRA, the investor cannot claim a foreign tax credit.

- **Stock markets in other countries are closed when the U.S. stock market is open:** Most of the world's stock markets are closed when the U.S. stock market is actively trading international ETFs because of time differences. The NAV (actual value of the underlying securities in an ETF), calculated when the home market closes, quickly becomes stale, especially if the market is volatile or currency is fluctuating, and the ETF price on the U.S. market might vary widely from the NAV. Many U.S. investors think the U.S. market price for an international ETF is incorrect because of this, but it is more likely that the price on the U.S. stock market reflects the true value of the underlying securities more accurately than the NAV at that particular moment. If the markets were open in the home countries, the real-time NAV of the securities underlying the ETF would resemble the ETF pricing. Global market participants are able to use ETF prices to "discover" what the prices of the underlying stocks will be during the next trading day.

- **Volatility is compounded by currency fluctuations:** International-equity mutual funds and ETFs quote prices in U.S. dollars, but the underlying stocks might be valued in another currency, such as Japanese yen. The Japanese price of a stock might not change, but its value in U.S. dollars will change if the value of the dollar goes up or down. Funds tracking Japanese market indexes such as the Nikkei can experience considerable price movements on the U.S. stock exchange, even when the stock price remains stable in Japan, because the stock markets are closed for the night. If the U.S. dollar falls in value relative to the yen, U.S. investors holding Japanese stock are hedged against the fall; the reverse is also true.

- **Foreign funds tend to have higher expenses:** Domestic funds tend to be less expensive than comparable foreign funds. Expense ratios for domestic broad-market ETFs range from 0.08 percent to

0.38 percent, while the expense ratio for iShares S&P Europe 350 (IEV) is 0.60 percent, and for PowerShares FTSE RAFI Developed Markets ex-US (PXF), it is 0.75 percent. Expense ratios for international ETFs average 0.53 percent and are as high as 1.25 percent for GS Connect S&P GSCI Enh Commodity TR ETN (GSC).

- **Liquidity:** You might not be able to buy or sell some foreign stocks quickly when you want to. The trading volume of the stocks underlying international funds and ETFs might not be large enough to allow rapid creation or redemption of fund shares if the market demand suddenly increases or decreases. There is increased risk that an international fund or ETF will continue to sell at a price above or below its NAV for extended periods.

- **Foreign companies are regulated by different laws and affected by economic factors different from those that affect business in the United States:** The information on the financial statements of foreign companies might not have the same meaning as the information on similar statements of U.S. companies. The International Accounting Standards Board (IASB) has adopted International Financial Reporting Standards (IFRS) that are now widely used in many countries. U.S. companies are still using Generally Accepted Accounting Principles (GAAP) standards, but the SEC is phasing in IFRS over the next decade. When researching a foreign company, be aware of the differences and how they might affect the information available on a company.

Terminology

Global funds or ETFs, also called world mutual funds, can hold U.S. stocks along with the international stocks.

International funds or ETFs, also called foreign, overseas, or ex-U.S. securities, hold only non-U.S. stocks. The prospectus of each ETF describes its methodology for selecting stocks.

Developed markets are economically and socially advanced countries with a GDP (gross domestic product) per capita of $20,000 or more. The developed markets include the United States, Japan, Western Europe, Canada, New Zealand, and Australia, and account for more than 80 percent of the market capitalization in the global equity market.

Emerging markets are developing countries that have maintained sustained economic growth throughout several years and exhibit good economic potential. They might not have a mature economy, stable securities market, or advanced banking system, and have a GDP lower than $20,000 per capita. Examples of emerging markets are China, India, Mexico, Brazil, Chile, much of Southeast Asia, South Asia, countries in Eastern Europe, the Middle East, parts of Africa, and Latin America. More than 150 economies meet at least some of the criteria for emerging markets; over 100 of them have stock exchanges. Emerging markets carry additional political, economic, and currency risks. Nevertheless, they often exhibit low correlation with developed markets, and can be used to lower the overall risk of a portfolio.

BRIC is an acronym for "Brazil, Russia, India, and China." In 2003, Goldman Sachs published a paper arguing that the rapidly developing economies of these four countries would be wealthier than most of the current major economic powers by 2050. The BRIC theory suggests that China and India will become the world's dominant suppliers of manufactured goods and services, respectively, while Brazil and Russia will become dominant as suppliers of raw materials.

Foreign indexes

The **MSCI Emerging Markets Index**, an index created by Morgan Stanley Capital International (MSCI) to measure stock market performance in global emerging markets, included (as of June 2007) 25 countries: Argentina, Brazil, Chile, China, Colombia, Czech Republic, Egypt, Hungary, India, Indonesia, Israel, Jordan, Korea, Malaysia, Mexico, Morocco, Pakistan, Peru, Philippines, Poland, Russia, South Africa, Taiwan, Thailand, and Turkey. MSCI evaluates companies according to GDP, local government regulations, foreign ownership limits, capital controls, and perceived investment risk. The index is market-capitalization and free-float — weighted. As of March 2008, the top five countries in the MSCI Emerging Markets Index were Brazil, China, South Korea, India, and Russia, accounting for more than 60 percent of total weight in the benchmark.

The **S&P Emerging Markets Indexes** and their underlying database, which S&P purchased from International Finance Corporation (IFC) in 2000, now cover more than 2,000 companies in established markets.

Index providers might differ in the way they make the distinction between an emerging market and a developed market. Countries such as South Korea, Taiwan, Israel, and Czech Republic, which have now developed beyond the emerging market phase, might be kept in an index to maintain continuity. Small countries can be excluded from an index, because their market liquidity is limited, and substituted with a larger neighbor in the same region.

Country risk factors

In addition to the market risk factors affecting domestic investments, there are special risks associated with investing in specific foreign countries.

Currency risk is the risk that the value of a foreign currency will rise relative to the U.S. dollar, causing the investment to lose value in U.S. dollars, even though the price of the stock remains the same. The reverse is also true: If the value of a foreign currency falls against the U.S. dollar, the value of an investment will increase.

Sovereign risk is the risk that a foreign government will default on its bonds. The U.S. government guarantees repayment of its bond obligations, based on its authority to tax the people of the United States. Other governments might not have the same authority, or their economies might become so constrained that they do not have the resources to meet their obligations.

Political risk is the risk that political developments such as civil strife, war, a change of government, or a coup d'état will weaken an economy or undermine contractual agreements. Examples include the destruction of infrastructure by war, nationalization of private companies by a government, and corruption.

Banking risk is the risk associated with foreign banks and includes the possibility that banks in other countries might fail due to bad management or poor fiscal policy, or that the banks in a foreign country might not have enough liquidity in U.S. dollars to make payments to American investors.

Economic structure risk is the risk that the economic structure of a country will jeopardize the development of its economy, or that changes in economic structure will affect business. For example, as the economy grows in a developing country with low-wage manufacturing, salaries begin to increase until eventually the manufacturing industry is no longer able to compete with other low-wage economies.

What to look for

The purpose of investing internationally is to expose your portfolio to new avenues of potential growth and to reduce overall risk with investments that will compensate for downturns in other areas of the market. Choose international investments for your portfolio using the same principles you followed for your domestic investments: Seek diversity and minimize costs. A single global fund or ETF can meet diversity requirements, but investing in individual market sectors or regions offers greater potential returns. If a portfolio is large enough, it should divide international investments by style as well as market.

To minimize the risks inherent in international investing, research each fund or company carefully. Information about international funds and their holdings is readily available through their prospectuses and the Web sites of fund providers, stock exchanges, and brokers. News media and articles by financial advisors provide valuable insight into the political and economic circumstances of each geographical region.

Examine the political and corporate governance, attitude toward corruption and the process of law, and fiscal discipline of a country or region. Developed markets are characterized by advanced banking structures, mature legal and political systems, and the existence of good working relationships with other countries and regions. They often have safeguards in place to protect the assets of private investors. Emerging markets are considered much more volatile, entailing greater risk but promising the possibility of rapid growth and expansion into new markets. Could impending political unrest disrupt the financial markets in the region? What is the possibility of a bank failure or a change of government that could dramatically alter the economic structure of a country?

High prices could mean a sector or region has already attracted a lot of investment and stocks might be overvalued. The best time to enter a foreign stock market is when prices are low, but there are signs that the economy is recovering and political problems are coming to an end.

Adding international funds or ETFs to your portfolio does not automatically ensure diversity. Large, multinational corporations that are active in the United States will be subject to the same economic fluctuations as American companies. An international fund might be weighted towards an industry sector in which your domestic portfolio is already heavily invested. Look at the fund prospectus to see what its top ten securities are and how they are weighted. The top ten provides a useful snapshot of the fund as a whole.

Many international funds and ETFs have more than half their total assets concentrated in the top five or six companies, increasing exposure to company-specific risk. International funds might also contain a large proportion of small-cap companies.

Look closely at the index tracked by an international fund to get a clear understanding of the markets in which it is investing. For example, several broad-market ETFs track the MSCI Europe, Australia, and Far East Index (EAFE), which contains 21 developed countries. The index weights the stock markets of each country by their market value so that 50 percent of its weight goes to just two countries: Japan and the United Kingdom. Smaller countries, such as Singapore, Ireland, and Indonesia, which have potential for rapid growth, make up only a small percentage of the index weight.

You can find statistics on world financial markets in the Bank for International Settlements, Quarterly Review Statistical Annex (**www.bis.org/ publ/qtrpdf/r_qa0812.pdf**). EmergingMarkets (**www.emergingmarkets. org**), sponsored by Euromoney Institutional Investor PLC, provides analysis, news, and articles on foreign markets.

Rebalancing Your Portfolio

Once your portfolio has been established, it should be rebalanced at regular intervals to maintain diversity. When you first created your portfolio, you decided what percentage of your assets to allocate to each type of investment, based on the amount of risk you could afford. For example, you might have decided to place 30 percent in bonds, 30 percent in U.S. stocks, 28 percent in foreign stocks, and the remainder in commodities and market-neutral funds.

As time passes, one area of your portfolio might do very well and grow rapidly in value, while the value of another area declines. Though the overall value of your portfolio has increased, its volatility and risk might also have increased because one type of investment is overtaking the others. Rebalancing is necessary to restore the original percentages of each type of investment.

You do not need to rebalance strategic investment plans such as life-cycle IRAs and target-date funds because they automatically adjust asset allocations for you. IRA custodians that offer a limited selection of funds ask you to assign a percentage of your portfolio to each fund and maintain those percentages until you change them.

You need to actively rebalance your portfolio if you are managing a variety of investments and making your own selections. Remember that your IRA investments are only a part of your overall portfolio if you have other retirement plans, stock options, taxable investment accounts, own real estate or a business, or receive income from an inheritance, and that you should balance the risk of all of these.

How often should a portfolio be rebalanced?

Most financial professionals agree that a portfolio should be examined once a year and rebalanced if it has deviated significantly from your original asset allocations. If it is rebalanced at longer intervals, there is a risk the portfolio will become heavily overbalanced in one direction. If it is rebalanced more frequently, you run the risk of lowering your returns by interrupting rallies (the periods during which prices of a particular stock are on an upswing) too often.

More frequent rebalancing also results in more trades and therefore more expenses. If your portfolio is only slightly out of balance, consider how much you will spend in trading fees or brokerage expenses before taking action. A general rule is that if the trading costs are going to be more than 0.5 percent of your total purchase, it is better to wait another year before rebalancing.

How do I rebalance a portfolio?

The division between stocks and bonds has the greatest influence on portfolio risk, so it is most important to maintain your fixed income allocation. If the percentage of your portfolio allocated to bonds drops below your original target, increase it by using cash from dividends and earnings, or from contributions to purchase additional fixed income assets. You can also sell some shares of stock or equity funds that are performing poorly.

There are times when it is prudent to sell.

It is common sense to keep an eye on the market as a whole for drastic changes that might signal more than a normal fluctuation in a market sector. For example, technology stocks began to take off late in 1997 and increased rapidly in value until April 2000. By the end of December 2000, they had lost 45 percent; by the end of December 2001, they had last another 30 percent; and by the end of December 2002, they had fallen another 38 percent. From news coverage, it was evident that factors such as inexperience, overspending, and ill-conceived business plans doomed many technology start-ups. A well-read investor would have realized by the end of 2000 that technology stocks should not occupy a large portion of his portfolio, but many fund managers held on, hoping for a reversal.

Taking Money Out of Your Roth IRA

When you withdraw cash from your Roth IRA, the IRS distribution rules say the first amount to come out is your contributions, followed by conversions and then earnings. Only the earnings in a Roth are subject to income tax or early withdrawal penalties. Amounts converted from another IRA or retirement plan might be subject to penalties if they are withdrawn within five years of the conversion. If you are older than 59½ and have held the Roth for more than five years, you do not need to be concerned with distribution order.

Distribution rules refer only to the value of contributions and earnings, not to specific assets. You can sell any asset in your IRA and count its value as part of your contributions, until all of your contributions have been distributed. When you withdraw cash from your IRA, choose the assets that will be liquidated carefully. Your goal is to keep the investments in your Roth IRA growing, even while you are taking money out. Sell stocks that have performed poorly or bonds that have reached maturity, or take the cash from a short-term money market account. Compare the cost of liquidating different assets. If you are cashing out of mutual funds, you might pay exit fees; sales of stocks or ETFs incur trading fees, and bond sales could involve brokerage fees. Be sure to maintain your asset allocation as you liquidate some of your holdings. The custodian of an IRA with a structured investment plan might do all of this for you, maintaining your asset allocations while distributing cash. Some Roth IRAs are structured to provide a certain amount of cash on a regular basis while investments in the account continue to bring in earnings.

Managing Your Portfolio Online

In addition to mailing out quarterly or biannual statements, many IRA custodians offer the ability to log in, view your portfolio holdings, and change your asset allocations online. Take advantage of this opportunity to monitor your portfolio and educate yourself about your investments. Resist the temptation to "play the market" with your IRA or make frequent changes to your asset allocations because this will incur fees and trading costs that will wipe out some of your earnings.

Banks and financial management applications allow you to view your IRA accounts along with taxable investment, credit card, and bank accounts, and might offer suggestions or tax advice. You will have to enter log-in information and passwords so these applications can automatically update your information. These applications help with budgeting and financial planning and give you a picture of your overall portfolio.

Doing the Research

Where to Look for Information

Whether your IRA contains two or three broad-market mutual funds or an array of individual stocks, bonds, ETFs, and other financial instruments, you should understand how your money is invested. The sales literature your IRA custodian hands you is only the starting point. Though you can order prospectuses to be mailed to you and find Morningstar guides and other reference books in the public library or local bookstore, the Internet instantly puts a vast amount of information at your fingertips, and much of it is updated daily and even hourly.

Always look for information from at least three sources. Start with the sales literature, check the official sources such as stock exchanges and the SEC, and type the name of a fund or stock into a search engine to find articles and reviews from business magazines and financial commentators. In less than an hour you will have a good understanding of a particular investment. Sites like Morningstar.com (**www.morningstar.com**), Motley Fool (**www.fool.com**), and Seeking Alpha (**www.seekingalpha.com**) offer analysis and insight. *See Appendix A for a list of Web sites where you can find more helpful information.*

The SEC and other stock exchange and financial Web sites contain educational materials, such as tutorials and glossaries, to help you get started. If you are puzzled by terminology, type the term in a search engine and find alternative explanations. Do not stop looking until you are satisfied your questions are answered satisfactorily.

Mutual Funds

The majority of IRA custodians offer a selection of mutual funds representing broad financial markets as well as specialized funds dedicated to particular market sectors or investment styles. Large banks and financial institutions sometimes create mutual funds especially for IRAs. You can find information about an individual mutual fund on the fund provider's Web site or printed prospectus, and many business magazines and financial newsletters rate mutual funds and track their performances.

The U.S. Securities and Exchange Commission's (SEC) Electronic Data Gathering, Analysis, and Retrieval system (EDGAR) performs automated collection, validation, indexing, acceptance, and forwarding of submissions by companies and others who are required by law to file forms with SEC. Search for information on a mutual fund through EDGAR's mutual fund portal (**www.sec.gov/edgar/searchedgar/mutualsearch.htm**).

The Financial Industry Regulatory Authority Inc. (FINRA®) fund analyzer (**http://apps.finra.org/fundanalyzer/1/fa.aspx**) offers information on more than 18,000 mutual funds, exchange-traded funds (ETFs), and exchange-traded notes (ETNs). It estimates the value of the funds and impact of fees and expenses on your investment, and also allows you to look up applicable fees and available discounts.

The Mutual Fund Education Alliance (MFEA) is a national trade association of mutual fund companies that offer funds directly, through supermarkets or third parties and financial advisors. Collectively, the companies in Alliance memberships are responsible for nearly $6 trillion in mutual fund investments. The MFEA Web site (**www.mfea.com**) provides valuable resources and useful links.

ETFs and Stocks

The first place to look for information about an ETF or a company stock is on the Web site of the exchange on which it is trading. Most stocks trade either on the American Stock Exchange (AMEX) (**www.amex.com**), the New York Stock Exchange (NYSE) (**www.nyse.com**), or NASDAQ (**www.nasdaq.com**). Barclays Bank ETFs trade on the London Stock Exchange (**www.londonstockexchange.com**). ETF and stock options trade on the Chicago Board Options Exchange (CBOE) (**www.cboe.com**). Futures contracts trade on two futures exchanges, the Chicago Mercantile Exchange (CME) (**www.cme.com**) and OneChicago (**www.onechicago.com**). If you do not know where a particular ETF or company stock is trading, you can begin with one of the brokerage or investment information sites, such as Morningstar (**www.morningstar.com**), ETF Guide (**www.etfguide.com**), or Yahoo! Finance (**www.finance.yahoo.com/etf**), where there are complete listings broken down by style and sector.

If you want to know more about the index an ETF is tracking and the information is not on the fund sponsor's Web site, you can visit the Web site of the index provider. Sites like **www.indexuniverse.com**, **www.etfconnect.com**, **www.finance.yahoo.com/etf**, **www.indexinvestor.com**, and **www.etfzone.com** publish commentary and articles written by financial analysts, investment advisors, and individual investors, some of whom might be promoting their own strategies. A review of several articles about an ETF will alert you to potential risks and give you a better understanding of its methodology and the risk it carries.

The SEC's EDGAR database (**www.sec.gov/edgar.shtml**) contains registration statements, periodic financial reports, and documents filed by all companies, domestic and foreign, trading in the United States. EDGAR is intended to increase the efficiency and fairness of the securities market by making time-sensitive information available quickly to the public.

Introduction to researching public companies through EDGAR:
A Guide for Investors.

Excerpt from The SEC Web site
(**www.sec.gov/investor/pubs/edgarguide.htm**):

The SEC's EDGAR database provides free public access to corporate information, allowing you to quickly research a company's financial information and operations by reviewing registration statements, prospectuses, and periodic reports filed on Forms 10-K and 10-Q. You also can find information about recent corporate events reported on Form 8-K that a company does not have to disclose to investors.

EDGAR also provides access to comment and response letters relating to disclosure filings made after August 1, 2004, and reviewed by either the Division of Corporation Finance or the Division of Investment Management. On May 22, 2006, the staffs of the Divisions of Corporation Finance and Investment Management began to use the EDGAR system to issue notifications of effectiveness for Securities Act registration statements and post-effective amendments, other than those that become effective automatically by law. These notifications will be posted to the EDGAR system the morning after a filing is determined to be effective.

Bonds

Bonds are bought and sold primarily in secondary markets, and there is no central exchange where you can find bond information. Many financial advisors and brokerages offer education and investment tools on their Web sites, and they often provide access to prospectuses, sales literature, and other information about each bond they sell. Remember that these sites are created as sales vehicles, and double-check the recommendations they make by comparing them with comparable offerings on other sites.

The Securities Industry and Financial Markets Association (FINRA) offers bond price information on its Web site, Investinginbonds.com (**http:// investinginbonds.com**). Created under the auspices of the SEC, the Trade Reporting and Compliance Engine (TRACE) (**http://cxa.marketwatch. com/finra/BondCenter/Default.aspx**) offers price information on bond sales within 15 minutes of a trade. You can use TRACE to find the last price at which a particular bond traded. TRACE information is also displayed on other brokerage and financial sites. Many bonds trade infrequently, so the price information could be months old and might not reflect the current price at which the bond would sell.

Electronic Municipal Market Access (EMMA), sponsored by the Municipal Securities Rulemaking Board (MSRB) (**www.emma.msrb.org**), makes available official statements for most new offerings of municipal bonds, notes, 529 college savings plans, and other municipal securities since 1990, and provides real-time access to prices at which bonds and notes are sold or bought.

Incapital, LLC (**www.incapital.com**) underwrites and distributes fixed-income securities and structured notes through more than 900 broker-dealers and banks in the United States, Europe, and Asia. Their Web site offers investment tools and an educational program for bond investors (**www.bondschool.com**).

Morningstar, Inc. (**www.morningstar.com**) has its own ranking system for hundreds of bond funds, and a bond calculator that allows you to compare two or more bonds.

MuniNetGuide (**www.muninetguide.com/nfma.php**) is an online research guide and directory to municipal-related content on the Internet with a unique emphasis on municipal bonds, state and local governments, and public finance.

NYSE provides a trading platform for bond traders (**www.nyse.com/bonds/nysebonds/1127299875444.html**) and an online dictionary of bond terms.

Electronic Municipal Statistics (**www.emuni.com**) provides free access to all municipal bond official statements submitted to it for publication by bond issuers and underwriters. If the terminology is abbreviated or unfamiliar, use an investment glossary, or simply type the term into a search engine until you find a definition you can understand.

Financial news media and publications

Financial news, business magazines, and investment Web sites and blogs provide invaluable information on the economy and the stock market. Read about the latest investment products, industries, and market sectors that are experiencing growth or encountering difficulties; newly emerging trends; changes in IRS rules; and highly-rated stocks and bonds. Be aware of the source of the information; some sites are marketing specific products. Many financial publications offer online classes, educational articles, and practice portfolios. Some of the best-known financial Web sites are:

- Business Week (**www.businessweek.com**)

- CNN Money (CNN, *Fortune, Money* magazine) (**http://money.cnn.com**)

- *Forbes* (**www.forbes.com**)

- Index Universe (**www.indexuniverse.com**)

- Investment News (**www.investmentnews.com**)

- Investopedia (**www.investopedia.com**): Sponsored by Forbes, this Web site provides tutorials, educational materials, and a glossary of investment terms

- Kiplinger.com (**www.kiplinger.com**)

- Market Watch (**www.marketwatch.com**)

- Moneychimp (**www.moneychimp.com**)

- Morningstar (**www.morningstar.com**)

- National Association of Securities Dealers (**www.nasd.com**)

- Seeking Alpha (**www.seekingalpha.com**)

- Smart Money (**www.smartmoney.com**)

- Social Investment Forum (**www.socialinvest.org**)

- The ETF Guide (**www.etfguide.com**)

- The Motley Fool (**www.fool.com**)

- TheStreet.com (**www.thestreet.com/life-and-money/etfs/index.html**)

- Value Line (**www.valueline.com**)

- *The Wall Street Journal* (**www.wsj.com**)

- Yahoo! Finance (**www.finance.yahoo.com/etf**)

What to Look For

Stocks

When you look at the financial pages in a newspaper, listings on a stock exchange Web site, or the "stock screeners" on various online brokerage and financial sites, you will find the same basic information presented in different ways. Financial analysts are paid hefty salaries to spend their days examining financial statements and market data and identifying the best companies to invest in. You cannot hope to duplicate their efforts, but you can glean important information about a company and determine whether or not it belongs in your portfolio.

Metrics and ratios provide a snapshot of a company's current situation, but to get an accurate picture, you need to look at these numbers over time. The previously listed Web sites contain charts and graphs of a stock's performance over time, as well as historical comparisons and comparisons with other companies in the same industry. Data should also be looked at in connection with other information about the company and about the industry as a whole.

The following are some terms you might encounter:

Ticker or symbol: The three- or four-letter acronym by which a stock is identified in the stock exchange.

Trading volume: Trading volume is the number of shares of a company's stock that have been traded over a period of time. A high trading volume is a sign of investor confidence in a company. A stock with a high trading volume has a high liquidity, meaning it can be sold quickly. A high trading volume can also be an indicator that a company's stock is overpriced because it is in high demand.

Risk: Risk is an indicator of a stock's volatility. *Measures of risk such as a stock's beta and Sharpe and Treynor ratios were discussed in Chapter 6.*

Market cap: Market capitalization represents the total value of a company in the stock market. It is calculated by multiplying the price of a share times the number of outstanding shares. As explained in Chapter 5, market capitalization is used to categorize a company by size. Companies of different sizes are affected in different ways by changes in the economy. Companies with a large market cap tend to be more stable, while mid- and small-cap companies are associated with more risk but experience more growth.

Shares outstanding: The number of shares of a company's stock that are held by investors, including company employees and officials as well as the public.

Price-to-earnings ratio (P/E): The price-to-earnings ratio is a measure of the price of a stock relative to its return. A low P/E might be an indicator that a stock is undervalued and therefore has good potential for growth. A high P/E means investors value the stock because they believe the company will grow rapidly in the future, but there is no guarantee of this.

Earnings per share (EPS): The amount the company has earned over a period of time for each share of stock. It is calculated by dividing the company's net income, minus dividends paid on preferred stock, by the average number of outstanding shares during a financial period. A high EPS indicates a company is making a healthy profit for its stockholders. It should be examined, however, in the context of other factors, such as the company's market capitalization.

Price-earnings-growth ratio (PEG): PEG is calculated by dividing a company's P/E ratio by the growth in its earnings per share over a year. It is an indicator of whether a company's share price accurately reflects its value. A PEG higher than 1 indicates the company is overvalued by the stock market.

Price: Current price-to-sales, price-to-earnings, and price-to-book ratios are compared to the average long-term ratio for that industry. If the stocks for that industry are selling above their historical average, they are avoided; if they are selling below historical average, they are desirable.

Financial statements: Publicly-traded companies are required to file annual financial reports with the SEC and send annual reports to their shareholders. In addition, they must file forms to report a variety of significant events whenever they occur. All of this information is available to the public through EDGAR (**www.sec.gov/edgar.shtml**).

Many investors look at the bottom line of a company's income statement to see whether it made a profit or a loss over a financial period, but the line items on the report, the footnotes, and accompanying explanations contain important information.

Debt: A decrease in a company's debt relative to its equity is a sign of good management and proper use of capital.

Cash flow: Free cash flow indicates the company is earning a profit and will be able to pay dividends.

Liabilities: A company that is involved in litigation or has committed itself to long-term purchase contracts has an uncertain future, even if it is currently doing well.

Accounting practices: Look for indications that a company is deviating from generally accepted accounting practices (GAAP). This is an indication that the company is misrepresenting its true financial situation. Terms like "pro forma" and "EBITDA" (earnings before interest, taxes, depreciation, and amortization) are signs a company is bending the rules on its financial statements.

Bonds

If you are selecting individual bonds for your IRA, look for bonds that match your investment strategy. Bonds are typically regarded as a trade-off: a lower rate of return in exchange for a stable income and protection of your capital. Though not as volatile as stocks, bonds can default under certain circumstances. Before selecting, look at:

Maturity: When a bond reaches maturity, your principal is returned and you stop earning interest income. Choose bonds that will mature when you need cash or when another investment opportunity is available. A bond with a long maturity carries the risk that inflation will wipe out the value of earned interest.

Interest rate: The interest on a bond is your earnings from your investment. How will the rate of return fit in with your investment strategy? Bonds with higher interest rates typically involve greater risk.

Credit rating: Bonds with high credit ratings are considered safer but typically offer lower interest rates. A high credit rating makes a bond easier to sell. A bond with a very low credit rating, or no credit rating, has a high risk of default.

Tax status: Interest from certain types of bonds, such as municipal bonds, is not taxed as income. These bonds do not belong in your IRA portfolio because they are already tax-advantaged.

Mutual funds

Mutual funds are the mainstay of many IRAs. The name of the mutual fund usually tells something about its investment strategy and the type of assets it holds. Look at:

Assets in the fund: Your goal is a diverse and well-balanced portfolio. Look carefully at the type of investments in a fund before buying it. You do not want to duplicate another fund or investment already in your portfolio. For example, if you already have a broad market fund, you will want to buy a growth fund or a fund that offers exposure to international stocks.

Index: The backbone of your portfolio should be funds with market indexes. Custom indexes and specialized investment strategies should make up only a small portion of your holdings. *Market indexes and custom indexes were discussed in Chapter 6.*

Expenses: Mutual funds charge various fees, including load, exit, management, and custodial fees. There might also be fees associated with transactions within the fund, such as stock trades.

Experts have identified these expenses as a major deterrent to growth in retirement accounts. Look closely at the expenses associated with a fund before you buy it. Ideally, expenses should be less than 2 percent. Do not look only at expenses, but also at returns. It might be worthwhile to pay a little more in expenses if the returns of a fund are higher.

ETFs

ETFs resemble mutual funds, but their shares are sold like stocks on the stock exchanges. Many ETFs have only been in existence for one or two years, so there is little historical data for comparisons. ETF listings on stock exchange and brokerage Web sites allow you to conveniently compare important data for all the ETFs of a particular style or market sector, or to select ETFs using different criteria such as expense ratio or fund group. Look at:

Fund provider: The fund provider or fund sponsor is the company that has created the ETF. Some fund providers are well-known financial institutions with established reputations, while others are relative newcomers.

Expense ratio: The percentage of an ETF's average net assets used to pay its annual expenses. Over time, these expenses eat into returns, so a lower expense ratio is more desirable. ETFs following broad market indexes have lower expense ratios than those following custom indexes or specializing in specific asset classes. Higher returns from a more aggressive investment strategy might justify the increased expenses.

Inception date: The date on which an ETF was launched. The inception date is important because it tells you how long the fund has been on the market. Many ETFs are so new that there is little data available to evaluate their performance relative to the broad market.

Market price return: The annualized return is the average return of a fund for each year of a multi-year period. If available, annualized returns are usually shown for one-, three-, five-, and ten-year periods. Annualized return takes into account the reinvestment of dividends and capital gains as well as the change in the price (NAV) of the ETF over a specific period of time.

A consistent return over long periods of time indicates lower volatility and less risk. Only a few ETFs have been in existence long enough to supply meaningful data. Some ETF providers analyze the past performance of the index on which an ETF is based to make projections about future performance.

Year-to-date return: The year-to-date (YTD) return shows how an ETF is performing in the current market. A comparison of the YTD returns of ETFs in different industry sectors provides a snapshot of broad market performance. The NAV YTD of an ETF shows the performance of the underlying stocks in an index and can vary from the performance of the ETF itself.

Average market capitalization: The average market capitalization is an indication of the size of the companies included in an ETF. Most brokerage and financial Web sites classify ETFs by styles and sectors. Just as with mutual funds, it is important to look at the assets in an ETF in relation to the other holdings in your portfolio. Use ETFs to add to your asset allocations, but be careful about duplicating your mutual fund holdings.

Self-directed IRAs

The IRAs at most banks, brokerages, and financial institutions offer a selection of mutual funds, ETFs, bonds, stocks, and money market accounts. IRS rules, however, permit an IRA to hold almost any type of investment with a few restrictions. An IRA can invest in more than 40 asset classes, including commodities, precious metals, real estate options, tax liens, rental properties, and even land or businesses. If you have experience with these other types of investments, you can put your knowledge to work and use the tax advantages of a self-directed IRA to achieve maximum growth with them. You can become a landlord or manage your own business and have all the profit go into your Roth IRA, where earnings can grow tax-free.

When the stock market goes into decline, your rate of return on equity investments could be much lower than the average 7 percent, and you could even lose some of your capital. It takes months for the stock market to recover — and years for you to recover from your losses. A two-year slump early in your working career could mean there will be substantially less in your IRA when you are ready to retire. Management fees for mutual funds and fees for stock transactions also eat into your returns. If you are knowledgeable and willing to involve yourself in actively managing your IRA, a self-directed IRA can be a valuable tool for accumulating wealth.

The "self-directed IRAs" many financial institutions advertise are simply IRAs that allow you to choose which stocks, bonds, and mutual funds to invest in. A completely self-directed Roth IRA offers the flexibility to invest in many types of assets, including real estate and business ownership. To distinguish themselves, some companies advertise a "truly self-directed IRA," meaning they are prepared to handle many types of investments and put you in charge of managing them. An IRA with "checkbook control" is an arrangement that lets you handle the financial transactions associated with your investment.

The Major Players

To prevent misuse of the tax benefits offered by a Roth IRA and the manipulation of clients by financial institutions, the IRS has strict rules governing the way in which a self-directed IRA can be structured. For example, only a bank or an approved financial entity can hold the assets in your IRA, and it must submit annual reports to the IRS. This financial entity cannot interfere in investment decisions. You are not allowed to directly carry out transactions such as buying and selling the assets in an IRA; this must be done by a professional intermediary. While a custodian might manage an IRA invested in mutual funds, stocks, and bonds, a self-directed IRA typically requires the additional services of an administrator or trustee. The responsibilities of each are different:

Custodian

Your IRA custodian is the bank or financial institution that holds your IRA account. The custodian is responsible for keeping the accounts and reporting to you and to the IRA. According to IRS rules, an IRA custodian must remain neutral in regard to investment decisions, taking direction from the IRA owner and not attempting to influence or advise him or her. According to federal law, only a bank, savings and loan, credit union, or an institution or individual who has received approval from the IRS may act as an IRA custodian.

Trustee

A trustee represents a trust that holds assets on your behalf and has the authority to act on your behalf in certain matters. A trustee is obligated by law to act in your best interests.

Administrator

An IRA administrator handles the administrative details of an IRA account and acts as an interface between the IRA owner and the custodian or trustee. An administrator does not hold assets or have fiduciary authority over assets in the IRA — an administrator carries out the process of opening and closing an IRA account; receives contributions; executes rollovers, transfers, and distributions; and conveys the account holder's instructions regarding transactions.

Choosing an administrator

An IRA administrator is typically a company employing a staff of accountants, lawyers, and finance professionals. It might be a small company with a handful of employees, or a large firm serving thousands of clients. It is important to choose an administrator that is equipped to handle transactions for the types of investments you plan to include in your self-directed

IRA. You do not want to do the extra work of changing administrators later on when your investment plans are underway.

You can find potential administrators by typing "self-directed IRA" in an online search engine, inquiring at banks and brokerages, or asking professionals and friends for recommendations. There are several questions that can help you select the right administrator:

- **What kind of transactions can you handle?**

  Most administrators of self-directed IRAs can handle real estate transactions, but if you are interested in owning a business, buying and selling mortgage notes, or investing in precious metals, make sure the company is equipped to support you.

- **What is your typical turn-around time for funding a transaction?**

  Some investment opportunities, like the purchase of tax liens, require immediate action. IRS rules prohibit temporary borrowing from personal funds to pay for an IRA investment, so funds in the IRA must be easily available for such transactions. A company with a large number of clients might take days to respond to an order, resulting in the loss of investment opportunities.

- **What are the credentials of your staff?**

  An ideal administrator will have lawyers, accountants, and certified real estate professionals on staff. They should have experience as IRA advisors and receive ongoing training to keep abreast of the changes in IRS rules. The penalty for engaging in a prohibited transaction is severe; even if the transaction represents only a small portion of your Roth IRA, the entire IRA will be deemed distributed and you will have to pay income tax on earnings and (if applicable) an early withdrawal penalty that tax year. Your administrator should be able to alert you to any possible contradictions of IRS rules.

- **How long have you been in business?**

    A company that has been in business for a long time will have an established reputation and a large, experienced staff. On the other hand, a smaller company might offer more personal attention and a faster response to your requests. It is important to know the background of a new business; its founders might have a wealth of experience or they could be newcomers to the field.

- **Is your company involved in any current, ongoing, or pending litigation?**

    A company that is being sued for mishandling someone else's investments is not a good choice for yours. Ask if the company is bonded for theft or fraud and insured for errors and omissions. Ask to see the company's annual financial statements.

- **Whom do you consult when you need expert advice?**

    A good administrator will have access to experts outside the company who can give legal advice and answer questions when a situation is unclear.

- **Do you provide education for investors?**

    Some administrators provide newsletters, information, and classes on their Web sites, or the services of a financial advisor to help you get started.

- **Can you automatically transfer unused cash into a money market account?**

  Some IRA administrators automatically place unused cash into a money market account at the end of each day so it can earn interest until it is needed.

- **What is your fee structure?**

  Administrative fees for a typical IRA are less than $100 per year, while fees for a self-directed IRA can range from several hundred to more than $1,000 a year for a $100,000 account, reflecting the additional services provided. A self-directed IRA incurs fees both from the IRA custodian and the administrator. Custodians generally charge a fee for each transaction and might also charge an annual fee. A fee-based administrator charges either a flat annual fee or a fee for each service or transaction, in addition to the custodian's fee. An asset-based administrator charges an annual fee based either on the value or the number and type of assets in the IRA. Some administrators charge a flat annual fee along with a fee for each transaction. There might also be a termination fee when you close your account or transfer to another IRA.

> *Paying fees with outside funds means more money stays in your IRA.*
>
> Many IRA owners pay IRA administrators' fees with outside funds in order to preserve as much cash as possible inside the IRA.

- **Can I access my account online?**

  Many IRA administrators offer the ability to make changes to an account and submit orders online. It is helpful to be able to view your account details easily whenever you need them.

- **What kind of customer service do you offer?**

    If you want someone to be available to answer your questions, try calling the company customer service telephone number to see how responsive the staff is. Some administrators offer live chats online with customer service representatives. Not everyone needs to consult with their IRA administrator on a regular basis, but if you do, make sure you will be able to do so easily.

Funding a self-directed IRA

The amount available for investment in a self-directed IRA is restricted by annual contribution limits ($5,000 per year; $6,000 if you are over 50). You might have a substantial amount to invest if you are rolling over a traditional IRA, 401(k), or other retirement plan. A self-employed individual establishing an SEP IRA is allowed to contribute 25 percent of his or her wages (or up to 20 percent of Schedule C income), up to a maximum of $49,000 (in 2009). Before setting up a self-directed IRA, confirm that the amount in your account will be sufficient for the type of investment you are planning.

If your account has a small balance, you might be able to increase it by making some short-term investments with quick returns. You can leverage the money in your IRA by creating and investing in your own limited liability company (LLC), which then takes out a mortgage or a business loan to be paid back with rent or business income.

Your Roth IRA can also buy a partial interest, or partnership, in a company that is otherwise established with outside funds, or in collaboration with a spouse or other family member. You will manage the company, but only the IRA's share of the profits can be deposited into the IRA account.

> ### *All expenses must be paid from IRA funds.*
>
> IRS rules do not allow the use of personal funds to pay expenses associated with an investment your IRA owns. If cash is needed to pay for maintenance, supplies, or service charges associated with real estate or a business owned by your IRA, you must ensure there is enough cash in your IRA account to cover these needs.

Checkbook control

One of the limitations of a self-directed IRA is the owner must instruct the IRA custodian to carry out financial transactions on his or her behalf, resulting in delays, extra paperwork, and custodian transactional fees. To get around this difficulty, the owner of a self-directed Roth IRA can set up a LLC that he or she manages, and instruct the IRA custodian to invest in it. This is known as "checkbook control." The IRA owner has sole signing authority for the bank accounts of the LLC and can carry out financial transactions without the involvement of the IRA custodian. The profits of the LLC go directly to the IRA. This structure was officially sanctioned by a tax court case, Swanson v. Commissioner of Internal Revenue, 106 T.C. 76 (1996). James Swanson, owner of Swanson's Tools, set up a company called Worldwide to export tools abroad. All shares of Worldwide were owned by an IRA set up by James Swanson, and the company received commissions for its export sales and paid dividends to the IRA. The IRS characterized this arrangement as "self-dealing" and declared these to be "prohibited transactions." Swanson appealed, and the court declared that the payment of dividends to the IRA, by a company wholly owned by the IRA, benefited the IRA and did not directly benefit James Swanson. This ruling set a precedent for self-directed IRAs to own a business managed by the IRA owner and receive dividends from that business without losing their tax-deferred status.

The IRA owner finds a custodian that allows self-directed IRAs, sets up the LLC, and directs the custodian to purchase membership interest in the LLC and transfer funds to the LLC bank account. The IRA owner writes a check from the LLC to purchase an investment, which he or she then manages.

The IRA custodian is a non-discretionary trustee, meaning it does not offer legal or tax advice, or ensure that legal requirements are met. The IRA owner is responsible for making sure all codes, regulations, and legal requirements are complied with. It is essential that the owner of a self-directed IRA who sets up an LLC seek out the independent advice of accountants, lawyers, and business advisors who are not affiliated with the IRA custodian and who understand the IRS rules concerning IRAs.

Managing risk

Any type of business has some risk associated with it. In the bond markets and credit markets, when there is a greater risk that borrowed capital might not be paid back, the borrower offers a higher rate of return as an enticement to investors to take a chance. Financial institutions rank bond issuers and assign credit ratings to try to quantify this risk. Investment in a risky enterprise is often justified with the saying, "The greater the risk, the greater the potential reward." In business, there is no logical basis for this statement. Risk is not associated with reward. A business entailing a great deal of risk might offer only a minimal reward, and a relatively "safe" business can be extremely profitable. As the person responsible for your self-directed IRA, you are dealing with specific investment opportunities, not generalized statistics. It is up to you to use your common sense, your knowledge and experience, and the resources at hand to carefully evaluate a business opportunity and decide whether you can profit from it.

An IRA has some restrictions that make it different from a taxable investment account and that require additional business planning. Funds from outside the IRA cannot be used for expenses, and assets the IRA owns cannot personally benefit the IRA owner. *See the following section on prohibited transactions for more information.* If IRS regulations are violated, an IRA runs the additional risk of immediately becoming fully taxable.

There are several steps you can take to minimize the risk associated with your IRA investments and ensure your efforts increase your wealth and fulfill the purpose of the account.

Due diligence

Due diligence is the process of thoroughly investigating every aspect of a business opportunity. It includes everything from research and financial analysis to a physical inspection of the business's property and assets. Before jumping into an investment, learn all there is to know about it. Investigate its history and the history of similar businesses. Evaluate contracts, pending liabilities, patents, and exclusive rights. Analyze a business's potential to succeed. If you are unable or unwilling to do this yourself, have it done by professionals. Do not leave any eventuality unexplored or any question unanswered.

Have a business plan

Never lose sight of your purpose, which is to increase your wealth by utilizing the tax advantages of your IRA. Plan exactly how you will enter an investment, how it will be managed, how long you will hold it, and when and how to exit. Whether you are looking for short-term profits or long-term increase in value, you should know your estimated return on investment (ROI). The business plan is based on the research from the "due diligence" phase and includes how much you are willing to pay for the investment, where the funds will come from, and the point at which you expect to realize a profit. Once your plan is established, you are responsible for following it and achieving the desired results. If you find the outcome of your investment is deviating too far from your business plan, revaluate to determine whether it will still be profitable for you and what changes should be made.

Protect yourself from loss

Take all the precautions necessary to protect yourself from loss. By exercising due diligence, you should be able to detect possible fraud, such as the overvaluation of property or the concealment of a defect or weakness. Purchase adequate insurance and set aside enough cash for contingencies. Be flexible and seek alternative solutions when a funding or cash-flow problem threatens your IRA.

Real estate

A self-directed IRA can be invested in many types of assets, but the most common investment vehicle is real estate. Carefully managed real estate transactions can produce much higher returns than the stock market. During the real estate boom that occurred from 2003 through 2007, home prices were escalating at a dizzying rate, enticing investors to put their money into real estate. When the subprime mortgage bubble burst in 2007 to 2008, many investors lost everything, and some found themselves in irrecoverable debt. Even in difficult economic times, however, real estate presents some solid investment opportunities if due diligence is carried out. Real estate is particularly appealing when the stock market has lost so much value that many investors have found the value of their IRAs almost halved.

A self-directed IRA is a good vehicle for real estate investment because all the income generated from rent and from the sale of property goes untaxed directly back into the IRA, where it can be reinvested. Capital gains taxes on property sold by a Roth IRA can be eliminated.

An IRA can hold almost any type of real estate investment: single-family houses, apartment and office buildings, shopping centers, hotels, storage facilities, boat slips, tax-lien certificates, and undeveloped land.

Purchasing real estate with a self-directed IRA

There are three ways in which wealth can be generated from investing in real estate:

1. **Rental property**: You can purchase a property and become a land-lord, using the rent received from your tenants to pay the mort-gage, taxes, and maintenance expenses, and put the excess income back into the IRA.

2. **Appreciation in value over time**: Real estate typically increases in value as time passes. You can buy a property, rent it out for several years or decades, and sell it for considerably more than you paid for it.

3. **Quick profit**: You can search for properties that are undervalued, buy them, make some improvements, and sell them again a short time later for a profit.

A number of other real estate investment options are listed below.

Real estate-backed promissory notes

A self-directed IRA can be used to purchase mortgages, or it can underwrite new loans. A real estate-backed note is a loan for which a piece of property is the collateral. The borrower promises to make regular payments of principal and interest until the note is eventually paid off. If the borrower defaults on the note, the lender becomes owner of the property.

Real estate-backed notes are sold in both primary and secondary markets. Notes originate in the primary market when the borrower and original lender sign an agreement. At any time before the loan is paid back, the lender can sell the note on the secondary market. If carefully researched and constructed, real estate-backed notes can generate a quick profit. Several factors affect the value of a note and the price that will make it attractive on the secondary market:

- **Loan-to-value ratio (LTV)**: A note's LTV is calculated by dividing the balance of the loan by the market value of the property. The lower the LTV, the less risk the note entails for the lender.

- **Creditworthiness of the borrower**: Creditworthiness is an evaluation of the probability that the borrower will repay the loan according to the terms of the note. Information on the borrower's income and credit history play a part, but the judgment is largely subjective.

- **Interest rate**: The percentage of the loan balance that the borrower agrees to pay to the lender.

- **Term**: The lifespan of the note. A mortgage note is typically written for a duration of five, ten, 15, 20, or 30 years. On the secondary market, the term is the length of time remaining on the note.

Notes should be held only for relatively short periods.

A real estate-backed note is a contract to pay back principal and interest at a specified rate over a period of time. Because the average annual inflation rate of 3 percent gradually reduces the buying power of the borrowed capital, it is better not to hold a note for more than three years.

The two major types of risk associated with real-estate backed notes are the risk that the property used as collateral has been overvalued and is not worth the full amount of the loan, and the risk that the borrower will not be able to repay the loan and will go into foreclosure. Both of these risks can be mitigated through due diligence. A title insurance company can ensure the property is not under any legal encumbrances. If the property does go into foreclosure, all is not lost because the property can be sold to another buyer. It will involve some extra work and aggravation, but if the market is right, the property can be sold for more than it was originally worth.

The burst of the real estate bubble in 2007-2008 created a foreclosure crisis.

The overselling of subprime mortgages from 2000 to 2007 created a wave of foreclosures in a market with few buyers. Home prices dropped, and banks and lenders were unable to recover their investments. To protect your IRA, research a note carefully before buying it. A home buyer who has already paid off a good part of a mortgage is less likely to stop making payments and walk away from the home than someone who has only paid off a few thousand dollars.

Real estate options

A real estate option is a contract granting the exclusive right to purchase a property for a specific price on a specific date. A self-directed IRA can be used to purchase real estate options. If the property is not bought by the date specified in the option, the price of the option is forfeited, and the owner of the property is free to sell it to someone else. If you know a property is undervalued and you can sell it quickly to another buyer for a higher price, a real estate option is a good way to turn a quick profit.

Buying and selling distressed properties

You have probably seen ads promising quick profits from the purchase and sale of foreclosed or bank-owned properties, or hand-written signs by the roadside offering "cash for houses." The basic principle is to buy a property for less than it is worth, sell it quickly for its market value, and pocket the difference. A distressed property is one that is selling for less than its market value because the owner has been unable to make mortgage payments or owes taxes on the property, or because a property has fallen into disrepair. While money can be made from buying and selling distressed properties, the process is full of pitfalls, and success requires careful attention and a thorough knowledge of the market, in addition to a good understanding of the rules and restrictions governing IRA transactions.

Foreclosures and REOs

Foreclosure is the process by which a borrower who is unable to pay off a mortgage relinquishes title to the property, which is then repossessed and resold by the lender. The foreclosure process offers several opportunities to make a profit:

- The owner of a property that is about to go into foreclosure might be willing to sell his or her equity for less than it is worth, allowing the buyer to pay off the rest of the mortgage and acquire the property for less than its market value.

- To avoid foreclosure, a lender might allow a property to be sold for the less than the amount outstanding on the mortgage and accept the proceeds as satisfaction of the debt. This is known as a short sale and is another way to acquire a property at a bargain price.

- Foreclosed properties are sold at foreclosure sales, or auctions, in which the minimum bid includes the balance of the mortgage plus all expenses and attorneys' fees. Often the property is not sold because the minimum bid exceeds the market price, but sometimes a bargain can be found. Properties in such sales are sold "as is," and a prospective buyer does not have access to the property to conduct an inspection. Full payment might be required within a day or two. A foreclosed property might still be occupied by the previous owners, and eviction proceedings could be necessary.

- A property that does not sell at a foreclosure sale becomes the property of the bank or lender and is known as "real estate owned" (REO). REO properties are sold "as is," but a prospective buyer is able to inspect the property. REOs are often listed with real estate brokers and are priced to reflect any defects.

Tax sale certificates and tax liens

When property owners fail to pay property taxes, the tax jurisdiction, after exhausting all its recourses to collect the outstanding taxes, sells tax lien certificates to investors. The investors pay the back taxes and buy the right to collect the taxes plus costs and interest or foreclose on the property after a specified waiting period, called the redemption period. The property owner can redeem the certificate at any time during the redemption period by paying the back taxes, interests, and costs. If at the end of the redemption period the certificate has not been redeemed, the investor becomes the owner of the property. At minimum, the investor will collect interest on the taxes. If the certificate is not redeemed, the investor acquires a property for the low price of the tax lien certificate, realizing a very large return on the initial investment. During the redemption period, the certificate holder must continue to pay taxes on the property.

Tax lien certificates are not without risk. A property might have multiple tax liens against it if it has been subdivided or rezoned. If the property owner has a pending bankruptcy or owes federal income taxes, those claims take precedence over a property tax lien. Tax districts charge various fees for participating in tax certificate sales. There is almost no opportunity to inspect a property before buying the certificate.

Seeking the assistance of professionals

Successful investing in real estate, especially in complex investments such as commercial properties or construction and development, requires expertise and experience in numerous areas. Even if you have a thorough knowledge of your investment, it is prudent to develop a network of reliable professionals to whom you can turn when you are starting a new venture or have unanswered questions. The benefits of a sound legal structure and detailed financial analysis will be worth the money you pay for their services. Some of the professionals whose services you might need when you invest in real estate with a self-directed IRA are:

- **Real estate agent**
  A real estate agent can help you locate properties that could be good investments and perform many of the tasks associated with purchasing real estate. These include researching the market prices of similar properties in the area and local rental rates, drawing up contracts, acting as your representative in negotiations, overseeing inspections, and helping to arrange financing. A real estate agent who knows the local market and is experienced with real estate investment is well worth the expense of a commission.

- **Licensed home inspector**
  The services of a licensed home inspector might cost a few hun-

dred dollars, but a thorough inspection will ensure that the property is sound and that there are no serious problems.

- **Title insurance company**

  A title insurance company researches the property to ensure that
  it is free of any liens or encumbrances and that the title deed is
  free of any legal defects. Title insurance companies offer insurance
  to pay for the resolution of any problems that might arise if their
  research is incorrect.

- **Property manager**

  A property manager is an individual or company that does the
  day-to-day work of cleaning and maintaining a property, finding
  tenants, checking their credit and creating rental contracts, and
  collecting rent.

- **Loan officer or mortgage broker**

  IRS rules allow the borrowing of money to purchase assets inside
  a Roth IRA, subject to some restrictions. Only the property being
  purchased with the mortgage can be used as security for the loan;
  if the loan is unpaid, the lender cannot attach other assets in the
  IRA or belonging to the IRA owner. You will need to locate a
  lender whose policies allow it to loan money to an IRA and whose
  terms are acceptable. The loan officer at your bank might be able
  to help or you can search for a mortgage broker. Some mortgage
  brokers now specialize in self-directed IRA investments.

- **Lawyer**

  An attorney with IRA and tax experience can be a valuable asset
  and can help protect you from running afoul of IRS regulations.
  You will need a lawyer to review real estate contracts, particularly
  if your investment is complex, such as a shopping center or retail
  property with multiple tenants. A lawyer can also act as an escrow

agent, help in the performance of due diligence, and assist in locating investment opportunities.

- **Accountant**

  A good accountant with tax and IRA experience can help with IRS compliance and the evaluation of potential investments. An accountant can also analyze the cash flow of complex businesses and provide insight and advice on business opportunities.

Evaluating a real estate investment

Because an IRA owner is not permitted to use a property owned by the IRA as a residence, any real estate an IRA purchases will have to be rented out until it is sold. The property will produce income from two sources — rent and the profit from the sale of the property. A property will also require maintenance, payment of property taxes, and possibly mortgage payments. To analyze the potential return on a real estate investment, you must consider several factors:

- The cash-on-cash return is calculated by dividing the net income on the property by the amount invested in it. The net income is equal to the annual revenues from the property minus the annual expenses. The cash-on-cash return is expressed as a percentage; a two-digit percentage is considered desirable, but a percentage in the high single digits is acceptable if other factors are favorable.

- The rate at which a property is expected to appreciate in value is typically determined by looking at the historical rate of appreciation for the area and considering changes such as nearby development or deterioration of the economy. A property that has a single-digit cash-on-cash return but a high expected appreciation rate is still a good investment. The sum of the cash-to-cash return and the appreciation rate gives an annualized ROI for the property.

- Examine the vacancy rate for rental properties of the same type in the same area. A high vacancy rate is an indicator that there will be times when the property might not have tenants and there will be no rental income.

Unrelated business income tax (UBIT)

Income from property an IRA purchases with a mortgage is subject to the UBIT, originally conceived for charities that make money from businesses unrelated to their central purpose. It is reported on IRS Form 990T, and further information is available in IRS Publication 598 (**www.irs.gov/pub/irs-pdf/p598.pdf**). Income from the portion of the property the mortgage finances that exceeds $1,000 is taxed at the trust rate. If the amount of the annual tax will exceed $500, quarterly estimated payments should be made. When the property is sold, the UBIT will apply to the capital gains if the investment has been associated with debt any time during the 12 months preceding the sale. The best way to avoid this is to pay off the mortgage at least 12 months before selling the property.

UBIT is payable on investments in a Roth IRA.

UBIT applies to any property an IRA owns and purchased with a mortgage, whether it is traditional IRA or a Roth IRA.

Disadvantages of owning real estate in a self-directed IRA

- The strict IRS rules regarding real estate owned by an IRA mean some of the benefits investors in real estate normally enjoy are not available to IRA owners.

- The tax deductions usually available for real estate cannot be taken for real estate an IRA owns.

- An IRA owner cannot use a house the IRA owns as a primary residence, vacation home, or business site. The property cannot be rented to a parent, grandparent, child, or member of an immediate step-family.

- An IRA cannot purchase property previously owned by members of the family.

- The IRA custodian, not the IRA owner, must buy the property and will charge a fee for this service. Custodians' fees vary widely.

- The IRA must pay all the expenses associated with the property, including maintenance and property taxes. Enough cash must be available in the IRA to cover these costs.

- The regulations governing ownership of real estate in an IRA are complicated, and the penalty for breaking them is severe.

- When you want to take money out of your Roth IRA, it might be necessary to sell some of the property your IRA owns.

Loans

Many owners of self-directed IRAs originate loans for personal acquaintances or individuals with good references who are not able to get an ordinary bank loan at favorable rates. For example, interest rates are higher for bank loans on undeveloped property or vacation homes than for loans to purchase primary residences. A financially responsible person might not have a good credit history because he or she has never used credit cards or taken out a loan before. A loan can be issued through your IRA custodian or administrator. Peer-to-peer lending Web sites such as LendingClub.com (**www.lendingclub.com**) make it possible to formalize a loan for a relative, friend, employee, or a complete stranger who has accepted your bid.

Loans from an IRA must be made at market rates.

The IRS stipulates that the primary purpose of any transaction carried out with funds from your IRA must be to benefit the IRA. Loans made with funds from an IRA must be offered at market rates. You cannot do someone a favor by giving them a low-interest loan.

Direct investing with dividend reinvestment plans (DRIPs)

More than 1,300 U.S. and international companies and closed-end mutual funds offer dividend reinvestment plans (DRIPs) that allow existing shareholders to use cash from dividends to buy additional shares directly from the company, bypassing brokers and trading fees. DRIPs are well-suited for IRAs because they are offered by dividend-paying companies and promise long-term growth. According to Ibbotson Associates (Morningstar), 40 percent of investment returns since 1920 have been produced by dividends. Most of these plans also allow investors to make optional cash payments (OCPs) to these plans of as little as $10 and sell fractional shares. The owner of a fractional share is entitled to that fraction of the dividend from a whole share. OCPs allow small investors to make small, regular contributions and to purchase an interest in highly desirable blue-chip stocks whose prices would otherwise be unaffordable. You can build a diversified portfolio entirely of DRIPs or use them to expand an existing portfolio of stocks and funds.

Many custodians of self-directed IRAs are brokerage firms that rely on trading fees or commissions, so they do not allow you to invest in DRIPs. A self-directed IRA administered by a bank or other financial institution will be more accommodating. Some companies, including Exxon, offer DRIP IRAs. In order to enroll in a DRIP, you must be a stockholder of record, meaning that you must own at least one share in the company, and it must be registered in your name, not the name of a brokerage. Once you have selected a company and determined that they offer a DRIP, you can pay a one-time trading fee to purchase a share through a broker. Some companies, such as McDonald's, Procter & Gamble, Exxon, and Texaco, have direct-purchase programs that allow investors to purchase shares directly from the company instead of going through a broker. If a friend or family member holds stock in the company you want to invest in, ask them to transfer one share into your name. You can then request a prospectus and an application from the company. Specialists in DRIPs such as Temper of the Times Investment Services (**http://temperofthetimes.com**) perform the enrollment for you. You can find a directory of companies that offer DRIPs on the DirectInvesting.com Web site (**www.directinvesting.com/ advanced_drip_search.cfm**). DRIP Central (**www.dripcentral.com**) offers tutorials and resources for investing in DRIPs, including a list of banks and financial institutions that administer DRIPs.

Before signing up for a DRIP, find out if the plan charges any fees and if the company requires you to own a minimum number of shares before you can participate. Even if fees are charged, the cost of buying and selling shares in a DRIP will be nominal compared to broker trading fees. Ask about the timing of the DRIP reinvestments: Some companies purchase stock monthly, some quarterly or weekly, and some at a specific time of the month. Arrange for any contributions to be made before stock is purchased.

Precious metals

A self-directed IRA can be used to purchase gold, silver, and platinum. The IRA owner cannot take possession of these assets; the administrator must arrange for them to be stored in a secure repository. The precious metals can be held until their prices go up and then sold for a profit. Gold is considered to have little correlation to the stock market, and the demand for it increases when the stock market slumps. Investors often buy precious metals as a hedge against stock market losses. Late in 2009, following historic stock market losses in 2008 and unsteady performance afterward, the price of gold reached a record high.

The time to buy precious metals is not when their prices are high.

A slump in the stock market typically results in increased demand for precious metals, raising their prices. When the price has already risen, it is not a good time to buy gold. As soon as the stock market improves, the price will start to decline. Your goal is to buy when the price is low and sell when it is high.

When deciding how much to invest in precious metals, consider the annual administration fees for the account. If the fees equal more than 2 percent of the total amount invested, you might not realize enough returns to justify the investment. Do not invest in precious metals unless you can afford to invest enough to offset annual administrative costs and still realize a profit.

Administration costs must be paid with outside funds.

Precious metals do not generate any cash income until they are sold; they simply sit in a vault. You will have to pay annual administration costs out of other funds.

Prohibited transactions

Self-directed IRAs are in particular danger of violating IRS rules regarding prohibited transactions. *See Chapter 2 for more information on IRS rules.* The IRS stipulates that every transaction in a self-directed IRA must be for the primary benefit of the IRA. The purpose of a Roth IRA is to use tax privileges to generate retirement income for the owner, not to provide concessions or tax breaks to the IRA owner and his or her immediate family. Your IRA custodian, trustee, and administrator are also prohibited from using your IRA for their personal benefit.

You cannot pay yourself a salary from a company your IRA owns unless the company is structured so someone else decides your compensation. You are not allowed to commingle your personal funds with IRA funds or to loan money to your IRA. This means you cannot pay any expenses for property your IRA owns out of your personal bank account. A business your IRA owns cannot furnish free goods or services to you or your administrator. The penalty for a prohibited transaction is the immediate distribution of all assets in the IRA and the loss of its tax-free status.

Consult an attorney to ensure your IRA investments are structured in a way that does not violate IRA rules. You can limit the risk by creating a separate IRA for your business venture and keeping the rest of your retirement savings in another IRA.

Excerpt from Internal Revenue Service Publication 590, Traditional IRAs

(www.irs.gov/publications/p590/ch01.html#en_US_publink10006397).

Accessed June 22, 2009.

Prohibited Transactions

Generally, a prohibited transaction is any improper use of your traditional IRA account or annuity by you, your beneficiary, or any disqualified person.

Disqualified persons include your fiduciary and members of your family (spouse, ancestor, lineal descendant, and any spouse of a lineal descendant). The following are examples of prohibited transactions with a traditional IRA:

- Borrowing money from it.

- Selling property to it.

- Receiving unreasonable compensation for managing it.

- Using it as security for a loan.

- Buying property for personal use (present or future) with IRA funds.

Fiduciary

For these purposes, a fiduciary includes anyone who does any of the following:

- Exercises any discretionary authority or discretionary control in managing your IRA or exercises any authority or control in managing or disposing of its assets.

- Provides investment advice to your IRA for a fee, or has any authority or responsibility to do so.

- Has any discretionary authority or discretionary responsibility in administering your IRA.

- Has an effect on an IRA account. Generally, if you or your beneficiary engages in a prohibited transaction in connection with your traditional IRA account at any time during the year, the account stops being an IRA as of the first day of that year.

- Has an effect on you or your beneficiary. If your account stops being an IRA because you or your beneficiary engaged in a prohibited transaction, the account is treated as distributing all its assets to you at their fair market values on the first day of the year. If the total of those values is more than your basis in the IRA, you will have a taxable gain that is includible in your income.

- Borrows on an annuity contract. If you borrow money against your traditional IRA annuity contract, you must include in your gross income the fair market value of the annuity contract as of the first day of your tax year. You may have to pay the 10 percent additional tax on early distributions, discussed later.

- Pledges an account as security. If you use a part of your traditional IRA account as security for a loan, that part is treated as a distribution and is included in your gross income. You may have to pay the 10 percent additional tax on early distributions.

Roth IRAs and Your Estate

E arlier in this book, you learned three important principles to follow if you want to maximize the tax benefits of your IRA: Contribute early and often, keep expenses low, and understand IRS rules so you can minimize taxes and maximize growth.

You have read about several strategies for getting the greatest benefit from your Roth IRA's tax-free status, including constructing a well-balanced portfolio by applying sound investment principles, regularly reviewing and adjusting your asset allocations, and using your personal experience and know-how to manage your own investments. Income tax has already been paid on your Roth IRA contributions and conversions, and earnings can be withdrawn tax-free, so there is no required minimum distribution (RMD) every year after you reach the age of 70½ as there is with a traditional IRA or 401(k). If you do not need the funds for retirement income, you can leave them in your Roth IRA to accumulate tax-free earnings. When you die, your IRA might be the most valuable asset you leave for your heirs. To extend the benefits of your Roth IRA to them, you must do two things: Keep assets in the account generating tax-free earnings for as long as possible and minimize estate taxes.

While the U.S. government intends for your Roth IRA to fund your retirement, it recognizes that your surviving spouse might rely on income from your IRA for his or her old age. There are several rules and provisions that allow assets to remain and continue to grow in your IRA long past your death. By understanding these rules and setting up your IRA correctly, you can ensure your IRA can be passed on to your heirs and can continue to grow for as long as possible.

Every family's situation is unique and often complicated by changing financial circumstances, multiple marriages, and sometimes the early death of a beneficiary. Consult an experienced tax advisor or estate planner who can evaluate your situation and help you set up your IRAs so your wishes are carried out and your family does not suffer unexpected tax consequences. An experienced professional will be familiar with the most recent tax laws and IRS rulings on situations similar to your own.

The IRS has built in several benefits for surviving spouses and heirs of Roth IRAs, but these are often lost because the beneficiaries were not properly designated by the owner, or because they did not know what to do with the inherited account. The following section explains the steps you can take to prolong the benefits of your IRA for your survivors. You will learn which types of investments belong in a tax-deferred account and which do not, how to plan for your spouse and your heirs, and when you might need to consult a professional financial advisor or a lawyer.

Your IRA and Your Will

Many people are under the mistaken assumption that when they die, most of their assets will be distributed according to their will. The fact is that many important assets do not pass through a will. If a deceased person has a joint bank account or brokerage account with a spouse, the entire account goes to the surviving spouse. A home owned jointly with a spouse goes directly to that spouse, no matter what the will says. The proceeds of a life insurance policy go directly to the beneficiary. An IRA or retirement account goes directly to the named beneficiaries, regardless of the provisions in a will.

The IRS rules governing the distribution of IRAs take precedence over the provisions of a will. Assets that do not pass to heirs by designation or ownership are subject to probate, a legal process in which assets are collected, outstanding debts are paid, and a court verifies that an estate is properly distributed to the heirs. The probate process can tie up assets for months and incur court costs and attorneys' fees that must be paid out of the estate. There is also a possibility that a relative might contest the provisions of the will. Normally an IRA bypasses the probate process by passing directly to a named beneficiary or beneficiaries. If there is no named beneficiary, the IRA passes to the estate and is subjected to probate. All assets must be withdrawn and income tax paid, and the tax benefits of an IRA end there.

Naming your beneficiaries

Naming a beneficiary or beneficiaries for your IRA is the single most important action you can take to protect your heirs and ensure your wishes are carried out after your death. It is almost like writing a special will for your IRA. The beneficiary or beneficiaries you name for your Roth IRA will determine what can be done with the IRA after your death.

Each of your qualified retirement plans and IRAs has a retirement account beneficiary form, the document that guarantees that the person(s) you name will get your IRA when you die. It is important you fill out this form when you open a retirement account and that you update it whenever a marriage, birth, death, or divorce changes your circumstances. This form should be on file with the custodian of your account, and you should keep a copy in a safe place in case the original is lost. An IRA might have existed for several decades when the owner dies and the custodian might have changed filing systems, making it difficult to locate the original form.

You could disinherit a loved one by failing to update your retirement account beneficiary forms.

If you fail to update your beneficiary form after a divorce, your IRA could end up going to your ex-spouse instead of to your current spouse and children. If a child who is your beneficiary dies before you do, his or her children might not get a share of your IRA because you did not add them as beneficiaries.

Who can be a beneficiary?

Anyone can be the beneficiary of an IRA, including a minor child, but a spouse who is a sole beneficiary has certain privileges that are not available to any other beneficiary. You can also name a charity or a trust as a beneficiary. If this is done on the beneficiary form, the assets in the Roth IRA can pass directly to the charity without going through probate. Some company retirement plans require your spouse or another family member be named as beneficiary.

Spouse as sole beneficiary

Naming your spouse as the sole beneficiary of your Roth IRA will allow him or her more latitude in deciding what to do with your IRA after your death and might also affect the amount he or she must withdraw annually after your death.

After you die, a spouse who is a sole beneficiary can leave your Roth IRA in your name and wait until the year that you would have turned 70½ before starting to take a RMD based on his or her own life expectancy, keeping assets in the tax-advantaged account for as long as possible. This applies even if the spouse was already older than 70½ in the year you died.

A spouse who is a sole beneficiary also has the option of rolling over the assets from your IRA into his or her own IRA. RMDs can then be deferred until he or she is 70½ years old. Non-spouse beneficiaries are not allowed to roll over assets from your IRA plan into their own IRAs. *See Chapter 11 for more information on the options available to spouse beneficiaries.*

For tax purposes, the IRS does not recognize same-sex marriages.

Even if you live in areas where same-sex marriages have been legalized, the IRS treats same-sex partners as single for tax purposes. An unmarried or same-sex partner is treated as a non-spouse beneficiary. This might change in the future.

Primary and contingent beneficiaries

Your primary beneficiary is the person or entity you name to receive the benefits of your Roth IRA when you die. You can also name contingent beneficiaries who will receive the benefits of your IRA if, and only if, a particular event occurs that disqualifies the primary beneficiary. The disqualifying event is usually the death of the primary beneficiary, but it could be something else, such as a divorce. Naming contingent beneficiaries is another way of ensuring your IRA goes where you want it to go. For example, if you recently remarried, you might want to make your spouse your primary beneficiary, but your children from an earlier marriage the contingent beneficiaries if you and your spouse should divorce or if your spouse should die. This will ensure your IRA does not go to your spouse's relatives if he or she dies soon after you do.

When you name your children as beneficiaries, their children can be named as contingent beneficiaries who will receive the benefits of your IRA if one of your children dies before you do. If you do not name grandchildren as contingent beneficiaries and their parent dies before you do, they might be disinherited, and the IRA might be divided among the surviving named beneficiaries.

If the death of the primary beneficiary is the event that would pass the IRA on to the contingent beneficiaries, the naming of contingent beneficiaries has no effect on distribution rules. If the primary beneficiary could be disqualified for any reason other than death, the primary and contingent beneficiaries together are regarded as multiple beneficiaries.

Multiple beneficiaries

You can name several primary beneficiaries for your IRA, including charities or trusts. If the balance in your IRA is small or you anticipate that your beneficiaries will cash out your IRA soon after your death, you do not need to be concerned about naming multiple beneficiaries. If your intention is to keep assets growing in your tax-deferred IRA long after your death and to have them distributed in small amounts over as long a period as possible to minimize the income tax your heirs will pay, you should understand the consequences of naming multiple beneficiaries.

IRS rules for distributing an IRA vary depending on the type of beneficiary. For example, a spouse who is named as a co-beneficiary with your children will lose the benefits allowed for a spouse who is a sole beneficiary (see the previous section) and will be treated as a non-spouse beneficiary. A spouse who is one of several beneficiaries will not be able to roll the IRA over into his or her own IRA, to defer distributions until the year you would have turned 70½, or to use an applicable distribution period (ADP, which is an estimate of the number of years a person is expected to live) from the Single Life Table to take smaller annual RMDs.

Make sure the percentages add up.

Many IRA owners name multiple beneficiaries and assign a percentage of the IRA to each one, instead of allowing the IRA to be divided into equal parts. Often upon examination, the percentages do not add up to 100, particularly if the beneficiary form has been updated after a birth or death. When you assign percentages in your beneficiary form, be sure they add up to 100 percent.

Designated beneficiary

IRS rules for the distribution of an IRA distinguish between a "designated beneficiary" and other types of beneficiaries. A designated beneficiary must be either a natural person or a qualified trust. If you name a charity, a corporation, a nonqualified trust, or your estate as a beneficiary, you are considered to have no designated beneficiary for distribution purposes. If you name one of these entities as a co-beneficiary with your family members or a qualified trust, your IRA is still considered to have no designated beneficiary.

An IRA might have a designated beneficiary even if you did not name one.

An IRA with a custodial agreement that makes surviving family members beneficiaries by default will have a designated beneficiary, even if the owner never named one.

If your IRA has no designated beneficiary it must be entirely distributed within five years of your death. A large IRA balance distributed over five years could have considerable tax consequences for your heirs. When an IRA has a designated beneficiary, distributions can spread over the life expectancy of the beneficiary, starting with the year after your death.

Life expectancy for multiple beneficiaries

When an IRA has multiple designated beneficiaries, the life expectancy of the oldest beneficiary must be used to calculate the annual RMD, which is then divided among the beneficiaries in proportion to the interest each holds in the account. That means that if your spouse and children were all beneficiaries, your spouse's life expectancy would be used to calculate the distribution for all of them. If each was the beneficiary of a separate account, the younger children could use their own life expectancies and take smaller distributions.

After you die, your beneficiaries will have until December 31 of the following year to split your IRA into separate accounts and retain the ability to take minimum distributions over their life expectancies. There is always a risk that this might not be done in time if the family is in turmoil or unaware of the problem. Some IRA custodians will agree to treat each beneficiary's share as a separate account, but most are unwilling to do this. The easiest solution is to create a separate IRA for any beneficiary that cannot be a designated beneficiary. A charity is not required to pay income tax and will probably want to take the assets out of an IRA as soon as possible, while family members will probably want to stretch the IRA distributions over many years.

Qualified trust

There are no tax advantages gained by making a trust your IRA beneficiary, but there might be personal reasons for naming a trust as your beneficiary. By setting up a trust, you can maintain some control over what happens to the assets in your IRA after you die. You might set up a trust to make regular distributions to a disabled dependent or someone who is financially irresponsible. You could also use a trust to ensure your beneficiaries extend your Roth IRA's tax-free status as long as possible by only taking the RMD every year.

A trust can be a designated beneficiary of your IRA if it fulfills these conditions:

- The terms of the trust must be legal according to state law.

- You must identify the beneficiaries of the trust by name or by a description, such as "spouse," "child," "issue," or "grandchild."

- The trust must be irrevocable or become irrevocable after your death. If the trust is revocable during your lifetime, you must provide the IRA custodian with a copy of any changes that are made to it.

- You must give a copy of the trust to your IRA custodian or trustee. Instead of submitting the entire trust agreement, you can give your custodian a list of the beneficiaries with the amount each is to receive and the conditions under which they will receive the benefits. A copy of the trust agreement must be submitted to the IRA custodian by October 31 of the year following your death.

Trusts set up as beneficiaries of Roth IRAs must take into account all the IRS rules governing distributions. The trust must take RMDs just as a human beneficiary would. If a trust fails to take all or part of an RMD, it must pay the same 50 percent penalty as an IRA owner. The trust must calculate RMDs and file a tax return every year, creating extra paperwork and management costs.

A trust cannot usually separate the accounts of multiple beneficiaries in the way that an IRA can be split, so the age of the oldest beneficiary will be used to calculate the RMDs. If for any reason the trust fails to qualify as a designated beneficiary, the beneficiaries will lose out on the opportunity to stretch out their RMDs over their own life expectancies. The entire IRA will be paid out in five years.

Charities

You can make a charity or other organization the beneficiary of your IRA. Charities do not qualify as designated beneficiaries and are therefore required to withdraw all IRA assets by December 31 of the fifth anniversary year of the owner's death.

As explained earlier, when a charity is named as beneficiary of an IRA along with persons or qualified trusts that would otherwise qualify as designated beneficiaries, they lose the option to stretch the IRA distributions over their own life expectancies. If you want your beneficiaries to be able to keep assets in your IRA as long as possible, it is wise to create a separate IRA account with the charity as beneficiary.

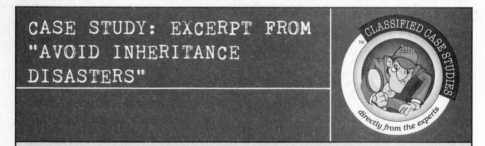

CASE STUDY: EXCERPT FROM "AVOID INHERITANCE DISASTERS"

Bob Carlson is editor of the monthly newsletter Retirement Watch (*http://retirementwatch.com*), providing independent, objective research covering all the financial issues of retirement and retirement planning, and chairman of the Board of Trustees of the Fairfax County Employees' Retirement System. He is the author of Invest Like a Fox...Not Like a Hedgehog, The New Rules of Retirement, and numerous other books and reports, including Tax Wise Money Strategies, Retirement Tax Guide, How to Slash Your Mutual Fund Taxes, Bob Carlson's Estate Planning Files, and 199 Loopholes That Survived Tax Reform.

Make sure your heirs know their options. Part of your estate planning should ensure that your heirs know what to do — and what not to do — with the IRA. Do not expect that they will get good advice from the IRA custodian, or just any accountant, or financial professional. We are in the early stages of the first generation to inherit IRAs, and many advisors are not up-to-speed on the rules. IRA custodians are not in the business of advising beneficiaries of their best moves. You need to get good advice and pass it on to your heirs.

Here are the key inherited IRA mistakes and how to avoid them:

Disappearing documents. Your will or living trust has no effect on an IRA. Only the beneficiary designation on the form held by the IRA custodian determines who inherits the IRA. IRA owners often make the mistake of not designating a beneficiary or not updating the form after a beneficiary passes away, or there is some other change in circumstances. Another common mistake is the heirs misplacing or not being able to find the designation form. They have to depend on the custodian to have a current copy. Custodians do not always have a copy, especially if it was filed many years ago or the original firm has merged one or more times. In any of those cases, the custodian's rules (if it has any) determine the beneficiary. It might be your estate, which is the worst result from a tax standpoint. Or it might be a spouse when you intended the IRA to go to your children.

Keep copies of your beneficiary designation forms in a file that is easy to find, and keep the designations up-to-date. Let your executor and heirs know where the forms are.

Ignoring spousal benefits. When a surviving spouse inherits an IRA, a special option is allowed.

The inheriting spouse can elect to treat the IRA the same as any other beneficiary can. Or, the spouse can use a special option to roll over the inherited IRA into a new IRA in his or her own name. The rollover allows the surviving spouse to start a new required minimum distribution schedule based on his or her own age. It also allows the spouse to name new beneficiaries. ...Your spouse should know that he or she has options, and the consequences of each choice can be very different. Ensure that a good advisor is available to your spouse, or leave some suggestions and guidelines for the spouse to follow.

Rolling over an IRA or changing the title. Non-spouse beneficiaries do not have the same options as surviving spouses. For example, if your children inherit the IRA and roll it over into their own IRAs ... the children would be treated as though the inherited IRA were distributed directly to them in cash. They might owe a 6 percent excess contribution penalty for each year the money sits in their IRAs. [Instead, they should] roll over the inherited IRA to new, separate IRAs in their own names ... Yet, many IRA custodians simply ask the heirs what they want to do with the IRA and do not explain fully the consequences of the actions.

Spending down the IRA. Despite all their parents' planning, an extremely high percentage of non-spouses who inherit IRAs take the balances as lump sums and spend them. That is too bad. ...Instead of spending the IRA on whatever their current needs are, heirs should let the IRA continue to compound tax deferred. They would end up with significantly more wealth than they would by taking a distribution. If your beneficiaries are likely to spend the entire IRA after inheriting, consider leaving them other property if you have it. It would be better to leave the IRA to other beneficiaries or charity. Heirs that plan to spend the inheritance quickly are better off receiving non-IRA assets, if that option is available to you... Some heirs fail to begin taking the RMDs, so they pay penalties. Others take the RMDs under the wrong schedule and take larger distributions than they need to. Be sure your heirs who will not spend the IRAs have good information about how to determine the RMDs that will stretch the IRA the most.

Not splitting the IRA. An inherited IRA can be split into separate IRAs for each of the beneficiaries. Then, each beneficiary makes individual investment decisions and takes required distributions based on his or her own life expectancy. If splitting an IRA is what your heirs are likely to do, then check with your IRA custodian. Though the tax law allows IRAs to be split, the custodian does not have to allow it. Be sure the custodian will allow a split and will not charge fees or penalties for the split. If it won't, move the IRA to another custodian now.

Also, be sure your heirs know their options, the consequences, and the deadlines. IRAs are the prime assets in many estates. They are surprisingly complicated financial accounts — especially when it is time to take distributions. Few people know how to handle them. Be sure your beneficiaries have the information they need to make the right decisions.

Your custodial agreement

When you open an IRA with a bank, brokerage, or financial institution, you are asked to sign a custodial agreement. Each IRA custodian has its own rules concerning what it will and will not allow you to do with your IRA. These rules might be more restrictive than IRS rules, and the IRA custodian might not allow you to do something that is otherwise legal. Before opening an IRA account, make sure the IRA custodian will allow you to carry out your plans. Most custodians allow multiple beneficiaries, and some allow you to file customized beneficiary forms. Some do not allow a beneficiary to name his or her own beneficiary for the account after you die. This is a drawback, because if your beneficiary dies soon after you do, the balance of the IRA would immediately pass into his or her estate instead of being paid out over many years.

Many custodial agreements include a default clause stipulating what will happen to the account when you die if there is no named beneficiary or if the beneficiary is deceased. A typical default clause states that the IRA will go to the estate if there is no named beneficiary. Some IRA custodial agreements make the spouse and then the surviving children default beneficiaries if there is no named beneficiary. Ask whether the custodial agreement has a "per stirpes" provision, meaning that a deceased beneficiary's share of an IRA automatically passes to his or her heirs. Otherwise, your grandchildren could be disinherited if their parent dies before you do and the IRA is shared among the surviving beneficiaries. If there is no per stirpes provision, it is even more important that you regularly update your beneficiaries.

If you want to name a trust as a beneficiary, make sure the IRA custodian allows this. Find out if a beneficiary who is not your spouse would be allowed to transfer the IRA to another custodian. Ask whether your beneficiaries will be allowed to "stretch" your IRA by continuing to take your

RMDs until the balance is depleted. It is also important to know what will happen if you and your beneficiary die at the same time, particularly if you or your spouse have children from a different marriage.

> *The terms of your IRA custodial agreement take precedence over your will.*
>
> The default clause in your custodial agreement takes precedence over your will in dictating who will get your IRA when there is no named beneficiary.

Tax consequences of inheriting an IRA

Several things can happen to your Roth IRA when you die. Your beneficiary can take RMDs based on his or her life expectancy and continue to keep assets in the Roth for years to come. A spouse who is a designated beneficiary might opt to treat the IRA as his or her own. Your spouse and children might decide to cash out the IRA. If your IRA does not have a beneficiary, it could pass directly into your estate, in which case it would be liquidated. You may also make a charity the beneficiary of your IRA.

Income tax

Unlike a traditional IRA, a Roth IRA does not impose income tax burdens on your heirs. A Roth will only incur taxes or penalties if earnings or conversions are withdrawn from it before it is five years old. This can easily be avoided; if you die before your Roth IRA has been established for five years and your heirs decide to liquidate it, they can simply wait until the end of the five-year holding period. If they decide to stretch the IRA and take RMDs, it is highly unlikely that any earnings will be disbursed during the five-year holding period because IRS rules require contributions to be disbursed first. Even if your Roth was established by converting a traditional IRA or retirement plan and is not yet five years old, RMDs taken by heirs of an IRA are not subject to the 10 percent early withdrawal penalty.

Estate tax

In response to the economic slump of 2000, in June 2001, President George W. Bush signed the Economic Growth and Tax Relief Reconciliation Act of 2001 (EGTRRA). Until then, any estate of up to $1 million had been exempt from estate tax. Amounts larger than $1 million were taxed at rates ranging from 41 percent to as high as 60 percent for amounts between $10,000,000 and $17,184,000. State governments were allotted a percentage of the estate tax. EGTRRA limited the highest taxation rate to 45 percent and gradually raised the exemption to $3,500,000, phasing it out entirely in 2010. The generation-skipping "transfer tax" (GSTT) imposed on property transferred to someone more than one generation younger, such as a grandchild, was also scheduled to be phased out in 2010. In compliance with the Congressional Budget Acts of 1974 and 1990, which require the vote of 60 senators to pass a bill that results in a decrease of annual fiscal revenue for more than 10 years, EGTRRA included a "sunset provision" that returned the estate tax exemption to $1 million again in 2011. In the meantime, some states that did not want to give up income from the estate tax created their own state estate taxes.

In 2011, Congress will again vote on the estate tax. Its future is unclear. The effects of the economic recession of 2008 and the tax policies of the current President Barack Obama administration could result in the reinstatement of an estate tax, but almost certainly with a higher exemption. A historically unprecedented transfer of wealth began in the United States as members of the World War II generation began to pass away and leave their hard-earned savings to their children. The growing role of IRAs in funding retirement will ensure the working population will continue to hand substantial savings down to future generations.

Your IRA is part of your estate. When the value of all your assets, including your IRA, exceeds the estate tax exemption ($3,500,000 in 2009, phased out in 2010 and possibly reinstated in 2011), your beneficiaries have to pay estate tax of up to 45 percent on all or part of your IRA.

If the value of your estate is less than $3,500,000 you do not need to concern yourself with estate tax. If you have a large estate, you should consult a professional estate planner and take steps to protect the assets in your IRA. You can employ various strategies to reduce the size of your taxable estate and to keep assets in a tax-deferred IRA as long as possible.

The unlimited marital deduction and the estate tax exemption

When an estate tax is in effect, every individual has the right to pass on a certain amount of assets free of estate taxes ($3,500,000 in 2009). A married couple often loses one of their estate tax exemptions because of another estate tax provision, the unlimited marital deduction. When one spouse dies, the surviving spouse can inherit unlimited assets without paying estate tax on them. When the second spouse dies, however, he or she could only leave $3,500,000 (in 2009) free of estate tax to their children. The estate tax exemption for both spouses can be claimed by splitting an IRA into two accounts: one equal to the amount of the estate tax exemption, naming the children as beneficiaries; and the other account holding the balance of the IRA with the spouse as beneficiary. When the IRA owner dies, the first IRA will go directly to the children free of estate tax, and when the spouse dies, the children can receive a second amount free of estate tax.

Protect your estate with life insurance

To ensure assets stay in your Roth IRA for as long as possible, consider purchasing life insurance with your heirs as beneficiaries. Proceeds from a life insurance contract are generally not taxed as income. The death benefit from a life insurance policy can be used to cover the expenses of settling your affairs and avoid the need to make a withdrawal from your Roth IRA for this purpose. Life insurance might be difficult to obtain if you are older or in poor health, and the premiums will be higher. If you are still working, you might be able to obtain life insurance through your employer. Professional associations sometimes offer life insurance to their members.

Death benefits from a life insurance contract are included in your estate. If you are wealthy and your estate will be subject to estate tax, establish an irrevocable life insurance trust (ILIT) to purchase the life insurance policy. Because the trust owns the life insurance policy, the death benefit will not be part of your estate and will not be subject to estate taxes. An ILIT can be designed for a special purpose, such as to take care of a special needs child. You will pay an attorney or financial planner's fee to set up the trust and will have to designate a trustee. If the trustee is not a family member, you might need to pay an annual management fee. Cash to purchase premiums must be gifted to the trust. You can gift up to $12,000 per year for each beneficiary without paying a gift tax. The trustee must then notify each beneficiary that they have the right to withdraw the gift money from the trust within the next 30 days. After 30 days, the money becomes the property of the trust and can be used to pay the life insurance premium. Beneficiaries should not withdraw the gifted money from the trust.

Wealthy people often use an ILIT to pay estate taxes so that the estate itself can be left intact. There are some restrictions to consider before buying a life insurance policy through an ILIT:

- The trust is irrevocable; once a life insurance policy has been purchased by the trust, you cannot take it out.

- You cannot change the beneficiary of your life insurance policy.

- You cannot take out a loan against the cash value of the life insurance policy, because the trust owns the policy.

- You cannot take out a loan against the cash value of the life insurance policy, because the trust owns the policy.

Stretching an IRA

When you die, IRS rules allow your designated beneficiary to take RMDs from your Roth IRA using his or her own life expectancy from the Single Life Expectancy Table. *See Appendix E for the Single Life Expectancy Table.* This is called "stretching" an IRA, and it has two benefits. The assets in your IRA can remain there longer, continue to grow in value, and produce tax-free earnings. By taking only the minimum required amount out of your IRA year-by-year, your beneficiaries can continue to generate income in it. An IRA has a lifespan; eventually all the assets in it must be distributed. The longest an IRA can be stretched is 82.6 years, the average deferral percentage (ADP) for a newborn baby in the Single Life Expectancy Table.

If your designated beneficiary dies before the Roth IRA is completely depleted, his or her beneficiary will continue to take the RMDs based on your designated beneficiary's life expectancy.

IRS rules regarding distributions to a designated IRA beneficiary are detailed. Your beneficiaries might have difficulty stretching your IRA if you do not set it up correctly or if they are not well-informed. You know your beneficiaries better than anyone else, and it is up to you to set up your IRA so that your wishes will be carried out. There are several factors to consider.

How large is the balance in your IRA?

The benefits of stretching an IRA are minimal if the balance in it is small. Your beneficiary will probably prefer to withdraw the whole amount rather than deal with the paperwork and report it on an income tax return every year. The five-year rule requires your beneficiary to withdraw the full amount within five years of your death.

Roll over your 401(k)s and other retirement plans into a Roth IRA

Although IRS rules permit the designated beneficiary of a qualified retirement plan to take RMDs over his or her own life expectancy, many employers require beneficiaries to withdraw the entire balance upon the death of the original plan owner. Employer plan administrators do not want to take on the additional accounting work or the possible liability if a mistake is made. The rules of retirement plans take precedence over IRA rules. If an employer goes out of business, your beneficiary could have difficulty contacting them regarding your retirement plan. If your intention is for your beneficiaries to stretch your retirement account, roll it over into a Roth IRA with a financial institution or brokerage as soon as you leave your employer.

Confirm that your retirement plan administrator will allow your beneficiary to take RMDs

IRA custodians have their own rules and restrictions regarding how an IRA will be distributed to beneficiaries. If you want your heirs to stretch your Roth IRA, choose an IRA custodian that will allow your wishes to be carried out.

Name your beneficiaries carefully

The section on naming your beneficiaries earlier in this chapter emphasized the importance of naming and updating your beneficiaries on a beneficiary information form to ensure your wishes are carried out. Only a designated beneficiary will be able to stretch an IRA by taking RMDs over his or her own life expectancy. An IRA can have only one designated beneficiary who must be either a person or a trust that identifies a person as its beneficiary. A charity or any other type of trust cannot be a designated beneficiary. If you name a charity as co-beneficiary for your IRA with your spouse and children, the IRA will be considered not to have a designated beneficiary and the total balance will have to be withdrawn within five years. If you want to leave part of your IRA to charity, it is wise to create two or more separate IRAs: one for the charities that do not qualify as designated beneficiaries and one for the people who will be the beneficiaries of the rest of your IRA.

A sole beneficiary who is a spouse has special privileges; he or she can wait until the year after you would have turned 70½ to start taking RMDs, and the amount of those RMDs can be calculated more favorably using the Single Life Expectancy Table. *See Appendix E.* A sole spouse beneficiary can also roll the IRA over into his or own IRA, and beneficiaries of that IRA can stretch it instead. Instead of naming your spouse and children as co-beneficiaries, you can name your spouse as primary beneficiary and your children as contingent beneficiaries who will become beneficiaries of the IRA when your spouse dies.

When you name several beneficiaries for your IRA, you must stipulate how you want the IRA to be distributed among them, such as "equal shares" or percentages. Directions given in your will cannot be carried out unless they are reflected on the beneficiary form filed with your IRA custodian.

When an IRA has more than one beneficiary, the IRS will use the life expectancy of the oldest beneficiary to calculate the RMD for all of them. If you name your sister and your children as beneficiaries, the younger children would have to take their RMDs based on your sister's age. Your beneficiaries will have a certain time period to split the IRA after you die so they can each use his or her own life expectancy. To make sure this is done properly, you can split your IRA into a separate IRA for each beneficiary. *See Chapter 11 for more information on the rules regarding an inherited IRA.*

Inform your beneficiaries

Inform your beneficiaries of your intentions and make sure they understand the benefits of keeping assets in your Roth IRA as long as possible. Keep copies of your beneficiary forms in a safe place where family members can find them easily and on file with your executor. Few people have a thorough understanding of IRA rules. Beneficiaries should be advised about any steps they need to take after your death and about the tax consequences of withdrawing money from your IRA.

Beneficiaries can make their own decisions.

Once you are gone, your beneficiaries can make their own decisions about whether to split and stretch your IRA by taking RMDs over a period of time or to withdraw all the assets at once. If you have a large IRA and feel strongly about keeping it active for as long as possible, you can create an irrevocable trust to receive the RMDs from your IRA and pass them on to your beneficiaries. A trust will entail the additional cost of an attorney to set it up and management fees, but it will ensure your plans are carried out.

Make sure your beneficiaries do not need to use cash from your IRA for expenses

To protect the assets in your Roth IRA, arrange for cash from other sources to cover funeral costs, the expenses associated with administering your estate, settlement of outstanding debts, and any estate and income taxes. This can be done by purchasing life insurance or arranging for the liquidation of assets outside your tax-deferred accounts.

Keep all your IRA documents in one place

IRS rules regarding the distribution of IRAs are complicated enough without your heirs having to search through old tax returns to identify your IRA custodians. You might own more than one IRA, either because you are keeping an account an old employer sponsored, you inherited an IRA, or you opened separate IRAs for your beneficiaries. The IRS allows until September 30 of the year following your death for a designated beneficiary to be named for each IRA, and until December 31 of the year following your death for your IRA to be split into separate accounts for multiple beneficiaries. In the turmoil following your death, your bereaved spouse and children might find it difficult to concentrate on detailed financial matters. Make it easier for your beneficiaries by keeping copies of IRA custodial agreements and beneficiary forms for all your IRAs in one safe place.

Life expectancy for beneficiaries

A beneficiary must begin taking RMDs in the year following the death of a Roth IRA owner. If the beneficiary is not a spouse, or there are multiple beneficiaries, the beneficiary uses the life expectancy next to his or her age in Table I: Single Life Expectancy to calculate only the first RMD. *See Appendix E.* Each year after that, one year is simply subtracted from the first life expectancy. A surviving spouse who is the sole beneficiary will be able to recalculate by returning to the Single Life Expectancy Table each year and using the life expectancy for his or her age to determine the RMD. A sole spouse beneficiary of a Roth IRA owner who dies before reaching the age of 70½ will be required to start taking RMDs from the IRA in the year of the owner's RBD if he or she had lived.

Convert to a Roth IRA

You can avoid creating a tax burden for your beneficiaries with your IRA or retirement plan by converting it to a Roth IRA and paying the income tax yourself. Your beneficiaries will have to take the RMDs every year, but they will not have to pay income tax on the distributions. In the past, income limits prevented owners of very large IRAs from converting to a Roth IRA, but as of 2010, anyone could convert to a Roth. If you have a very large balance in your retirement account, you probably have a large estate that might be subject to estate tax. Paying the income tax on a Roth conversion could help to lower the size of your estate.

When You Inherit a Roth IRA

I nheriting a Roth IRA is not like inheriting a house, an investment account, or money in the bank. You own the money in the IRA, but you have a tax obligation and are required to follow IRS rules by taking money out every year. If you fail to comply with the rules, you will be penalized, just as the owner of a traditional IRA would be penalized.

IRS rules give you several options for managing an inherited Roth IRA, and surviving spouses are given special privileges because they presumably shared an income with the deceased. After the owner of an IRA has died, there are deadlines to be observed and legal steps that must be taken to preserve the tax-deferred benefits of the IRA. This chapter will cover the available options and the steps that are necessary to carry them out.

Consult an experienced financial advisor when you inherit an IRA.

After the death of a loved one, you might not feel emotionally prepared to deal with financial matters, but the clock is ticking for an inherited IRA. Consult an experienced financial advisor or attorney who can assess your tax obligations, explain the possible courses of action, and make the necessary legal arrangements for you before the IRS deadlines.

What Are Your Tax Liabilities?

A distribution from a Roth IRA is tax-free income. You are not required to pay income tax on it, but you are required to take a required minimum distribution (RMD) every year and report it to the IRS. Because the main purpose of a Roth IRA is to provide retirement income for its owner, the U.S. government wants to ensure that its tax-free status does not extend indefinitely beyond the owner's death. You can always withdraw more than an RMD whenever you wish, but remember that the excess withdrawals cannot be applied to the next year's RMD.

If your inherited Roth IRA account is not at least five years old, you will have to pay income tax on any earnings you withdraw from it before it reaches its five-year anniversary. Because contributions are always distributed before earnings, this rule will probably not affect you unless you decide to completely empty the Roth before the five years are up.

Naming a Designated Beneficiary

IRS rules for the distribution of a Roth IRA are based on the age of the designated beneficiary, who must be named by September 30 of the year following an IRA owner's death. *See Chapter 10.* A designated beneficiary must be either a person or a trust that has a person as its beneficiary (qualified trust). If a charity, a corporation, a nonqualified trust, or the owner's estate is listed as a co-beneficiary in the IRA custodial agreement, the IRA is considered to have no designated beneficiary for distribution purposes. You have at least nine months to remove a nonqualified beneficiary from the Roth IRA, either by cashing out its share of the Roth IRA or by splitting the IRA into different IRAs for designated beneficiaries and nonqualified beneficiaries.

Life Expectancy Rule

The designated beneficiary takes required minimum distributions (RMDs) from the IRA every year using his or her own life expectancy from the IRS Single Life Expectancy Table. *See Appendix E.* The first distribution must be taken by December 31 of the year following the IRA owner's death. The first year, the beneficiary looks up the applicable distribution period (ADP) for his or her age in the Single Life Expectancy Table and calculates the RMD by dividing the balance of the account on December 31 of the year the IRA owner died by the ADP. Each year afterward, the beneficiary subtracts one from that ADP and divides it into the IRA balance as of December 31 of the previous year.

A beneficiary who fails to take an RMD or who does not take the full RMD will have to pay a penalty at tax time of 50 percent of the amount that should have been withdrawn. The IRS might waive the penalty if it was an innocent mistake, but it will be necessary to attach a special letter of explanation, requesting a waiver, to the tax return.

If a Roth IRA has more than one beneficiary, the RMD will be calculated using the age of the oldest beneficiary to look up the ADP. The longest period of time over which RMDs could be extended is 82.4 years, the ADP for a newborn baby in the Single Life Expectancy Table. Extending RMDs over the life expectancy of a beneficiary is known as "stretching" an IRA.

How Large is Your Inherited IRA?

Because IRAs were only introduced in 1974, and contribution limits were relatively low until 2001, IRAs with large balances have only begun to emerge in significant numbers in the last decade. If there is only a modest balance in your inherited IRA, or your share of an inherited IRA is small, you might simply want to cash it out now and go on with your life. You will not need to receive paperwork and report an RMD on your tax return every year. The benefit of a Roth IRA is that the assets in it can continue to grow tax-free. You will not be able to contribute anything more to an inherited IRA unless you are a spouse and sole beneficiary, and you are still earning income from work.

There are several reasons for keeping a large Roth IRA intact and continuing to take annual RMDs from it. If you have been left a large IRA, chances are you have inherited other substantial assets and do not need cash from the IRA for your living expenses. Earnings in a large IRA will continue to be significant if they are left to grow tax-deferred.

If cash is not available from other sources to pay for funeral costs and the expenses of settling the deceased's estate or your own affairs, you might have no choice but to make a withdrawal from the IRA. Once the money has been taken out of an IRA, it can never be replaced.

The First Step: Name a Successor Beneficiary

The first thing to do when you inherit an IRA is name a successor beneficiary who will receive the balance of the IRA if you die before it is completely depleted. In Chapter 10, you learned that an IRA without a beneficiary passes directly into your estate. That is exactly what could happen if you should die shortly after inheriting an IRA and have not named a successor beneficiary. The successor beneficiary of an inherited IRA, however, can continue to take the RMDs that you would have taken if you were still alive and stretch the IRA over the remainder of your life expectancy.

Spouse sole beneficiary

A spouse who is the sole beneficiary of an IRA is given several options that are not available to any other beneficiary:

- The spouse can leave the IRA in the IRA owner's name and begin taking distributions the year after the IRA owner would have turned 70½, using his or her own life expectancy from the Single Life Expectancy Table to calculate the RMD. Instead of subtracting one from the ADP each subsequent year, the spouse goes back to the Single Life Expectancy Table, looks up the ADP for his or her age, and divides it into the balance of the IRA on December 31 of the previous year.

  The following table illustrates the advantage a sole spouse beneficiary has over a non-spouse beneficiary in calculating RMDs. It shows what would happen to an IRA with a balance of $100,000 if a beneficiary began taking distributions at the age of 70½. A non-spouse beneficiary (left) would be forced to take larger distributions and deplete the IRA balance more rapidly. This example is only hypothetical because it does not allow for the growth that would add to the balance of the IRA throughout several decades. Assets held in a large IRA and allowed to grow for two or three more decades could produce substantial returns.

Comparison of RMDs for spouse and non-spouse beneficiaries

Age	ADP	Annual RMD for a Roth IRA with a balance of $100,000 on Dec. 31 of year the spouse turned 70 ½	Age	ADP	Annual RMD for a Roth IRA with a balance of $100,000 on Dec. 31 of year the spouse turned 70 ½
		Annual RMD calculated using the Single Life Expectancy Table by a non-spouse beneficiary who begins taking distributions at the age of 70 ½			*Annual RMD calculated using the Single Life Expectancy Table by a spouse sole beneficiary who begins taking distributions at the age of 70 ½*
70	17	$5,882.35	70	27.4	$5,882.35
71	16	$5,882.35	71	26.5	$5,774.09
72	15	$5,882.35	72	25.6	$5,699.58
73	14	$5,882.35	73	24.7	$5,584.05
74	13	$5,882.35	74	23.8	$5,465.24
75	12	$5,882.35	75	22.9	$5,342.89
76	11	$5,882.35	76	22	$5,216.68
77	10	$5,882.35	77	21.2	$5,044.22
78	9	$5,882.35	78	20.3	$4,911.48
79	8	$5,882.35	79	19.5	$4,729.58
80	7	$5,882.35	80	18.7	$4,544.10
81	6	$5,882.35	81	17.9	$4,309.87
82	5	$5,882.35	82	17.1	$4,120.42
83	4	$5,882.35	83	16.3	$3,880.87
84	3	$5,882.35	84	15.5	$3,641.31
85	2	$5,882.35	85	14.8	$3,401.75
86	1	$5,882.35	86	14.1	$3,162.19
87		$0.00	87	13.4	$2,879.01
88		$0.00	88	12.7	$2,604.81
89		$0.00	89	12	$2,339.92
90		$0.00	90	11.4	$2,084.65
91		$0.00	91	10.8	$1,804.03
92		$0.00	92	10.2	$1,546.31
93		$0.00	93	9.6	$1,311.00
94		$0.00	94	9.1	$1,097.58
95		$0.00	95	8.6	$883.42
96		$0.00	96	8.1	$720.68
97		$0.00	97	7.6	$560.53
98		$0.00	98	7.1	$428.64
99		$0.00	99	6.7	$331.85
100		$0.00	100	6.3	$240.31
Balance		$0.00			$456.58

- A sole spouse beneficiary can also elect to treat the inherited Roth IRA as his or her own IRA, or roll over the inherited IRA into his or her own existing Roth IRA. The spouse becomes owner of the Roth IRA and can make contributions to it as long as he or she has earned income. As the owner of the Roth IRA, a surviving spouse can also convert funds from other retirement accounts to it and name any beneficiary he or she wants for the new IRA. The new owner is not required to take RMDs and can leave funds untouched in the IRA for as long as he or she wishes.

Most spouse beneficiaries roll over inherited IRAs, but there are cases in which it is desirable to leave the inherited IRA in the name of the original owner. If you inherit a Roth IRA from your spouse when you are younger than 59½ and need cash, you will pay a 10 percent early withdrawal penalty and income tax on any earnings you withdraw from your own Roth before you reach 59½. On the other hand, you could leave the Roth IRA in the name of your deceased spouse and begin taking RMDs right away. The inherited Roth IRA does not have to be rolled over into an IRA at any particular time. The spouse beneficiary can leave it in the original owner's name for several years before rolling it over.

A spousal rollover into a new IRA cannot be reversed.

Once a spouse beneficiary has rolled over an inherited IRA into his or her own Roth IRA, the decision cannot be reversed.

- A spouse can also take over an IRA by failing to take a RMD. Under the life expectancy rule, a Roth beneficiary should take the first RMD by December 31 of the year after the IRA owner's death. If a spouse beneficiary does not take a distribution by December 31 of that year, the spouse automatically becomes owner of the Roth IRA.

Non-spouse beneficiary

A beneficiary who is not a spouse does not have the option of taking over an inherited Roth IRA as his or her own and must use the life expectancy rule and take RMDs as explained earlier in the chapter.

The IRS allows a non-spouse beneficiary to transfer the inherited Roth IRA into a new Roth IRA, but it must still be established in the name of the deceased. The beneficiary might make such a transfer to take advantage of better investment opportunities or lower fees another IRA custodian charges. The transaction must be carried out as a trustee-to-trustee transfer.

Non-spouse beneficiaries cannot roll over an inherited IRA.

A non-spouse beneficiary is not permitted to roll over assets from an inherited IRA into his or her own IRA, because the RMD could then be deferred until he or she turned 70½. Any such transfer of assets is considered a direct withdrawal of funds from the IRA; the full amount will be treated as a disbursement and the earnings will be subject to income tax. The beneficiary might be able to treat the transfer as his or her own tax-deductible contribution to an IRA, but any amount in excess of the contribution limit is subject to a 6 percent penalty.

Re-naming an IRA account

Many IRA custodians do not like to maintain an account in the name of someone who is deceased, yet the IRA must remain in the name of the original owner. To comply with IRS requirements, an IRA account is often given a new title that includes the name of the deceased and the name of the beneficiary, such as "Joe Doe, deceased, for the benefit of (FBO) Fred Doe." A non-spouse beneficiary is not allowed to transfer the IRA into his or her own name exclusively. Doing so would cause the assets in the account to be considered fully distributed and fully taxable in the current tax year.

Multiple beneficiaries

When an IRA has multiple beneficiaries, the oldest becomes the designated beneficiary, and all the other beneficiaries must take RMDs based on that person's life expectancy. The first year, the RMD is calculated by looking up the oldest beneficiary's ADP in the Single Life Expectancy Table. For every year after that until the account balance is depleted, one year is subtracted from the previous year's ADP. Each year's RMD is distributed among the beneficiaries according to the provisions in the beneficiary form, usually equal shares or percentages.

Any of the beneficiaries may cash out his or her entire share of the IRA at any time, and the remaining beneficiaries can continue to take their shares of RMDs until the balance is depleted.

Only a designated beneficiary can take distributions from an inherited IRA over his or her life expectancy. If even one of the IRA beneficiaries is a charity or other type of organization, the IRA is considered not to have a designated beneficiary and the entire balance must be distributed in the year following the IRA owner's death.

If the designated beneficiary is older than you are, your life expectancy will be used to calculate the distributions.

According to IRS rules, the RMD for multiple beneficiaries is ordinarily calculated using the life expectancy of the oldest beneficiary. If the oldest beneficiary is older than the deceased IRA owner, then the remaining life expectancy of the IRA owner will be used instead.

Changing the Beneficiaries

Changes can be made to the beneficiaries of an IRA after the IRA owner has died. IRS rules do not require a designated beneficiary to be named until September 30 of the year following the death of the IRA owner, which gives the beneficiaries at least nine months to decide how they want to take distributions. New beneficiaries cannot be added to an IRA after the owner is deceased, but existing beneficiaries can remove themselves, or the IRA can be split into a separate IRA for each beneficiary.

Disclaiming an IRA

An IRA beneficiary can decline the IRA by signing a disclaimer, a legal document stating that the beneficiary renounces all rights to the IRA. The IRA will then go to the other named beneficiaries or pass into the estate of the deceased. For example, a spouse who does not need the income from a Roth IRA might disclaim it in favor of children who are the contingent beneficiaries or in favor of a charity. A wealthy sibling might renounce his or her share of an IRA in favor of less prosperous brothers and sisters.

Removing a beneficiary

Beneficiaries such as charities or trusts that do not qualify as designated beneficiaries can be removed by distributing their interests in the IRA before September 30 of the year following the death of the IRA owner. Once the charity's portion of the IRA has been withdrawn, it is no longer included among the beneficiaries. The remaining beneficiaries, who qualify as designated beneficiaries, can then take RMDs until the balance of the IRA is depleted.

Splitting into several IRA accounts

When all the beneficiaries of an IRA are designated beneficiaries on September 30 of the year following the IRA owner's death, the IRS allows the IRA to be split into separate accounts for each beneficiary. The beneficiaries have until December 31 of that year to separate their shares of the IRA account. Splitting the IRA into separate accounts allows each beneficiary to use his or her own life expectancy to calculate annual distributions from his or her share. This is of special benefit if one or more of the beneficiaries is much younger than the others. Splitting accounts also simplifies accounting and allows beneficiaries to make their own investment decisions regarding the assets in the IRA.

The oldest beneficiary's life expectancy is used to calculate the RMD for the first year after an IRA is split.

Each individual beneficiary does not use his or her own life expectancy until the year after the IRA has been split into separate accounts. The first year, the ADP of the oldest beneficiary is used.

Death of an IRA Beneficiary

When the beneficiary of a Roth IRA dies before the IRA balance is depleted, the beneficiary's beneficiary becomes the successor beneficiary and continues to take distributions according to the schedule established at the original IRA owner's death. Some IRA custodians do not allow a successor beneficiary to continue taking RMDs and require the whole IRA to be disbursed within five years after the original beneficiary's death.

If the original beneficiary was a sole spouse beneficiary, the first year's RMD is computed using the ADP for the spouse beneficiary's age in the Single Life Expectancy Table. For following years, one year is subtracted from the previous year's ADP.

An Extra Amount Withdrawn One Year Cannot be Credited to a Later Year

You can withdraw as much as you want from an inherited Roth IRA; the RMD is only the amount that you must withdraw every year. If you withdraw more than the minimum required distribution, you cannot include the extra amount as part of the minimum required distribution in another year. Your RMD for the next year will be calculated using the balance in your IRA on December 31 of the previous year.

Penalty for Failure to Take Your RMD

The penalty for not taking your RMD is severe. If an IRA owner older than 70½ fails to take the RMD, the amount that should have been distributed but remained in the account is referred to as an "excess accumulation." The IRA owner must pay a penalty equal to 50 percent of the excess accumulation. The excess accumulation tax is calculated and reported on IRS Form 5329.

If the excess accumulation is due to an honest mistake and the IRA owner takes steps to remedy the insufficient distribution by making a withdrawal, he or she can request that the tax be waived by attaching a statement of explanation to a completed Form 5329. Instructions can be found under "Waiver of Tax" in the Instructions for IRS Form 5329.

Many people fail to take their RMDs on time.

The most common reason is a lack of understanding of IRA rules or of the penalties for breaking them. Some people are not aware they must begin withdrawing funds the year after the death of the IRA owner. Others are in poor health and unable to manage their financial affairs or receive faulty information from a financial advisor. A surviving spouse might not understand when RMDs are due to begin from an IRA. The IRS is relatively forgiving when there is a genuine misunderstanding, and the situation can usually be salvaged.

Reporting Distributions From an Inherited IRA

After an IRA owner dies, the IRS requires IRA custodians to file IRS Form 5498 for each beneficiary. The form reports the deceased IRA owner's name, the beneficiary's name and social security number or tax ID, and the amount of the beneficiary's share of the IRA at the end of the previous year. Form 5498 must be filed every year until the account is depleted.

IRA custodians are required by law to help IRA owners compute their RMD each year, but they are not required to do this for IRA beneficiaries. A beneficiary receives Form 5498 from the custodian, giving the balance in the IRA at the end of the previous year. The beneficiary is then responsible for calculating the required distribution every year, taking it, and reporting it on his or her income tax return.

Five-year Rule and Inherited IRAs

The five-year rule applies to withdrawals from a Roth IRA even after the death of its owner. Earnings withdrawn from a Roth IRA before the first day of the fifth taxable year after the Roth IRA was established are taxable.

A beneficiary who opts to stretch an IRA by taking RMDs starting in the year following the death of the IRA owner could be required to pay some income tax if the IRA was only recently established and earnings are part of the withdrawal. This is not likely to happen, though, because earnings are not distributed until after contributions have been the depleted. Earnings will make up only a small part of a new Roth IRA.

CHAPTER 12
TWELVE

Special Circumstances

Divorce or Separation

After a divorce or separation, your IRA might be the largest asset that has to be divided between you and your ex-spouse. Qualified retirement plans such as 401(k)s receive different treatment than IRAs under a divorce decree or separate maintenance agreement. A qualified company retirement plan is divided according to a qualified domestic relations order (QDRO) issued by a judge, under which an ex-spouse becomes an "alternative payee" and is entitled to receive a percentage of the account whenever plan rules allow it to be distributed, which could be years later. A QDRO cannot force a distribution of assets in a retirement plan if such a distribution is contrary to plan rules.

An IRA is divided according to the terms of the divorce or separate maintenance decree. To avoid early withdrawal penalties, all or part of an IRA can be transferred to the ex-spouse's own IRA or a new IRA in his or her name. These funds should be moved only by a trustee-to-trustee transfer. The participant can also direct the IRA custodian to change the title of the IRA to an IRA in the name of the ex-spouse. The IRA custodian should receive a copy of the divorce decree before any funds are transferred. The transfer to the ex-spouse's account must be done within 60 days. After this deadline has passed, you might have to pay income tax on the earnings taken out of your Roth IRA and an additional 10 percent early withdrawal penalty if you are less than 59½ years old.

Once funds from your Roth IRA have been transferred to a Roth IRA in the name of your ex-spouse, that IRA is treated as though the ex-spouse is the original owner. Your ex-spouse will pay the income tax when distributions of earnings are made prematurely and will be liable for the 10 percent early withdrawal penalty if he or she withdraws funds before reaching the age of 59½.

Only the IRA owner can initiate the transfer of funds to an ex-spouse's IRA. The ex-spouse cannot initiate the transfer or take possession of IRA funds before they have been deposited in an IRA in the ex-spouse's name.

Does your divorce lawyer or financial advisor understand how to split an IRA?

Some divorce lawyers and financial advisors are not well-informed about the IRS rules and the tax consequences of splitting an IRA after a divorce. If necessary, consult more than one advisor to be sure that your IRA is accurately divided according to the terms of the divorce or separate maintenance decree. Your advisor should have an understanding not only of IRS rules, but of the nature of the investments in the IRA and how their value can change over time.

Paying alimony or child support from your IRA

After a divorce or separation, you might need cash to make regular alimony or child support payments. Your Roth IRA should always be a last resort, but if it is your only resource, you can avoid early withdrawal penalties and taxes on earnings by setting up a series of substantially equal periodic payments (SEPP), also known as a 72(t) for Section 72(t)(2)(A)(iv) of the

Internal Revenue Code. You will have to commit yourself to a payment schedule for at least five years. Failure to maintain the scheduled payments will incur a 10 percent penalty on all earnings withdrawn since the beginning of the plan.

Consult your IRA custodian to set up a 72(t). Once you have selected a distribution method, your plan should be committed to writing. Most IRA custodians have a form for this purpose. Your IRA custodian will report your 72(t) distribution every year on IRS Form 1099-R. If Box 7 on that form contains a two (meaning "early distribution, exception applies under age 59½"), you do not need to file any additional forms or documents. If Box 7 contains a one ("Early distribution, no known exception") or seven ("Normal distribution"), then you will need to file IRS Form 5329 to claim the exemption to the 10 percent penalty tax. Keep records of all your plan transactions and copies of the account statements that were used to calculate the first payment.

If you have more than one IRA, you can take 72(t) payments from only one of them without affecting your other accounts. Your annual payment will be calculated based only on the balance of that account. Many IRA custodians have special 72(t) accounts designed to accumulate enough cash for the annual distributions while keeping assets in the IRA growing as much as possible.

You could be penalized if your Roth IRA balance is depleted before the end of your holding period.

If you are unable to take all of a fixed annual payment because your IRA balance has been prematurely depleted, it will be regarded as a violation of the plan, and you will be required to pay the 10 percent penalty on the full amount that has been withdrawn. To prevent this, you can change to a required minimum distribution method that is based on your account balance. If it has already happened, you will need to request a private letter ruling (PLR).

What to Do When You Make a Mistake

The rules defining IRAs are strict, and the various IRS forms that your IRA custodian is required to file every year make it certain that any failure to take an RMD from an inherited IRA, or to report a contribution, will be detected. Sometimes rules are broken because an investor does not understand them correctly or because a financial counselor gives incorrect advice. A beneficiary might fail to take the first RMD after an IRA owner's death because of confusion surrounding his or her affairs. The IRS recognizes that most IRA mistakes are honest oversights or due to circumstances beyond the IRA owner's control, and there are means of rectifying errors.

Failure to take an RMD from an inherited IRA

Beneficiaries of a Roth IRA do not have to pay income tax on withdrawals, but they are required to take RMDs from the inherited Roth IRA beginning in the year after the original owner's death. It is not unusual for someone to miss taking the first RMD from an inherited IRA because he or she is not aware of the rules, or to withdraw less than the required amount because of a miscalculation. The penalty is steep — 50 percent of the amount not withdrawn — but the IRS is willing to waive it if an honest mistake has been made. You cannot correct the error by filing an amended tax return because you cannot take a withdrawal for a year that has already ended. Instead, take the withdrawals in the next tax year and report them on Form 1040. Report the amounts in Section VIII of Form 5329, Additional Taxes on Qualified Plans (Including IRAs) and Other Tax-Favored Accounts, but do not fill in the 50 percent penalty. Write "See attached explanation," and attach a letter explaining why you failed to take the RMD and requesting that the IRS waive the penalty. The IRS will decide whether to waive the penalty.

Excess contributions

There are several ways in which you might exceed contribution limits to a Roth IRA. You can only contribute earned income; if you contributed $6,000 to an IRA in 2009 but you and your spouse had combined earned income of only $4,000 that year, you have an excess contribution of $2,000 in your account. Income from rental property or stock dividends is not considered to be earned income. You might mistakenly roll over ineligible assets from another retirement plan; for example, you cannot roll over an amount that was taken as an RMD from a traditional IRA, or deposit a withdrawal from a Roth IRA into a traditional IRA. A rollover must be made with the same type of asset; if you withdraw cash from one IRA, you must make a cash deposit into a new IRA; if you withdraw stocks, you must deposit stocks. You cannot contribute to a Roth IRA if your income exceeds a certain limit; such contributions are also regarded as excess contributions. You might earn unexpected income at the end of the year that makes you ineligible after you have already contributed to a Roth IRA.

The excess contribution plus any earnings on it will be taxed at 6 percent if it is not withdrawn by the date your tax return is due the next year. If you file by April 15, you will be given an automatic six-month extension of the deadline (until October 15) for withdrawing the excess amount. Earnings on your excess contribution are figured by calculating the percentage of return on the IRA as a whole during the time the excess contribution was held in the account and then multiplying it times the amount of your contribution:

Earnings =

$$\frac{\text{Excess contribution x (Adjusted closing balance of IRA – Adjusted opening balance of IRA)}}{\text{Adjusted opening balance of IRA}}$$

The adjusted opening balance is the fair market value (FMV) of the IRA when the excess contribution was made, plus any transfer credits, contributions (including excess contributions being removed), and amounts recharacterized to the IRA. The adjusted closing balance is the FMV of the IRA when the excess contribution is withdrawn plus any transfer debits, distributions, and recharacterizations from the IRA. When the excess contribution and the earnings are withdrawn, the IRA custodian will issue a Form 1099-R reporting the distribution. The earnings will be taxable as income, and could be subject to the 10 percent early withdrawal penalty if you are younger than 59½.

Excess contributions are taxed at 6 percent for as long as they remain in your IRA. If you miss the deadline for withdrawing an excess contribution, you can include it in the next year's contribution.

Ineligible contribution to a Roth IRA

If you contribute to a Roth IRA and then earn enough income later in the year — for example from an employer bonus, to make you ineligible for a Roth IRA, or if you mistakenly open a Roth IRA when you do not qualify, — you can recharacterize it to a traditional IRA *See the section on recharacterization in Chapter 4 for more information.* You have until October 15 of the following year to recharacterize and submit an amended tax return. Once the deadline has passed, ineligible contributions to a Roth IRA are treated as excess contributions, subject to the 6 percent penalty.

If the excess amount in the Roth IRA is not large, you can simply withdraw the funds and forfeit the opportunity to contribute to a traditional IRA for that year.

Private Letter Ruling

If you are uncertain about your tax situation or about an IRA transaction, or you have inadvertently incurred a penalty because of an honest error, you can request a private letter ruling (PLR) from the IRS. A PLR is the IRS's written response establishing the tax consequences of a particular transaction and is applicable only to the taxpayer who requested it. If all the information about the transaction is accurate, a PLR is binding on the IRS. You can request a waiver of fees or penalties, extension of a deadline, interpretation of a tax regulation, or a ruling on a particular IRA question. You are entitled to a single conference with an IRS representative if it is necessary to resolve the situation. You should not request a PLR unless you seriously intend to carry out the transaction and are willing to abide by the IRS decision in order to avoid a tax audit.

Instructions for submitting a request can be found in Internal Revenue Bulletin, Bulletin No. 2009-1 January 5, 2009, Rev. Proc. 2007-4, page 118, Rulings and Determination Letters (**www.irs.gov/pub/irs-irbs/irb09-01. pdf**). The applicable fee might range from $380 to $9,000, depending on the type of transaction. All facts pertaining to the transaction should be included in the request and copies of relevant documents should be attached. When you receive the PLR from the IRS, you should attach a copy of it to your tax return.

PLRs are IRS rulings on specific individuals' situations and are not intended to establish legal precedents. The IRS is required to make PLRs available to the public after stripping them of all personal information. You can search a complete list on the IRS Web site (**www.irs.gov/app/picklist/list/ writtenDeterminations.html**). An experienced tax advisor will be familiar with PLRs that give an indication of the position the IRS is likely to take on similar cases.

Saving for Retirement in Difficult Times

CHAPTER

13

THIRTEEN

All discussions of risk and volatility talk about the behavior of the financial markets and of investment portfolios when the economy enters a decline. In 2008, after a decade of growth and prosperity, the stock market began a downward spiral, and banks and financial institutions began to fail. Well-established corporations shut their doors forever. One national government after another stepped in to bail out failing banks and industries with taxpayer dollars in an effort to stem a worldwide economic collapse. Suddenly, many of the economic "truths" of the past 50 years became obsolete or unsound. By early 2009, economists were announcing the deepest economic recession since the Great Depression of the 1920s and 1930s.

It is one thing to read about theories and another to personally experience the effects of an economic recession. The rapid decline of the value of the stock market and the failure of trusted financial institutions was especially cruel to people who relied on their investments for retirement income. In 2008, the portfolios of many IRA owners shrank to half of their previous values as the stock market lost 43 percent of its value. An elderly person with declining health cannot wait a decade for the economy to recover. Workers in their 50s and 60s experienced severe setbacks during the economic slump that might impede their ability to save enough, and younger families striving to set aside money for retirement saw much of their initial effort evaporate. The financial media is full of advice for confused investors, but no one has the answers, and no one can predict exactly what will happen in the next few years.

As the economy begins an expansion and the stock market starts to rise again, different areas of the global economy will respond at different times, and there will not be a smooth upward transition, but a gradual sequence of ups and downs. In making decisions about your investments and your IRA, it is important to maintain an awareness of the financial markets. Educate yourself. Read news and commentaries. Be flexible and think about the future. The rapid changes taking place might have altered time-honored truths, but they also present new opportunities.

Financial experts agree that you should not stop saving for retirement during a recession. Your IRA will probably be your largest source of retirement income, and you should not pass up any opportunity for tax-advantaged earnings. Contribute as much as you can to your Roth; remember that you have the option of withdrawing your contributions without penalty if you need emergency cash.

Save More

Widespread layoffs and job uncertainty have reawakened Americans to the importance of setting aside savings. The savings rate in U.S. households has risen from almost nothing in early 2008 to almost 4 percent in 2009. You will need to increase the amount you save annually in order to achieve the retirement goals you set before the economic recession.

If you are earning income, contribute as much as possible to your Roth IRA. Remember that if you need to tap your savings before you reach the age of

59½, you can always withdraw your contributions (but not your earnings) from a Roth IRA without the 10 percent early withdrawal penalty.

Adjust Your Goals

Many Americans are realizing they will have to work longer to save enough for retirement, or that early retirement is no longer an option. Revisit your financial plan and recalculate your goals based on the amount of savings you now have and a lower average rate of return from the stock market. You might have to adjust your expectations: retiring in a less expensive city or country, retiring later, working part-time after retirement, or spending less.

Review and Regroup

After your IRA has suffered substantial losses in a down market, you might be tempted to unload your stocks and stock funds in favor of bonds and money market accounts. Many investors are already doing the same thing; stocks will be undervalued because everyone is selling, and prices for bonds will go up because they are in demand. It could take several years for the stock market to recover, but eventually the stocks of many companies will regain value. Take a close look at the holdings in your IRA portfolio; some stocks might truly be write-offs, but others are solid companies and industries that are positioned for growth as the economy improves. When you make a contribution to your IRA, invest in these industries or market sectors.

The losses in your portfolio might have caused it to become unbalanced. Return your portfolio to its target asset allocations. You can do this by investing new contributions in weak areas; selling some of the assets that are too heavily weighted; and purchasing additional shares of funds, stocks, or bonds in other styles or industry sectors.

Watch the IRS Rules

Congress is likely to make changes to IRS regulations to help compensate for IRA losses during the recession. Do not wait until tax time to learn what the new rules might be. Check the IRS Web site (**www.irs.gov**) and watch for news articles in the financial sections of newspapers and on finance and tax-preparation Web sites.

One big change was the elimination of income limits in 2010 for conversions of traditional IRAs and 401(k)s to Roth IRAs. Many wealthier investors will have access to a Roth IRA for the first time. Income limits remain in place for contributing to a Roth, which means that individuals who exceed the income limit must first contribute to a traditional IRA and then convert it to a Roth. Congress might make changes to these rules in the near future.

Convert to a Roth

While the balance in your traditional IRA or 401(k) is diminished, convert to a Roth IRA. Not only will you pay less income tax on the lower balance, but if you are unemployed or your income has decreased because of the poor economy, you will be in a lower tax bracket. When the economy does pick up, earnings from the assets in your Roth IRA will be tax-free. The one-year exemption from income limits for IRA conversions in 2010 means that even if your income normally excludes you from opening a Roth IRA, you have an opportunity to convert while the stock market is down. When you open a Roth IRA, you might be able to transfer your stocks, mutual funds, and other assets from your traditional IRA or 401(k).

Do Not Do Anything

Do not hurry to do anything; sometimes the best action to take is no action at all. Become well-informed about investing. Take time to study your investments and compare them to similar investments and to other types of investments. Watch the market carefully and read the news to learn which companies have new contracts and new prospects, and which companies are declaring bankruptcy. Do not make any investment without thoroughly researching it first.

Get Back Into the Stock Market Gradually

This is a period of opportunity for long-term investors building up an IRA portfolio. Look for undervalued stocks and industries that are likely to experience growth in the next few decades. A stock market decline is an opportunity to add good-quality stocks and stock funds to your portfolio. If you have converted some of the stocks in your IRA to bonds or money market accounts, or if you are making a significant contribution to an IRA, do not buy into the stock market all at once. The stock market will probably not plunge lower than it already has, but stock prices rise and drop dramatically from day to day in response to economic news. To avoid becoming the victim of a sudden price drop the day after you purchase a particular stock or fund, invest your money in increments of a few hundred or a few thousand dollars over time to spread the risk.

Look for Solid Investments

Purchase stocks and stock funds in solid, wealth-generating industries. Avoid speculation, and do not put your money into any investment that you do not thoroughly understand. Be wary of funds with special invest-ment strategies because they tend to have higher management costs, and their results are not guaranteed. Choose investments in industries that you know something about.

Young and Working

If you are at the beginning of your career, you have many years of growth ahead of you. You can buy stocks and funds now at lower prices and let your earnings grow for several decades. Follow basic principles of investing: Create a diversified portfolio, choose solid investments and review them regularly, and be aware of new growth trends and opportunities.

Mid-career and Approaching Retirement

You will have to save more to meet retirement goals. To get the most out of the next decade, watch your portfolio closely. Remember to look at your whole financial picture, including mortgages, credit card debt, possible inheritances, and expenses such as a child's college education or medical expenses. You might have to adjust your retirement plans.

Already Retired

Try to avoid taking a withdrawal from your Roth IRA at this point unless it is absolutely necessary. Stocks and funds will regain value when the econ-omy starts to recover, so hold on to them as long as possible. When the economy begins to recover, you will probably need to shift a portion of your fixed-income assets to stocks to try to achieve more growth and make up for your losses.

Conclusion

Despite the losses suffered by investors in 2008, Roth IRAs are still the most advantageous vehicles for growing your retirement savings because they allow you to reinvest money you would otherwise have paid as taxes. Earnings are not taxed at all if you wait long enough before withdrawing them. You might need to make adjustments to your financial goals and to save more in order to achieve them, but do not pass up the opportunity to invest extra money.

After reading this book, you should have a good understanding of the IRS regulations governing Roth IRAs and of all the investment possibilities they offer. Put this knowledge to work for you and your family. Follow the basic principles of investing, and never stop using the many resources available to you through books, the media, and the Internet. Every question has an answer. Remember that saving is a steady, lifelong process, and make today the first day of your financial future.

APPENDIX A

Useful Web Sites

Regulatory and government agencies

Many government sites contain tutorials and information for private investors:

- Chartered Financial Analyst Institute (**www.cfainstitute.org**): The CFA Institute is the global, not-for-profit association of more than 90,000 investment professionals that confers the CFA and CIPM designations. The CFA Institute offers education and training and is a leading voice on global issues of fairness, market efficiency, and investor protection.

- Federal Reserve Internal Revenue Service Financial Industry Regulatory Authority (FINRA) (**www.finra.org**): FINRA is a merger of NASDAQ and the New York Stock Exchange's regulation committee, subject to oversight by the SEC. It oversees the operations of the stock exchanges and enforces federal securities laws and regulations. The FINRA Web site offers education for investors and numerous reports on individual companies and their compliance with the law.

- Municipal Securities Rulemaking Board (MSRB) (**www.msrb. org**): The Municipal Securities Rulemaking Board was established in 1975 by Congress to develop rules regulating securities firms and banks involved in underwriting, trading, and selling municipal securities. It sets standards for all municipal securities dealers and is subject to oversight by the SEC.

- National Futures Association (**www.nfa.futures.org**): The National Futures Association (NFA) is the industrywide, self-regulatory organization for the U.S. futures industry. It develops rules, programs, and services that safeguard market integrity and protect investors. The NFA Web site offers background checks on futures traders and education for investors.

- Securities and Exchange Commission (SEC) (**www.sec.gov**): Education for individual investors, laws, and regulations governing the financial markets, compliance information, registration, and background checks for brokerages.

- U.S. Commodity Futures Trading Commission (**www.cftc.gov**): Congress created the Commodity Futures Trading Commission (CFTC) in 1974 as an independent agency with the mandate to regulate commodity futures and option markets in the United States. The CFTC's mission is to protect market users and the public from fraud, manipulation, and abusive practices related to the sale of commodity and financial futures and options, and to foster open, competitive, and financially sound futures and option markets.

- U.S. Federal Reserve Board (**www.federalreserve.gov**): Information on monetary policy, banks and interest rates, and minutes of committee meetings.

- U. S. Internal Revenue Service (IRS) (**www.irs.gov**): The IRS Web site offers the complete tax code, instructions, forms, discussions, and education for taxpayers, as well as a complete list of private letter rulings.

- U.S. Treasury Department (**www.ustreas.gov**): The U.S. Treasury Web site is a vast resource of information on financial markets, the economy, international financial markets, taxes, and fraud.

Professional associations

Professional associations try to promote the business interests of their members by enforcing business standards and providing education for consumers:

- American Association of Individual Investors (AAII) (**www.aaii. com/bonds**): A non-profit membership association that provides free education and advice for individual investors, including sample portfolios.

- American Enterprise Institute for Public Policy Research (AEI) (**www.aei.org**): A private, conservative, not-for-profit institution dedicated to research and education on issues of government, politics, economics, and social welfare. Provides in-depth analysis of economic policy.

- American Institute of Certified Public Accountants (AICPA) (**www.cpa2biz.com**): Partners with the CPA2Biz Web site, which offers information and helpful articles on wealth planning.

- Government Finance Officers Association (GFOA) (**www.gfoa. org**): Information on recommended financial practices for state and local governments.

- International Accounting Standards Board (IASB) (**www.iasb. org**): Sets international standards for accounting practices.

- Investment Company Institute (**www.ici.org**): The national association of U.S. investment companies, including mutual funds, closed-end funds, exchange-traded funds (ETFs), and unit investment trusts (UITs) seeks to encourage adherence to ethical standards, and offers investor education about mutual funds.

- National Association of Tax Professionals (NATP) (**www.natptax. com**): Tax information and directory search for professional tax advisors.

- National Federation of Municipal Analysts (NFMA) (**www.nfma. org**): Established in 1983 to provide a forum for issues of interest to the municipal analyst community, its membership includes nearly 1,000 municipal professionals. It is a co-sponsor of EMMA (**www.emma.msrb.org**), a site offering extensive information on municipal bonds.

- Securities Industry and Financial Markets Association (SIFMA) (**www.sifma.org**): Represents more than 650 member firms of all sizes, in all financial markets in the U.S. and around the world. Sponsors Path to Investment (**www.pathtoinvesting.org**), an educational site for investors, and InvestinginBonds.com (**www. investinginbonds.com**).

Roth IRAs

- Lewis, Roy. The Motley Fool, "All About IRAs: Roth IRAs" (**www.fool.com/money/allaboutiras/allaboutiras04.htm**): This well-known investment Web site offers a series of detailed articles about Roth IRAs.

- Smart Money (**www.smartmoney.com/personal-finance/ retirement/?topic=roth-ira**): Information about Roth IRAs on the Web site of *Smart Money* magazine.

SEP and SIMPLE IRAs

- IRS Employee Plans Videos (**www.stayexempt.org/ep/manag- ing_ira.html**): The videos on this page were produced by the IRS Office of Employee Plans (EP). These videos provide useful infor- mation to help retirement plan sponsors choose and operate their plans and to help participants ensure their retirement benefits are protected. Participants will also learn more about the value of plans as a way to save for retirement.

Taxes

- Federal tax bracket calculator, MoneyChimp.com (**www.money- chimp.com/features/tax_brackets.htm**): This calculator shows you what tax bracket you are in and what percentage of your total income you will owe in income tax.

- National Association of Tax Professionals (NATP) (**www.natptax. com**): Tax information and directory search for professional tax advisors.

- IRS, Tax Information for the Retirement Plans Community (**www.irs.gov/retirement/index.html**): A clearinghouse of information on tax issues for employers and administrators of retirement plans.

- U.S. Internal Revenue Service (IRS) (**www.irs.gov**): The IRS Web site offers the complete tax code, instructions, forms, discussions, and education for taxpayers, as well as a complete list of private letter rulings.

Private letter rulings (PLRs)

- IRS Written Determinations (**www.irs.gov/app/picklist/list/writtenDeterminations.html**): A database of all private letter rulings.

- IRS, Retirement Plans FAQs relating to Waivers of the 60-Day Rollover Requirement (**www.irs.gov/retirement/article/0,,id=160470,00.html**): Information on circumstances under which the 60-day rollover requirement for IRAs and qualified retirement plans might be waived.

- Internal Revenue Bulletin, Bulletin No. 2009-1, January 5, 2009, Rev. Proc. 2007–4, page 118. Rulings and Determination letters (**www.irs.gov/pub/irs-irbs/irb09-01.pdf**): Instructions for submitting a request for a private letter ruling.

Legal and estate planning

- Legal Information Institute of the Cornell University Law School U.S. Code Collection (**www.law.cornell.edu/uscode**): An online presentation of the entire U.S, legal code, including the laws governing retirement plans.

- Smart Money, "Estate Planning With a Roth IRA" (**www.smart-money.com/personal-finance/retirement/estate-planning-with-a-roth-ira-7966**): An article from *Smart Money* magazine about using Roth IRAs for estate planning.

Mutual funds

- Commodity Mutual Funds, Money-zine.com (**www.money-zine.com/Investing/Mutual-Funds/Commodity-Mutual-Funds**).

- Mutual Funds Education Alliance, "Mutual Funds: Getting Started." (**www.mfea.com/GettingStarted**).

- SEC, "Invest Wisely: An Introduction to Mutual Funds" (**www.sec.gov/investor/pubs/inwsmf.htm**).

Stock exchanges

- CME Group (Chicago Mercantile Exchange) (**www.cmegroup.com**): Provides the widest range of benchmark futures and options products available on any exchange, covering all major asset classes.

- Chicago Board Options Exchange (**www.cboe.com**): The largest options market, trading index, equity, and interest rate options.

- NASDAQ (**www.nasdaq.com**): The largest electronic screen-based equity securities trading market in the United States, with the largest trading volume of any stock exchange in the world.

- NYSE Euronext (New York Stock Exchange, American Stock Exchange) (**www.ir.nyse.com**): Brings together six cash equities exchanges in seven countries and eight derivatives exchanges and operates the world ' s largest and most liquid exchange group and offers the most diverse array of financial products and services. NYSE Euronext is a world leader for listings, trading in cash equities, equity, and interest rate derivatives, bonds, and the distribution of market data.

- OneChicago (**www.onechicago.com**): An electronic exchange for futures on individual stocks, narrow-based indexes, and ETFs. It is a joint venture of IB Exchange Corporation and the world's premier options and futures exchanges: Chicago Board Options Exchange (CBOE) and CME Group (CME).

Bonds

- EMMA (**www.emma.msrb.org**): EMMA makes available official statements for most new offerings of municipal bonds, notes, 529 college savings plans, and other municipal securities since 1990, and provides real-time access to prices at which bonds and notes are sold to or bought.

- Incapital, LLC (**www.incapital.com**): Incapital underwrites and distributes fixed income securities and structured notes through more than 900 broker-dealers and banks in the United States, Europe, and Asia. Their Web site offers investment tools and an educational program for bond investors.

- Morningstar, Inc. (**www.morningstar.com**): Morningstar, Inc., a leading provider of information on investment products, has its own ranking system for hundreds of bond funds. Its bond calculator allows you to compare two or more bonds. Its subsidiaries include Morningstar Associates, LLC and Ibbotson Associates, Morningstar® Managed Portfolios, and Investment Services, Inc., a registered investment advisor and broker-dealer.

- MuniNetGuide (**www.muninetguide.com/nfma.php**): Online guide and directory to municipal-related content on the Internet with a unique emphasis on municipal bonds, state and local government, and public finance.

- New York Stock Exchange (NYSE) (**www.nyse.com/bonds/nyse-bonds/1127299875444.html**): The NYSE provides a trading platform for bond traders and an online dictionary of bond terms.

- Trade Reporting and Compliance Engine (**TRACE**) (**http://investinginbonds.com**) (**http://cxa.marketwatch.com/finra/BondCenter/Default.aspx**): Created under the auspices of the SEC, TRACE offers price information on bond sales within 15 minutes of a trade.

- Treasury Direct (**www.TreasuryDirect.gov**): Offers product information and research across the entire line of Treasury Securities, from Series EE Savings Bonds to Treasury Notes.

ETF providers

The following companies create and manage exchange traded funds. You can learn about their funds and investment strategies on their Web sites.

- Ameristock Funds (**www.ameristock.com**): Ameristock Funds offers ETFs that track the Ryan Indexes, the first daily bond indexes, which follow the most recently auctioned Treasury securities.

- Barclays Global Investors (BGI) (**www.iShares.com**) (**www.ipathetn.com**) (**www.iShares.ca**): Barclays Global Investors (BGI) is one of the largest asset managers in the world, with more than $2 trillion in assets (June 2007) for over 2,900 clients in more than 50 countries around the world. BGI created the first index strategy in 1971 and the first quantitative active strategy in 1978. It is the global leader in assets and products in the exchange-traded funds business, offering more than 190 funds, and is the world's second-largest manager of U.S. institutional tax-exempt assets.

- Claymore Securities (**www.Claymore.com/etfs**): Claymore Securities manages $18.5 billion in assets and offers a lineup of ETFs that track key market segments and indexes that seek to best capture the investment potential of unique strategies.

- Deutsche Bank (**www.DBCfund.db.com**): Partnering with PowerShares and State Street Global Advisors, Deutsche Bank is the sponsor of a series of ETFs tracking indexes in commodity and currency futures.

- Elements (**www.elementsetn.com**): Elements are exchange-traded notes designed to track the returns of commodity and currency indexes.

- Fidelity Management & Research Company (**www.nasdaq.com/oneq**): Fidelity Management & Research Company manages the "ONEQ" ETF tracking NASDAQ Composite Index, a market capitalization-weighted index representing the performance of over 3,000 stocks.

- First Trust (**www.FTportfolios.com**): First Trust ETFs track market segments and fundamentally weighted, quantitative indexes.

- FocusShares (**www.focusshares.com**): FocusShares ETFs follow custom indexes intended to target "real world" events.

- Greenhaven Commodity Services, LLC (**www.greenhavenfunds. com**): Sponsors the Greenhaven Continuous Commodity Index Fund (GCC), tracking the Continuous Commodity Total Return Index (CCI-TR), a basket of 17 commodities: wheat, corn, soybeans, live cattle, lean hogs, gold, silver, platinum, copper, cotton, coffee, cocoa, orange juice, sugar, crude oil, heating oil, and natural gas.

- HOLDRS (Merrill Lynch) (**www.holdrs.com**) (**www.totalmerrill.com**): A group of unmanaged sector portfolios in which the investor retains ownership benefits related to the underlying stocks.

- NETS Trust (**www.northerntrust.com**): NETS Trust also offers the NETS(TM) DAX(R) Index Fund (DAX), tracking the price and yield performance of the 30 largest and most actively traded companies in the German market.

- PowerShares Capital Management LLC (**www.PowerShares.com**) (**www.adrbnymellon.com/bldrs_overview.jsp**): Invesco PowerShares Capital Management LLC offers a family of 110 quantitative ETFs, including BLDRS, is a series of ETFs based on The Bank of New York ADR Index®.

- ProShares (**www.ProShares.com**): ProShares offers leveraged and inverse ETFs and are a unit of ProFunds Group.

- Rydex Investments (**www.Rydexfunds.com**): Rydex Investments offers a lineup of ETFs that track key market segments.

- SPA (**www.spa-etf.com**): SPA offers ETFs that track fundamentally driven indexes by MarketGrader.

- Select Sector Spidrs (**www.sectorspdr.com**): A site to diversify your portfolio by splitting up the S&P 500 into nine sectors.

- State Street Global Advisors (**www.SSGAfunds.com**): Manages a diverse lineup of ETFs tracking a variety of style and sector indexes. SPDR ETFs are managed by State Street Global Advisors.

- UBS (**www.ubs.com**): UBS sponsors the E-TRACS UBS Bloomberg CMCI Index ETN, tracking the UBS Bloomberg Constant Maturity Commodity Index, which measures long-term commodity performance.

- Van Eck Global (**www.VanEck.com**): Van Eck Global is a sponsor of Market Vectors ETFs tracking, global industry sectors, municipal bonds, and Chinese and Indian currencies.

- Vanguard (**www.Vanguard.com**): Vanguard ETFs are a share class of Vanguard index mutual funds.

- WisdomTree (**www.WisdomTree.com**): WisdomTree offers ETFs that fundamentally select and weight global equities.

- XShares (**www.xsharesadvisors.com**): XShares offers ETFs that track the Ryan Indexes, the first daily bond indexes, which follow the most recently auctioned Treasury securities.

- Ziegler Capital Management (**www.ziegler.com**): Ziegler Capital Management sponsors the NYSE Arca Tech 100 ETF, tracking a price-weighted index comprising 100 technology ADRs and common stocks listed on U.S. exchanges.

Brokers

To check the accreditation and legal status of brokers or financial advisors, look them up on the SEC (**www.sec.gov/investor/brokers.htm**) or FINRA (**www.finra.org/Investors/ToolsCalculators/BrokerCheck/index.htm**).

A major objective in getting the best performance from your portfolio is to keep expenses, trading fees, and commissions to a minimum. Discount brokerages charge a flat trading fee for each transaction and offer a variety of services. Their staffs do not receive commissions or solicit sales. You can easily open an account online or by visiting a local branch office. Competition for online customers has motivated these companies to offer increasingly sophisticated investment tools on their Web sites. A technical analysis center at TradeKing uses pattern-recognition technology to look for 60 different patterns in 22,000 publicly traded stocks. TD Ameritrade has a StrategyDesk program that allows investors to test trading strategies without making the trade and to set up programmed trades. Fidelity and Charles Schwab offer online classes to teach customers about investing. Fees now average $7 to $10 per trade and can be as low as $3 for automatic trades on specified days of the week. Shop around to find a brokerage that offers the services you need, and a Web site that you find easy to use. You can find reviews and charts comparing all the brokerages on financial Web sites such as SmartMoney (**www.smartmoney. com**), The Motley Fool (**www.fool.com**), and Stocks and Mutual Funds (**www.stocksandmutualfunds.com**).

Premium brokers (online trading and regional offices):

- E*Trade (**https://us.etrade.com/e/t/home**)
- Fidelity (**www.fidelity.com**)
- Vanguard (**www.vanguard.com**)
- Charles Schwab (**www.schwab.com**)
- T. Rowe Price (**www.troweprice.com**)
- T.D. Ameritrade (**www.tdameritrade.com**)

Discount brokers (online trading):

- TradeKing (**www.tradeking.com**)
- Scottrade (**www.scottrade.com**)
- Firstrade (**www.firstrade.com**)
- OptionsXpress (**www.optionsxpress.com**)
- Muriel Siebert (**www.siebertnet.com**)
- WallStreet*E (**www.wallstreete.com**)
- SogoInvest (**www.sogotrade.com**)
- Zecco (**www.zecco.com**)

Index providers

- American Stock Exchange (AMEX) (**www.amex.com**): The American Stock Exchange (AMEX) calculates and publishes a wide variety of indexes to support various index-based products such as ETFs, index options, and structured products. It also provides third-party index calculation services for custom indexes.

- Dow Jones and D.J. Wilshire Equity Indexes (**www.djindexes. com**): Dow Jones licenses over 3,000 market indexes, including the world's oldest stock indicator, the Dow Jones Industrial

Average. ETFs based on Dow Jones indexes include iShares industry and sector ETFs, and streetTRACKS large-, mid-, and small-cap ETFs.

Dow Jones publishes *The Wall Street Journal* and *Barron's*. In 2004, Dow Jones partnered with Wilshire Associates, a privately owned investment firm and index provider, to increase its depth in the market. The DJ Wilshire 5000 Index, established in 1974, was the first U.S. equity index to track the return of the entire U.S. stock market.

- Goldman Sachs (**www2.goldmansachs.com**): Goldman Sachs tracks a broadly diversified, unleveraged, long-only investment in commodity futures. Individual components qualify for inclusion in the S&P GSCI™ on the basis of liquidity and are weighted by their respective world production quantities. It is the basis for a variety of commodity ETFs.

- Morgan Stanley Capital International (**www.morganstanley. com**): Morgan Stanley Capital International provides a wide variety of indexes. Its indexes underlie the domestic and international Vanguard ETFs, and the Barclay iShares individual country ETFs.

- Morningstar Indexes (**www.morningstar.com**): Morningstar has 16 size and style indexes, based on the methodology used in their Morningstar Style BoxesTM, targeting 97 percent of the free-float U.S. equity market. Morningstar uses ten factors, five for growth and five for value, to define the style characteristics of a stock.

- NASDAQ (**www.nasdaq.com**): The NASDAQ Composite index tracks only companies that trade primarily on the NASDAQ and is the basis for the Fidelity NASDAQ Composite ETF (symbol:

ONEQ). The NASDAQ 100 tracks only companies that traded on the NASDAQ and excludes financial companies.

- New York Stock Exchange (NYSE) (**www.nyse.com**): The iShares NYSE Composite Index (symbol: NYC) tracks all the stocks that trade on the NYSE. The iShares NYSE 100 Index (symbol: NY) tracks the 100 largest companies on the NYSE.

- Russell U.S. Equity Indexes (**www.russell.com/Indexes**): The Russell 3000 Index measures the performance of the 3,000 largest U.S. companies, based on total market capitalization, and represents 98 percent of the United States Equity market. A number of Russell indexes are subsets of the Russell 3000, including the Russell 1000, tracking the 1,000 largest U.S. stocks, and the Russell 2000, tracking the next 2,000 largest U.S. stocks. The Russell Micro Cap Index is not a subset of the Russell 3000; it tracks the performance of stocks occupying the positions from 2,001 to 4,000 in size order.

- Powershares FTSE RAFI® (**www.invescopowershares.com/ rafi**): Unlike market-cap weighted indexes, PowerShares FTSE RAFI Portfolios incorporate the Fundamental Index® investment criteria of cash flow, book value, sales, and dividends to determine a stock's weight. Assigning weights based on the size of a stock's financial footprint can help to reduce the impact of price-distorting factors and provide a more objective representation of the market.

- Standard & Poors (**www.standardandpoors.com/indexes**): Standard & Poors, owned by McGraw-Hill, maintains hundreds of indexes, including the most famous market index of all, the Standard & Poors 500. More ETFs are based on indexes provided by S&P than by any other provider. S&P indexes include those used by the Barclay's broad-based international ETFs, Select Sector SPDRs that track various market sectors, and the iShares S&P Growth and Value ETFs.

Portfolio management

- Morningstar.com, "The Best Investments for Tax-Deferred Accounts" (**http://news.morningstar.com/classroom2/course. asp?docId=4444&page=1&CN=COM**): An online tutorial about making the most of tax-deferred accounts.

- Morningstar, Free Portfolio Manager (**http://portfolio.morningstar.com/NewPort/Reg/AddPortfolio.aspx**): A free online portfolio manager that tracks the up-to-the-minute performance of your investments and provides customized views of investment metrics.

Research, news, and commentary

- Bank for International Settlements, Quarterly Review Statistical Annex (**www.bis.org/publ/qtrpdf/r_qa0812.pdf**): Statistics on world financial markets.

- *Business Week* (**www.businessweek.com**): Articles and education on business, economy, and finance.

- CNN Money (CNN, *Fortune, Money* magazine) (**http://money. cnn.com**): Articles and education on business, economy and finance.

- EmergingMarkets (**www.emergingmarkets.org**): News, articles, and information on finance and economy in emerging market countries.

- Finra.org (**www.finra.org/index.htm**): The FINRA Web site offers education for investors and numerous reports on individual companies and their compliance with the law.

- Forbes.com (**www.forbes.com**): Articles and education on business, economy, and finance.

- Index Universe (**www.indexuniverse.com**): News, data, and research on ETFs and index funds.

- Investment News (**www.investmentnews.com**): Articles and education on business, economy, and finance.

- Investopedia (**www.investopedia.com**): Sponsored by Forbes, this Web site provides tutorials, educational materials, and a glossary of investment terms.

- Kiplinger.com (**www.kiplinger.com**): Articles and education on business, economy, and finance.

- Market Watch (**www.marketwatch.com**): Stock market quotes, business news, and financial news.

- Moneychimp (**www.moneychimp.com**): Education on investing and personal finance, financial calculators.

- Morningstar (**www.morningstar.com**): Stock market quotes, investor education, forums, articles, and calculators.

- Seeking Alpha (**www.seekingalpha.com**): Information and education for investors.

- Smart Money (**www.smartmoney.com**): Articles and education on business, economy, and finance.

- Social Investment Forum (**www.socialinvest.org**): Information, reports, and news about socially and environmentally responsible investing.

- The ETF Guide (**www.etfguide.com**): Information and articles on ETFs.

- The Motley Fool (**www.fool.com**): Information and education for investors.

- TheStreet.com (**www.thestreet.com/life-and-money/etfs/index.html**).

- Value Line (**www.valueline.com**).

- *The Wall Street Journal* (**www.wsj.com**): Articles and education on business, economy, and finance.

- Yahoo! Finance (**www.finance.yahoo.com/etf**): Articles and education on business, economy, and finance.

Calculators and tools

- 72(t) calculator (**www.bankrate.com/calculators/retirement/72-t-distribution-calculator.aspx**): Calculates your withdrawal amounts for a SEPP.

- Asset Allocator, Iowa Public Employees Retirement System (**www.ipers.org/calcs/AssetAllocator.html**).

- Correlation Tracker Select Sector SPDRs (**www.sectorspdr.com/correlation**).

- Effect of fund expenses on returns, TIAA-CREF (**www.tiaa-cref.org/calcs/expensegrowth/index.html**).

- Fidelity IRA evaluator (**http://personal.fidelity.com/products/ retirement/iraeval/popup.shtml.cvsr?refpr=IRAA0003**).

- Investment calculator for bonds, U.S. Treasury (**www.treasury-direct.gov/BC/SBCGrw**).

- Roth retirement calculator, MoneyChimp.com (**www.money-chimp.com/articles/rothira/roth_calculator.htm**).

- Federal tax bracket calculator, MoneyChimp.com (**www.money-chimp.com/features/tax_brackets.htm**).

Online savings accounts

- Capital One (**www.capitalone.com/directbanking**).
- ING Direct (**http://home.ingdirect.com/open/open.asp**).
- HSBC Direct (**www.hsbcdirect.com/1/2/1/mkt/savings**).

Budgeting applications

- Mint.com (**www.mint.com**).

- Quicken Online (**http://quicken.intuit.com/online-banking-finances.jsp**).

Saving for retirement and education

- AARP (**www.aarp.com**): Offers advice on personal finance, investing, and money management for retired persons.

- SavingforCollege.com (**www.savingforcollege.com**): Information, articles, and calculators for college savings.

APPENDIX B

Frequently Used Acronyms

ADP – Applicable Distribution Period

AGI – Adjusted Gross Income

AMEX – American Stock Exchange

BRIC – Brazil, Russia, India, China

CBOE – Chicago Board Options Exchange

CD – Certificate of Deposit

CESA – Coverdell Education Savings Account

CIP-U – Consumer Price Index-U

DRIP – Dividend Reinvestment Plan

EAFE – MSCI Europe, Australia, and Far East Index

EBITDA – Earnings Before Interest, Taxes, Depreciation, and Amortization

EDGAR – Electronic Data Gathering, Analysis, and Retrieval system

EGTRRA – Economic Growth and Tax Relief Reconciliation
Act of 2001

EIRA – Education IRA

EITC – Earned Income Tax Credit

EMMA – Electronic Municipal Market Access

ERISA – Employee Retirement Income Security Act (1974)

ESA – Coverdell Education Savings Account

ESOP – Employee Stock Ownership Plan

ETF – Exchange-Traded Fund

ETN – Exchange-Traded Note

Fannie Mae – Federal National Mortgage Association

FBO – For the Benefit Of

FDIC – Federal Deposit Insurance Corporation

FICA – Federal Insurance Contributions Act

FIFO – First In First Out

FINRA – Financial Industry Regulatory Authority, Inc.

FMV – Fair Market Value

Freddie Mac – Federal Home Loan Mortgage Corporation

GAAP – Generally Accepted Accounting Practices

Ginnie Mae – Government National Mortgage Association

GSE – Government-Sponsored Enterprises

GST – Generation-Skipping Transfer Tax

IASB – International Accounting Standards Board

IFRS – International Financial Reporting Standards

ILIT – Irrevocable Life Insurance Trust

IPO – Initial Public Offering

IRA – Individual Retirement Arrangement

IRC – Internal Revenue Code

IRS – Internal Revenue Service

LLC – Limited Liability Company

LTV – Loan To Value

MBS – Mortgage-Backed Securities

MFEA – Mutual Fund Education Alliance

MSCI – Morgan Stanley Capital International

MSRB – Municipal Securities Rulemaking Board

NASDAQ – National Association of Securities and Dealers Automated Quotation

NAV – Net Asset Value

NYSE – New York Stock Exchange

OCP – Optional Cash Payment

PE – Price-to-Earnings Ratio

PLR – Private Letter Ruling

PPA – Pension Protection Act of 2006

QDRO – Qualified Domestic Relations Order

RBD – Required Beginning Date

REIT – Real Estate Investment Trust

REO – Real Estate Owned

RMD – Required Minimum Distribution

ROI – Return on Investment

S&P – Standard & Poors

Sallie Mae – Student Loan Marketing Association

SDA – Self-Directed Roth Individual Retirement Arrangement

SEP – Simplified Employee Pension Plan

SEPP – Substantially Equal Periodic Payment

SIMPLE IRA – Savings Incentive Match Plan for Employees Individual Retirement Arrangement

QDRO – Qualified Domestic Relations Order

QHEE – Qualified Higher Education Expenses

ROI – Return on Investment

TDA – Tax-Deferred Annuity

TIPRA – Tax Increase Prevention and Reconciliation Act of 2005

TIPS – Treasury Inflation Protected Securities

TRACE – Trade Reporting and Compliance Engine

UBIT – Unrelated Business Income Tax

UDFI – Unrelated Debt Financial Income

TTCA-98 – Tax Technical Corrections Act of 1998

Internal Revenue Service and Federal Government Publications and Forms

APPENDIX C

Forms

Form 1040: U.S. Individual Income Tax Return (**www.irs.gov/pub/irs-pdf/f1040.pdf***)*

Schedule K-1 (Form 1065): Partner's Share of Income, Credits, Deductions (**www.irs.gov/pub/irs-pdf/f1065sk1.pdf**)

Form 1099-R: Distributions From Pensions, Annuities, Retirement or Profit-Sharing Plans, IRAs, Insurance Contracts, etc.

Form 4852: Substitute for Form W-2, Wage and Tax Statement, or Form 1099-R, Distributions From Pensions, Annuities, Retirement or Profit-Sharing Plans, IRAs, Insurance Contracts, etc. (**www.irs.gov/pub/irs-pdf/f4852.pdf**)

Form 5304-SIMPLE: Savings Incentive Match Plan for Employees of Small Employers (SIMPLE) — Not for Use With a Designated Financial Institution (**www.irs.gov/pub/irs-pdf/f5304sim.pdf**)

Form 5305-SEP: Simplified Employee Pension - Individual Retirement Accounts Contribution Agreement (**www.irs.gov/pub/irs-pdf/f5305sep.pdf**)

Form 5329: Additional Taxes on Qualified Plans (Including IRAs) and Other Tax-Favored Accounts (**www.irs.gov/pub/irs-pdf/f5329.pdf**); used to report early withdrawals and excess contributions

Form 8606: Non-deductible IRAs (**www.irs.gov/pub/irs-pdf/f8606.pdf**); used to report non-deductible contributions to a traditional IRA, distributions from a traditional IRA that include non-deductible contributions, or conversion of all or part of a traditional IRA with non-deductible contributions to a Roth IRA.
Instructions for Form 8606 (**www.irs.gov/instructions/i8606/ch01.html**)

Form 8880: Credit for Qualified Retirement Plan Contributions (**www.irs.gov/pub/irs-pdf/f8880.pdf**)

Form 8888: Direct Deposit of Refund to More Than One Account (**www.irs.gov/pub/irs-pdf/f8888.pdf**)

Government publications

Internal Revenue Bulletin, Bulletin No. 2009-1, January 5, 2009
(www.irs.gov/pub/irs-irbs/irb09-01.pdf).
Gives information about submitting requests for Personal Letter Rulings.

IRS Publication 505, Tax Withholding and Estimated Tax
(www.irs.gov/publications/p505/index.html)

IRS Publication 550: Investment Income and Expenses
(www.irs.gov/publications/p550/index.html)

IRS Publication 559 (2008), Survivors, Executors, and Administrators
(www.irs.gov/publications/p559/index.html)
Includes a discussion of IRD.

IRS Publication 571 (01/2009), Tax-Sheltered Annuity Plans (403(b) Plans)
For Employees of Public Schools and Certain Tax-Exempt Organizations
(www.irs.gov/publications/p571/index.html)

IRS Publication 575 (2008), Pension and Annuity Income
(www.irs.gov/publications/p575/index.html)

IRS Publication 590 (2008): Individual Retirement Arrangements (IRAs)
(www.irs.gov/pub/irs-pdf/f1065sk1.pdf)

IRS Publication 590, Roth IRAs, "How Do You Figure the Taxable Part?"
(www.irs.gov/publications/p590/ch02.html#en_US_publink10006526)

IRS Publication 3998, Choosing a Retirement Solution for Your Small Business
(www.irs.gov/pub/irs-pdf/p3998.pdf)

IRS Publication 4334, Simple IRA Plans for Small Businesses. U.S. Department of Labor's Employee Benefits Security Administration (EBSA) and the Internal Revenue Service (IRS)
(www.irs.gov/pub/irs-pdf/p4334.pdf)

IRS Publication 4484, Choose a Retirement Plan for Employees of Tax Exempt and Government Entities
(www.irs.gov/pub/irs-pdf/p4484.pdf)

IRS, *A Virtual Small Business Tax Workshop (VSBTW) DVD*
(www.irs.gov/businesses/small/article/0,,id=97726,00.html)
A ten-lesson tax workshop that helps small business owners and the self-employed understand and meet their federal tax obligations

"Overview of the Federal Tax System as in Effect for 2008." Prepared by the Staff of the Joint Committee On Taxation for Scheduled for a Public Hearing Before the Senate Committee On Finance on April 15, 2008 **(www.house.gov/jct/x-32-08.pdf)** Retrieved April 28, 2009

SEC, *Invest Wisely: An Introduction to Mutual Funds*
(www.sec.gov/investor/pubs/inwsmf.htm)

Glossary

401(k) plan – An employer-sponsored, tax-advantaged retirement savings plan.

Adjusted gross income (AGI) – Income minus certain deductions, as listed (including contributions to deductible retirement accounts, alimony paid by you); but not including standard and itemized deductions.

Administrator – A professional or agency that handles the administrative details of your IRA account.

After-tax dollars – The amount of income left after taxes have been paid.

Active management – Manipulation of asset classes and funds in a portfolio in an attempt to achieve higher returns than the market.

Active portfolio strategies – Methods used in the active management of a portfolio.

Aggregation rule – An IRS requirement that all IRAs owned by an individual must be treated as a single IRA when calculating withdrawals.

Annuity – A contract, usually sold by an insurance company, to make regular monthly, quarterly, semiannual, or annual payments over a period of time.

Applicable distribution period (ADP) – A specific time period over which distributions must be made, used to calculate the amount of an annual distribution.

Asset – Anything that has value, including shares of stock, bonds, notes, commodities, real estate, and cash.

Asset class – The style or type of an asset: fixed-income, equity, capitalization, growth, or value.

Automatic sweep – An IRA feature that regularly deposits earnings and excess cash into a money market account where it can earn interest.

Basis – The portion of an IRA that was contributed after taxes had been paid on it.

Beneficiary – The person who will receive the benefits from an IRA when the owner dies.

Beta – A popular indicator of risk that measures the volatility of a stock or a fund in relation to the volatility of the market as a whole, represented by the S&P 500 Index.

Buy and hold – A passive investment style in which investments are purchased and held untouched in a portfolio for long periods of time.

Call – A request for payment or redemption.

Callable bonds – Bonds that can be called in by the issuer prior to maturity date.

Capital gain – The profit realized from the sale of an asset such as stocks or real estate.

Capitalization – The value of a company's outstanding shares of stock.

Cash-on-cash return – The annual net income from a real estate property divided by the amount of money invested in the property.

Catch-up contribution – An additional amount that can be contributed to an IRA by an individual who is 50 or older.

Checkbook control – A structure in which a self-directed IRA invests in a LLC managed by the IRA owner, who is then able to conduct financial transactions without the involvement of the IRA custodian.

Closed investment trust, closed-end fund – A mutual fund that restricts the number of investors and does not create new shares. Shares can be traded on the stock market.

Commercial paper – Unsecured short-term (less than 270 days) loans to corporations.

Commodities – Products that are required every day, including food, such as livestock, grain, and sugar; and basic materials, such as steel and aluminum.

Compassionate revenue procedure – A waiver granted when an IRA owner has a legitimate reason for failing to complete a rollover in 60 days.

Compensation – Wages, salaries, tips, self-employment income, professional fees, bonuses, and other amounts received for providing personal services.

Conduit trust – A trust set up to receive money from an IRA and pass it on to a beneficiary subject to specified restrictions.

Contingent beneficiary – An individual or entity who becomes a beneficiary only if the primary beneficiary dies.

Contribution limit – The maximum amount that an individual can contribute to an IRA during a tax year, determined annually by the IRS.

Conversion – The conversion of a traditional IRA to a Roth IRA.

Correlation – The degree to which two investments move together in the market.

Correlation coefficient – A measure of how closely the standard deviations of two stocks follow each other.

Coverdell ESA – An IRA that allows parents and guardians to make Non-deductible contributions for a child under 18 and withdraw the funds tax-free to pay for qualified education expenses.

Custodian – An entity such as a bank, federally insured credit union, savings and loan association, or financial institution that is licensed to hold IRA assets on your behalf.

Custom index – A rules-based investment strategy.

Deemed IRA – A special IRA set by an employer with a qualified retirement plan to receive an employee's voluntary contributions.

Deferral period – The number of years over which the distributions from an IRA can be extended.

Deferred compensation – Income from a traditional IRA or qualified retirement plan that represents wages and employer contributions set aside in a tax-deferred account to be distributed at a later date, such as after retirement.

Defined benefit plans – A pension plan that guarantees specific benefits for particular events in an employee's life, such as retirement, death, or disability.

Designated beneficiary – A person who is named as the beneficiary of an IRA.

Disclaimer – The renunciation of property to which a person is entitled by law, by gift, or by the terms of a will.

Distribution – A payout of funds from an IRA to a beneficiary.

Distribution period – The number of years that an IRA owner is expected to take a RMD, calculated using IRS life-expectancy tables.

Dividend yield – The amount that a company pays out in dividends each year relative to its share price, expressed as a ratio.

Divorce decree – A legal document specifying the details of a divorce.

Dow Jones Average – A price-weighted average of the stock prices of 30 companies representing leading U.S. industries.

Due diligence – The process of thoroughly investigating every aspect of an investment opportunity.

Early withdrawal penalty – A 10 percent penalty imposed on funds withdrawn from an IRA before the owner reaches 59½.

Earned income – Wages, salaries, commissions, income earned from self-employment, nontaxable combat pay, alimony, and separate maintenance payments.

Earned income tax credit (EITC) – An amount deducted from income taxes for low and moderate-income working parents with two or more children.

Economic Growth and Tax Relief Reconciliation Act of 2001 – Legislation that raised the amount that could be contributed to an IRA and added catch-up provisions for workers over 50.

Efficient frontier – Certain portfolios or investment selections that optimally balance risk and reward.

Elective contribution – A contribution that an employee chooses to make to an employer-sponsored retirement plan.

Emerging market – Developing countries whose economies are beginning to expand.

Employee Retirement Income Security Act (ERISA) – The act of Congress that created IRAs in 1974.

Estate tax – A tax imposed on inherited assets.

Estimated withholding tax – A method of paying income tax in installments on income that is not subject to income tax withholding.

Excess accumulation – The amount of a RMD that is not withdrawn from an IRA before the end of the calendar year.

Excessive contribution – A contribution to an IRA that exceeds the annual contribution limits.

Expected return – The expected return from an investment after a certain time has passed, calculated using historical data over a given period.

Expected value – The expected value of an investment after a certain time has passed, calculated using historical data over a given period.

Expense ratio – The percentage of your investment in a fund or ETF that is consumed by management fees.

Exit fee – A one-time fee charged for cashing in an investment in a mutual fund.

Expense ratio – The percentage of a fund's average net assets used to pay its annual expenses.

Fair market value (FMV) – The price a willing seller could receive for an asset from a willing buyer in the current market.

Fiduciary – A person or institution with a legal responsibility of financial trust.

Five-tax-year rule – A rule that contributions must be held in a Roth IRA for five tax years before earnings can be withdrawn tax-free.

Fixed income assets – Assets such as bonds that return a fixed amount of interest on a regular basis.

Foreclosure – The process by which a lender repossesses a property after the borrower is unable to make payments on the loan.

Fractional shares – Shares of stock that are sold in portions to allow investment of smaller amounts.

Futures – Contracts to buy a commodity in the future at an agreed price.

Golden years – The early years of retirement when a person is healthy and active enough to enjoy freedom from the responsibility of work.

Grandfather provision – A provision in a new law that permits older laws or transitional laws to continue to apply in certain circumstances.

Growth stocks – Stocks whose value has been growing rapidly and is expected to continue growing.

Illiquid assets – Assets, such as bonds, that cannot be immediately redeemed for cash.

Income tax bracket – The highest percentage that you pay in taxes, based on your adjusted income.

Index fund – A mutual fund or an ETF that tracks the performance of an index.

Individual retirement arrangement (IRA) – A special type of savings account that increases the amount of money available to an individual in retirement by means of certain tax advantages.

Internal Revenue Service – The U.S. government agency responsible for the collection of income taxes and the administration of IRAs.

Investment Company Act of 1940 – An act passed by Congress to regulate the mutual funds industry, under which many ETFs are organized.

Investment trust – A company that receives funds for the purpose of investment.

Irrevocable trust – A trust that cannot be altered by its creator.

Irrevocable life insurance trust (ILIT) – An irrevocable trust created to own and pay premiums for a life insurance policy.

Junk bond – A corporate bond that is rated as less than investment grade and has a higher yield because of the increased risk of default.

Keogh plan (HR10) – A type of tax-advantaged plan established in 1963 to allow self-employed individuals to save for retirement.

Large-cap – Stocks are generally classified as large-cap if their market capitalization is over $5 billion.

Leverage – The use of borrowed capital, such as margin, or of financial instruments, such as futures contracts, to increase the potential return of an investment.

Life-cycle investing – An investment strategy in which an investor's portfolio is adjusted as he or she moves through different stages of life.

Load fee – A one-time entry fee charged by some mutual funds.

Market breadth – The ratio of the number of stocks whose price has gone up to the number of stocks whose price has gone down.

Managed fund – A mutual fund that uses a special investment strategy to try to outperform the stock market.

Market index – An index that follows the performance of a particular market.

Mechanical rotation strategy – A rules-based sector rotation strategy.

Micro-cap – Stocks with capitalization of less than $250 million.

Mid cap – Stocks are generally classified as mid-cap if their market capitalization is between $1 billion and $5 billion.

Modern portfolio theory (MPT) – A theory that evaluates the overall risk of a portfolio by calculating the risk of each investment in the portfolio in relation to all the other investments it holds; and tracks the performance of a portfolio as a whole.

Modified AGI – The adjusted gross income from the IRS tax return, with certain adjustments made, that is used to determine eligibility to contribute to a Roth IRA.

Money market fund – A low-risk, low-return mutual fund containing high-quality, short-term (less than one year) investments.

Mutual fund – An investment vehicle which allows investors to pool their capital in order to purchase a broad range of securities.

Net asset value (NAV) – A calculation of the value of a share in a mutual fund or an ETF, calculated by dividing the value of the underlying assets by the number of shares.

No-load fund – A mutual fund that does not charge a fee to become a shareholder.

Non-exclusion period – The five-tax-year holding period during which earnings from a Roth IRA cannot be withdrawn tax-free.

Net unrealized appreciation – The amount by which an asset which has not yet been sold has increased in value since it was purchased.

Nominal return – An unadjusted average of the changes in the price of an investment over time.

Non-callable bonds – Bonds that have no call provision and will not be redeemed until they reach maturity.

Non-deductible contribution – The difference between the amount contributed to an IRA and the amount deducted from taxable income for that year, when only a partial deduction is allowed.

Non-discretionary trustee – An IRA custodian that does not offer legal, business, or tax advice, but simply carries out the directions of the IRA owner.

Non-systemic risk – The risk associated with investing all of your capital in a single company or market sector.

NRSRO – Nationally Recognized Statistical Rating Organization, a designation given by the SEC to agencies qualified to provide objective, third-party assessments.

Open-ended mutual fund – A mutual fund that creates new shares as the demand for them arises.

Opportunity cost – The income lost when cash cannot be reinvested to bring in more returns, because it is tied up somewhere else.

Pass-through mortgage securities – Mortgage pools that pass both interest and principal repayments through to investors as they occur.

Passive investing – A strategy in which securities, ETFs, or mutual funds are simply purchased and held in a portfolio over time.

Passive management – A style of management in which the portfolio of a mutual fund or an exchange-traded fund mirrors a market index, rather than being manipulated by a fund manager.

Plain vanilla – The most simple, conservative, traditional form of a financial instrument.

Portfolio – A selection of investments.

Pretax dollars – Total income before income taxes are paid.

Preferred stock – A stock issue that pays fixed dividends and gives its owners priority over other shareholders.

Price transparency – The ability of investors to easily receive accurate price information.

Price-to-earnings ratio – The price of a share of a company's stock, divided by the company's earnings per share.

Principal – The amount of money which an investor initially invests in the stock market.

Private pension – A retirement pension funded and administered by a private company.

Probate – A legal process that distributes assets according to the terms of a will.

Prospectus – The official description of fund or an ETF which explains its objectives and methodology, and describes its holdings.

Qualified acquisition costs – The costs of buying, building, or rebuilding a home, and any usual or reasonable settlement, financing, or other closing costs.

Qualified dividend income (QDI) – Dividends paid by certain preferred stocks, which is taxable at the lower federal tax rate of 15 percent.

Qualified education expenses – Expenses incurred in attending school, such as tuition, fees, books, room, and board, that the IRS includes in calculating tax deductions for education.

Qualified plan – A retirement savings plan set up by an employer that conforms to Section 401 of the U.S. Tax Code.

Qualified trust – A trust that has a natural person as its beneficiary and therefore qualifies as a designated beneficiary of an IRA.

Real estate investment trusts (REITs) – Companies that hold portfolios of real estate properties, or assets related to real estate.

Real estate mortgage investment conduits (REIC, REMIC) – An investment vehicle that holds commercial and residential mortgages in trust and issues securities representing an undivided interest in these mortgages.

Real estate option – A contract to buy a property on a specific date for a specific price.

Real interest rate – The coupon rate of a bond adjusted for inflation.

Realized yield – The actual return on an investment over the period it is held, including returns on reinvested interest and dividends.

Rebalancing – The act of adjusting a portfolio to maintain its target asset allocations.

Recharacterization – The process of moving funds from a Roth IRA back to a traditional IRA, or from a traditional IRA to a Roth IRA.

Reconversion – The conversion of a Roth IRA that has been recharacterized as a traditional IRA back to a Roth IRA.

Redemption period – Waiting period during which a property owner can redeem title to the property by paying off back taxes and remove a tax lien.

Required beginning date – April 1 of the year following the year in which an IRA owner reaches age 70½.

Required minimum distribution (RMD) – The minimum amount that a person older than 70½ years must withdraw from his or her IRA annually.

Revocable trust – A legal arrangement that allows the creator of a trust to alter it, cancel it, or remove property from it.

Risk – The uncertainty that an investment produce its promised return.

Risk-adjusted return – A concept in which an investment's return is evaluated by measuring how much risk is involved in producing that return.

Rollover – The transfer of funds from one tax-advantaged account to another.

Roth IRA – An IRA to which contributions are made after income tax has been paid, and which distributes earnings tax-free.

Salary-deferral contribution – A contribution made by an employer to a retirement plan that would otherwise have been paid to the employee as part of a salary.

Self-dealing rule – An IRS rule that prohibits you from deriving personal benefit from any of the assets held in your IRA account.

Separate maintenance decree – A legal document specifying how a couple will divide their assets after a separation.

Serial bond – A single bond issue consisting of bonds with different redemption dates.

Settlement date – The day on which cash or securities are delivered to complete a transaction.

Short-term bonds – Bonds with maturities ranging from zero to two years.

Short sale – A sale of real estate in which the price paid for the property is less than the amount owed by the seller on the mortgage.

SIMPLE IRA (savings incentive match plan for employees) – A retirement savings plan used by small businesses in which the employer and employee both contribute to an IRA for each employee.

Simplified employee pension plan (SEP) IRA – A retirement savings plan used by small businesses and self-employed individuals in which an employer contributes to an IRA for each employee.

Sinking fund – An escrow account created to set aside funds for the repayment of a bond issue.

Sovereign risk – Risk associated with investing in a country whose political situation or fiscal policies may affect returns or cause losses.

Stable value fund – A mutual fund, typically containing a mixture of bonds and insurance contracts, that is guaranteed to produce a specific rate of return.

Standard deviation – A measure of a stock's volatility, the amount by which the returns of an individual stock deviate from its average return.

Stretch IRA – A process by which RMDs are extended over the life expectancy of a beneficiary after the death of the original IRA owner.

Structured investment plan – A plan managed by a financial institution that offers specific investment choices.

Subprime mortgage – A mortgage loan to a creditor with a low credit rating, usually at a much higher interest rate.

Substantially equal payments – An arrangement whereby an IRA owner begins withdrawing funds from an IRA before the age of 59½ by setting up a schedule of fixed annual distributions.

Systemic risk – The risk associated with the stock market and economy as a whole.

Sector rotation – An investment strategy in which an investor constantly shifts his assets to the best-performing sectors of the market.

Standard & Poors 500 – An index of 500 stocks selected based on market size, liquidity, and industry grouping, and other factors. The S&P 500 is one of the most commonly used benchmarks for the overall U.S. stock market.

Style – The characteristics by which a security is classified when it is evaluated for inclusion in a portfolio or index.

Tax-deferred annuity (TDA) – A retirement annuity plan for employees of public charities or schools which usually promises a monthly payout for life.

Tax lien certificate – A certificate granting the right to collect back property taxes and initiate foreclosure if they are not paid.

Taxable event – Any financial transaction that is subject to federal, state, or local taxes.

Tax shelter – An investment or account that meets IRS requirements for exemption from or deferral of taxes.

Tenancy in common – An arrangement in which the title to a real estate asset is held jointly by an individual and an IRA administrator.

Term-certain – A fixed, determinable period, such as a number of years, during which a legal arrangement must be carried out.

Treasury bills – U.S. Treasury bills with short maturities of four, 13, 26, and 52 weeks that though, technically not bonds, offer similar opportunities to investors.

Treasury bonds – Bonds issued by the U.S. Treasury with maturities of ten to 30 years.

Treasury inflation-protected securities – Securities issued by the U.S. Treasury that are protected against inflation by making adjustments to their face value in accordance with fluctuations in the Consumer Price Index.

Treasury notes – Notes issued by the U.S. Treasury with maturities of two, five, and ten years.

Trustee – A professional, agency, or financial institution that is authorized to act on your behalf in certain financial transactions.

Trustee-to-trustee transfer – The transfer of assets directly from one IRA custodian to another IRA custodian.

Turnover rate – The rate at which investments in a portfolio are liquidated and replaced with new investments.

Unit investment trust (UIT) – An investment company that offers a fixed, unmanaged portfolio, generally of stocks and bonds, and does not reinvest the dividends.

United States Treasury – The government executive agency responsible for advancing economic prosperity and ensuring the financial security of the United States.

Unlimited marital deduction – A federal tax provision that waives estate tax on assets inherited from your spouse.

Unrelated business income tax (UBIT) – A tax imposed on income from a business unrelated to the primary purpose of a charitable organization or an IRA.

Variable-rate bonds – Bonds with interest rates that are periodically reset, commonly in line with the market insurance rates on specified dates.

Value stocks – Companies whose size has remained steady, but whose stock is considered to be a good value compared to the stock of other similar companies.

Value-weighted index – An index containing a high proportion of value stocks.

Vested benefit – The amount of a retirement plan that an employee can take when leaving a company.

Volatility – The degree to which a stock or ETF price tends to fluctuate.

Waiver – An intentional dismissal of a penalty or a right.

World mutual funds – Mutual funds that may hold U.S. stocks along with the international stocks.

Yankee bonds – Corporate bonds issued by foreign companies but trading in U.S. dollars on U.S. exchanges.

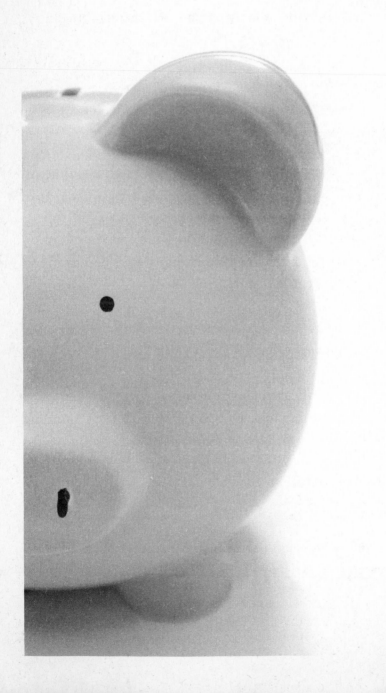

IRS Table I: Single Life Expectancy

This IRS table is used by beneficiaries of a Roth IRA to calculate the amount that must be withdrawn from an IRA each year.

Age	Life Expectancy (ADP)	Age	Life Expectancy (ADP)	Age	Life Expectancy (ADP)	Age	Life Expectancy (ADP)
0	82.4	28	55.3	56	28.7	84	8.1
1	81.6	29	54.3	57	27.9	85	7.6
2	80.6	30	53.3	58	27	86	7.1
3	79.7	31	52.4	59	26.1	87	6.7
4	78.7	32	51.4	60	25.2	88	6.3
5	77.7	33	50.4	61	24.4	89	5.9
6	76.7	34	49.4	62	23.5	90	5.5
7	75.8	35	48.5	63	22.7	91	5.2
8	74.8	36	47.5	64	21.8	92	4.9
9	73.8	37	46.5	65	21	93	4.6
10	72.8	38	45.6	66	20.2	94	4.3
11	71.8	39	44.6	67	19.4	95	4.1
12	70.8	40	43.6	68	18.6	96	3.8
13	69.9	41	42.7	69	17.8	97	3.6
14	68.9	42	41.7	70	17	98	3.4
15	67.9	43	40.7	71	16.3	99	3.1

Age	Life Expectancy (ADP)	Age	Life Expectancy (ADP)	Age	Life Expectancy (ADP)	Age	Life Expectancy (ADP)
16	66.9	44	39.8	72	15.5	100	2.9
17	66	45	38.8	73	14.8	101	2.7
18	65	46	37.9	74	14.1	102	2.5
19	64	47	37	75	13.4	103	2.3
20	63	48	36	76	12.7	104	2.1
21	62.1	49	35.1	77	12.1	105	1.9
22	61.1	50	34.2	78	11.4	106	1.7
23	60.1	51	33.3	79	10.8	107	1.5
24	59.1	52	32.3	80	10.2	108	1.4
25	58.2	53	31.4	81	9.7	109	1.2
26	57.2	54	30.5	82	9.1	110	1.1
27	56.2	55	29.6	83	8.6	111 and over	1

Bibliography

All URLs accessed December 1, 2009.

Bader, Mary and Steve Schroeder. "TIPRA and the Roth IRA New Planning Opportunity for High-Income Taxpayers." The *CPA Journal* (Online). May 2007. (**www.nysscpa.org/cpajournal/2007/507/essentials/p48.htm**).

Beacon Capital Management Advisors. "Solo 401(k)s." (**www.401ksolo.com**).

Carlson, Charles B. "All About DRIPs." DRIP Invester.com (**www.dripinvestor.com/FAQ/drip_faq.asp**).

Charles Schwab and Co., Inc. Investing Principles. (**www.schwab.com/public/schwab/planning/financial_guidance/investing_principles?cmsid=P-2448306&lvl1=planning&lvl2=financial_guidance&**).

Congressional Budget Office. "Legislative History of IRAs." Online Tax Guide. 2008. (**www.cbo.gov/OnlineTaxGuide/Text_2A.cfm##**).

CPMKTS℠ The Capital Markets Index, "Bond Market's Size Tops Equities for First Time Since '95," January 2, 2009. (**www.cpmkts.com/ press_20090102.php**).

Devilstower. "Whither Goest Thou, Stock Market?" Daily Kos. December 2, 2008. (**www.dailykos.com/ storyonly/2008/12/2/102214/940/743/668445**).

Employee Benefit Research Institute. "Workers Show Record Drop in Retirement Confidence, Health Care and Economy Are Major Concerns." 18th Annual Retirement Confidence Survey®. Employee Benefit Research Institute. April 9, 2008. (**www.ebri.org/pdf/ PR_796a_09Apr08.pdf**).

Fama, Eugene F. and Kenneth R. French. "How Unusual Was the Stock Market of 2008?" Fama/French Forum. May 4, 2009. (**www.dimensional.com/famafrench/2009/05/how-unusual-was-the-stock-market-of-2008.html**).

Fish, David. "Why DRIPs? Why Now?" The Moneypaper's Directinvesting.com. November 1, 2009. (**www.directinvesting.com/DRIP_Commentary.cfm**).

Joint Committee on Taxation Technical Explanation of the PPA. "Treatment of Distributions to Individuals Called to Active Duty for at Least 179 days (Sec. 72(t) of the Code)." Subtitle VII, Explanation 7. International City/County Management Association (ICMA) - Retirement Corporation (**www.icmarc.org/xp/rc/plansponsor/planrules/ppa/technicalexplanationC7.html?audience=contentonly**).

Holden, Sarah and Daniel Schrass. "The Role of IRAs in U.S. Households' Saving for Retirement, 2008." *Research Fundamentals* Vol. 18, No.

1. Investment Company Institute. January 2009. (**www.ici.org/pdf/fm-v18n1.pdf**).

Insure.com. "Irrevocable Life Insurance Trusts can Skirt Taxes, but Cost you Flexibility." Updated January 3, 2008. (**www.insure.com/articles/lifeinsurance/trusts.html**).

Internal Revenue Bulletin, Bulletin No. 2007-1, January 2, 2007, Sec. 4.02(7) (**www.irs.gov/pub/irs-irbs/irb07-01.pdf**).

IRS. Life Insurance & Disability Insurance Proceeds. FAQs. (**www.irs.gov/faqs/faq/0,,id=199751,00.html**).

IRS. "Lots of Benefits - When You Set up an Employee Retirement Plan." (**www.irs.gov/retirement/sponsor/article/0,,id=136475,00.html**).

IRS. Publication 590 (2008), Individual Retirement Arrangements (IRAs). Internal Revenue Service, U.S. Department of the Treasury. (**www.irs.gov/publications/p590/index.html**).

IRS. "Retirement Plans FAQs on Designated Roth Accounts." IRS.gov. February 25, 2009. (**www.irs.gov/retirement/article/0,,id=152956,00.html**).

IRS. SIMPLE IRA Plan. Internal Revenue Service, U.S. Department of the Treasury. (**www.irs.gov/retirement/sponsor/article/0,,id=139831,00.html**).

IRS. "The IRS Does Not Approve IRA Investments." Publication 3125 (8-98) Catalog Number 26091B. Internal Revenue Service, Department of the Treasury. (**www.irs.gov/pub/irs-pdf/p3125.pdf**).

IRS. Topic 610 - Retirement Savings Contributions Credit. (**www.irs. gov/taxtopics/tc610.html**).

Keebler, Robert S. "Eight Reasons to Convert to a Roth IRA." RothIRA. com. Jnuary 7, 2008. (**www.rothira.com/reasons.htm**).

Law Offices of Robert H. Glorch. Illinois Estate Tax 2009 Update. (**www. illinoisestateplan.com/sub/illinoisestatetaxupdate.jsp**).

Lesser, Gary S. *Roth IRA Answer Book*. New York: Aspen Publishers. 2006.

Marino, Vivian. "Using an I.R.A. to Buy Real Estate." *The New York Times*. April 17, 2005. (**www.nytimes.com/2005/04/17/ realestate/17assets.html?ex=1181361600&en=5728ecbef1662559&e i=5070**).

Miller, Mark. "Five things to remember if you lose your 401(k) match." Retirementrevised.com. April 22, 2009. (**http://retirementrevised.com/ money/five-things-to-remember-if-you-lose-your-401k-match**).

Money Blue Book. 2009 Federal Income Tax Brackets (Official IRS Tax Rates). (**www.moneybluebook.com/2009-federal-income-tax-brackets-official-irs-tax-rates**).

Pamuk, Humeyra. "Gold retreats from record high as dollar rebounds." *Forbes*. November 26, 2009. (**www.forbes.com/feeds/ reuters/2009/11/26/2009-11-26T164212Z_01_GEE5AP0ZD_ RTRIDST_0_MARKETS-PRECIOUS-UPDATE-7.html**).

Sahadi, Jeanne. "Have less than $25K in savings? Get in line." CNN-Money.com. April 11, 2007. (**http://money.cnn.com/2007/04/10/pf/**

retirement/ebri_survey_2007/index.htm?postversion=2007041108?c
nn=yes).

Shaw, Richard. "The Role of the U.S. in Overall Equity Allocation."
SeekingAlpha.com. November 17, 2008. (**http://seekingalpha.com/
article/106282-role-of-u-s-in-overall-equity-allocation**).

Short, Joanna. "Economic History of Retirement in the United States".
EH.Net Encyclopedia, edited by Robert Whaples. September 30, 2002.
(**http://eh.net/encyclopedia/article/short.retirement.history.us**).

Slesnick, Twila, John C. Suttle, and Amy DelPo. *IRAs, 401(k)s, & Other
Retirement Plans: Taking Your Money Out.* Berkeley, Calif: Nolo. 2006.

Sloan, Jim E. *How to Avoid HUGE Tax IRA Tax-Traps.* Calgary, Alberta,
Canada. Blitzprint. 2006.

Slott, Ed. *Your Complete Retirement Planning Road Map: A Comprehensive
Action Plan for Securing IRAs, 401(k)s, and Other Retirement Plans for
Yourself and Your Family.* New York, Ballantine. 2008.

Slott, Ed. *The Retirement Savings Time Bomb and how to Defuse it: A
5-step Action Plan for Protecting Your IRAs, 401(k) s, and Other Retirement
Plans From Near Annihilation by the Taxman.* New York: Viking. 2007.

Thomas, Kaye A. "Conversion Rule Changes: Recent Laws Change
the Rules." Fairmark.com. September 24, 2006. (**www.fairmark.com/
rothira/expand.htm**).

Thomas, Kaye A. *Go Roth! 2009 Your Guide to the Roth Ira, Roth 401k
and Roth 403b.* Fairmark Pr Inc. 2009.

U. S. Department of Labor, Employee Benefits Security Administration. "Private Pension Plan Bulletin Abstract of 2006 Form 5500 Annual Reports." December, 2008. (**www.dol.gov/ebsa/PDF/2006pensionplanbulletin.PDF**).

U.S. Securities and Exchange Commission. "Beginners' Guide to Asset Allocation, Diversification, and Rebalancing." SEC. May 2007. (**www.sec.gov/investor/pubs/assetallocation.htm**).

PRNewswire. "U.S. Senator William Roth to Celebrate Anniversary of Roth IRA With PFPC Inc." Source PFPC Inc. Wilmington, DE. Jan. 21, 1999. (**www2.prnewswire.com/cgi-bin/stories.pl?ACCT=104&STORY=/www/story/01-21-2000/0001120802&EDATE=**).

Zaritsky, Howard M. *Practical Estate Planning and Drafting After The Economic Growth and Tax Relief Reconciliation Act of 2001*. Valhalla, N.Y.: Warren Gorham & Lamont of RIA. 2001.

Author
Biography

Martha Maeda is an economic historian who writes on politics, ethics, finance, and modern philosophy. After graduating from Northwestern University, she lived and worked in Australia, Japan, Latin America, and several African countries, before settling in the United States. She has a particular interest in micro-economics and in the effects of globalization on the lives and businesses of people all over the world.

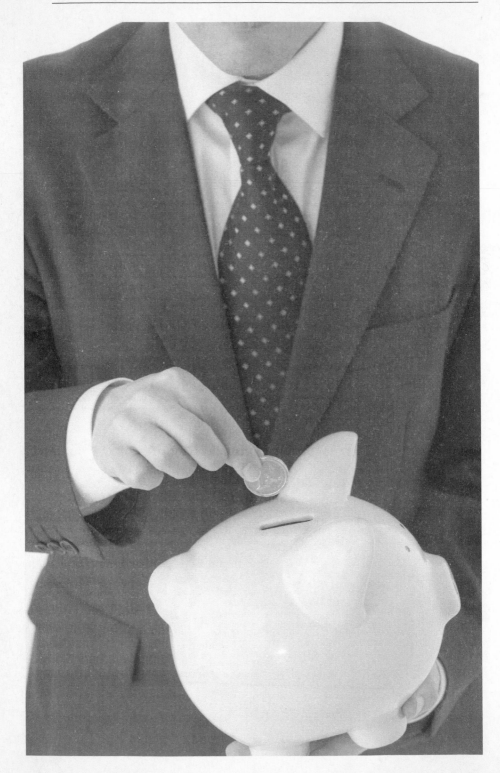

Index